International Business in
the Nineteenth Century

International Business in the Nineteenth Century

The Rise and Fall of a Cosmopolitan Bourgeoisie

Charles A. Jones

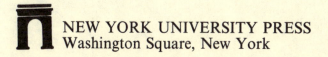

NEW YORK UNIVERSITY PRESS
Washington Square, New York

First published in the USA in 1987 by
NEW YORK UNIVERSITY PRESS,
Washington Square, New York, N.Y. 10003

© Charles A. Jones, 1987

Library of Congress Cataloging-in-Publication Data

Jones, Charles A., 1949–
  International business in the nineteenth century.

  Bibliography: p.
  Includes index.
  1. Commerce—History—19th century. 2. International
business enterprises—History—19th century. 3. Middle
classes—History—19th century. I. Title.
HF497.J66   1987   338.8'8'09034   87–11321
ISBN 0–8147–4172–X

Typeset in 11 on 12pt Times by
C R Barber & Partners (Highlands) Ltd, Fort William

Printed in Great Britain by
Billing & Sons Ltd, Worcester

For Jessie Anderson and Arthur Jones

Contents

Preface

This book has developed gradually, over a number of years, out of a Cambridge doctoral dissertation presented in 1974. I owe a great debt to Christopher Platt, not only for his careful supervision of that dissertation but also for the important part he played in the 1960s, gathering Anglo-Latin American business records and information about them. Through Platt I also first came into contact with many other historians working on Latin America, notably Bob Greenhill, with whom I worked closely in the early 1970s, and David Rock who, with his wife, Rosalind, helped introduce me to Argentina. Finance for this early research came from the Social Science Research Council. The same body financed a later research project devoted to the collection of records in Britain about Anglo–overseas enterprise. I am therefore doubly grateful. Many senior academic colleagues helped and encouraged me during these years, including Leslie Pressnell, Peter Lyon, John Lynch, R. A. Humphreys and until his premature death, Trevor Reese. These years—first at Cambridge then, successively, at the Institutes of Latin American and Commonwealth Studies of London University—brought me into contact with innumerable archivists and librarians all over Britain. They cannot all be named, but I owe special thanks to staff at University College, London, and at the National Register of Archives. Between 1970 and 1977 I was engaged, most of the time, in very specific empirical and archival research. I was therefore especially grateful during the middle 1970s, at the ICS, for the intellectual stimulus and broadening effect of the many seminar series housed there, and most of all

ix

the Southern African series then organised by Shula Marx.

In 1977 I was appointed to a lectureship in International Studies at the University of Warwick. I was made welcome by Fred Hirsch, the founder of the department, though he was already severely disabled by the disease that was soon to kill him. I gained a clear impression of his intention in founding the new department from his family, from papers relating to the courses he had introduced at Warwick, and from colleagues who had known him before he became ill and who helped to ensure that the department survived him: Peter Oppenheimer, Joy Gardner, Barry Buzan and David Fieldhouse. Naturally, the preparation of teaching in these inauspicious circumstances kept me away from research for some time. But to be forced into a variety of courses on intellectual history and international economic relations was what I needed at the time, and this book certainly would not have been as it is had I been appointed to an orthodox history department.

When I returned, four years ago, to the revised draft of the dissertation which I had shelved five years earlier on leaving London, a number of influences persuaded me to broaden its scope. Doctoral work at Birmingham by my wife, Linda Jones, on the interplay of public and private motivations and roles in nineteenth-century Birmingham made me more confident about my treatment of John Morris, Charles Morrison and their associates. Peter Cain's work on Cobden and Tom Tomlinson's papers on the development of Indian commercial structure also emerged from the Birmingham department at this time. They offered pointers to a possible synthesis. So too did my reading of the contemporary literature on multinational corporations.

Many firms kindly allowed me access to their archives. I am indebted to Ashurst Morris Crisp, Baring Brothers, Dalgety, Lloyds International, Balfour Williamson, the Sun and Phoenix insurance companies, Kleinwort Benson, and many other firms.

The manuscript was read by several colleagues and friends and by two anonymous readers. I am most grateful for their comments. Robert Skidelsky took more than ordinary care in this and exerted a further influence of a more general sort through years of stimulating and entertaining conversation in and out of the classroom at Warwick. I have profited greatly from teaching with him on the M.A. course in international political economy originally designed by Fred Hirsch.

The greatest intellectual debt is to my wife, Linda. We are both historians, and this has made it possible for each of us to read and judge the other's work critically. This working relationship has continued, and indeed developed, as we have moved into new fields increasingly removed from orthodox empiricist history.

Finally, my thanks are due to Joy and Graham Gardner, not only for their help in preparing the book for publication, but for their friendship and support since I came to Warwick, to the University of Warwick itself for providing an atmosphere in which it is easy to trespass across disciplinary boundaries, and to my daughters Kate and Ellen, for keeping it all in proportion.

Charles Jones

Moseley, September 1986

Verdaderamente, señores, el capital inglés es un gran personaje anónimo, cuya historia no ha sido escrito aún.

Bartolomé Mitre

1 Introduction

THE ARGUMENT

There are two books here. The first is a history of international business in the nineteenth century; the second is an historiographic essay about why such a book has not been written before. The remainder of the first section of this chapter is devoted to a summary of the narrative and the principal arguments in the text that follows, while the second and third sections provide a slightly more discursive introduction to the history and the historiography, respectively. But even before embarking upon the summary the central argument should be introduced. There was, in the nineteenth century, a widespread expectation, especially among those engaged in commerce, that free trade would bring to an end the era of despotism and war. Merchants trading internationally were inclined to see themselves, and to be seen by others, as agents of an individualistic and progressive liberal revolution. But economic and technological stimuli forced changes upon a reluctant bourgeoisie: changes—including the spatial concentration of managerial authority, enlargement of scale in business organisation, and a *rapprochement* with the state—which finally rendered this class incapable of fulfilling its original political mission. In the long run, survival in changing markets proved incompatible with maintenance of the social and cultural identity and political capability of the cosmopolitan bourgeoisie. This progressive class resolved itself into reactionary nationalist fragments and, in so doing, created cultural conditions in which the history of its rise and fall would remain obscure for decades to come.

1

The narrative structure of the text is soon described. This first chapter is followed by five chronological chapters. The first and second of these examine the international trading world from three vantage points—Buenos Aires, India and Britain—and cover the period from about 1770 to 1860. Their argument, in brief, is that severe dislocation of international trade during the Revolutionary and Napoleonic Wars and the breakdown of longstanding mercantilist systems, coupled with the development of machine-based manufacturing techniques, led to successive waves of retirements and bankruptcies among merchants trading abroad in the early decades of the period, brought new patterns of mercantile migration and finance, and encouraged, to an exceptional degree, the mixing of merchants of different nationalities. In this way there came into being, by the middle years of the nineteenth century, a truly cosmopolitan bourgeoisie trading internationally under British naval protection. This is the rise of economic liberalism viewed from below: not the legislative history, not even the national movement in Britain against the Corn Laws, but the mundane chronicle of mercantilist structures at the limits of European dominion in irreversible decline.

The next chapter outlines some perennial problems which had long plagued international business operations, before going on to examine new sources of disruption which appeared or accelerated during the last third of the nineteenth century, especially improved methods of transport and communications. These are regarded as having upset the institutional basis of international capitalism by altering economies of scale in almost every sector, though not always in the same direction. Established firms sought out market niches which utilised their substantial capital and credit. Frequently, this meant going into sectors in which information, proprietary technology, close contacts with a state, or an indivisible management team conferred monopolistic advantages. In these sectors, vertical integration followed, as predicted (retrospectively) by the modern neo-classical theory of the firm, because the extreme imperfection of markets for intangible assets favoured administrative relations over market transactions at the margin, and because new capital-intensive storage, processing and transport techniques markedly increased vulnerability to upstream or downstream market disruption, providing a further motive for integration.

But vertical integration had clear spatial implications. In a period when European imports of raw materials and foodstuffs were growing rapidly, integration back from manufacturing towards sources of raw materials led firms from Europe to the lands of European settlement and to Africa and Asia. Conversely, forward integration, in theory, led producers of raw materials into Europe. In fact, until the very end of the nineteenth century, these extreme cases were less frequent than integration by middlemen based in European or overseas ports, and Chapter 4 is devoted to an examination of the adaptive strategies of this group, taking the cases of Thomas Mort, Gibbs Ronald & Co., and Frederick Dalgety in Australia, Dwarkanath Tagore in Calcutta, Robert Shewan in Hong Kong, Baron Mauá in Brazil, the Wanklyn brothers and the Tornquists in Buenos Aires, and Thomas Russell in New Zealand.

Only in Chapter 5 are the strategies developed simultaneously by metropolitan merchants, pure financiers and industrial capitalists in response to the very same stimuli of improved transport and communications, changes in commercial law and new processing technologies superimposed upon the manoeuvres of these peripheral capitalists. Here, the variety of experience of metropolitan merchants is illustrated by reference to the Holt, Booth, Swire and Lockett families, and Balfour, Williamson & Co., all originating in Liverpool; Edward Ashworth and Ludwig Knoop from Manchester; James Finlay & Co. from Glasgow; and, from London, Shaw Wallace & Co., Knowles & Foster, and Samuel Samuel & Co.

It is argued that central location, preferably in London, conferred an advantage because of ease of access to the capital market, because of the commercial importance of London, and because of its position as the centre of national and imperial decision-making. It was also attractive to a provincial and colonial bourgeoisie with social pretensions. The consequent centripetal tendency, already illustrated in passing, is emphasised by reference to Wernher Beit, the Mosenthals, and the Günthers, all of whom are seen as transferring their family operations and allegiances from North Europe to London. From further afield came Dalgety, the Bolivian Suárez family, the Sassoons and the im Thurns.

The remainder of the chapter is given over to a study of the internal tensions that developed within spatially extended, vertically integrated business groups and corporations. These tensions are held to have led to a marginalisation of firms which continued to be based outside Europe. Such firms are regarded as having been nudged towards secluded but relatively stagnant sectors or to strategies of alliance with regimes pursuing economic nationalist policies in their home states in their efforts to counter the growing competitive advantages of British and European-based firms.

A short sixth chapter examines the effects of all these disruptions and adjustments of the later nineteenth century on the cosmopolitan mercantile bourgeoisie and concludes that this class was effectively destroyed. Its basic social *and* business unit had been the family, extending, more widely, to a connexion or cousinhood within which business was transacted, apprentice clerks exchanged and marriage contracted. This integrated vehicle for social and economic transactions ceased to be effective and gave way, in the sphere of business, to the corporation. There were two main reasons for this—growing capital requirements and the need for technically skilled management—and together they liberated the bourgeois family from business constraints and made it a strictly social institution. This made possible an alignment and intermarriage of merchant families with landed and ruling groups, and so provided a social analogue to the growing political alignment of capital with populist or imperialist regimes which was to characterise the age of imperialism.

It is one thing to summarise the narrative, quite another to lay bare its structure. There are, I believe, five themes of importance, which receive very unequal treatment.

First, most basic and least examined, is technological change. The evolution of more regular, speedier and more capital-intensive systems of transport and communication and new techniques for the storage and processing of raw materials and foodstuffs is seen as the root cause of the institutional changes with which the book is explicitly concerned. There is no discussion of the ultimate source of technological change in the book. My predisposition is towards explanations which treat it as endogenous to society and look for ultimately cultural determinants of change.

The second theme follows directly from the first, and centres upon the characterisation of the firm. Here I have been content, at the theoretical level, with the neo-classical account pioneered by Coase and currently represented in work of the Reading group and Alan Rugman among others.[1] Firms are viewed as administrative structures at the interstices of markets for factors and final goods. The frontier between firm and market is set by the points of convergence of marginal costs of administration and of market transactions. Where I have found myself parting company with the economists is over their anachronistic application of mid-twentieth-century descriptive categories to the nineteenth century and, more fundamentally, their implicit assumption that a uniform set of descriptive terms can be developed to describe institutional change over historical time. A good deal of the early part of the book is devoted, often implicitly, to showing the inappropriateness of twentieth-century legalistic concepts of the firm and of nationality (let alone crudely individualistic notions of rational self-interest) to a world in which the same widely dispersed structures of kinship and acquaintance were central to bourgeois social *and* economic relations. In short, the superficially neo-classical account I have given of integration and other forms of structural adaptation to markets is, in fact, constrained by the available social possibilities, and just as much of the drama comes from changes in the institutional constraints (from natural to artificial, private to public, customary to legal) as from changes in markets.

The third theme is the political context of business history. Here there are both neo-classical and Leninist assumptions to be brought out into the open. I have worked with an assumption in the back of my mind, drawn from Frederick Lane's work of the 1940s and 1950s, that the state is a special sort of firm.[2] Lane cast it as the producer of protection from violence, which he characterised as a fourth factor of production. This is needlessly elaborate. Lanean protection may be characterised as an impure public good. To some extent states are natural monopolists in its supply because of their territorial basis, but there are limits to this, and capitalists, especially mercantile capitalists, are at one and the same time more aware than other people of inter-state variations in protection costs and more able to take advantage of them by foreign investment and migration.

This is a very crude theory of the state.[3] Accepted, however tentatively, it provides a novel reading of Lenin's *Imperialism*. Liberal critics have sometimes crudely portrayed the Marxist theory of the state as a relationship between basic economic forces and a political superstructure: the state as executive committee of the bourgeoisie. But if we now accept the neo-classical theory of the firm as an island of administration and hierarchy at the interstices of market relations and accept, too, the neo-classical theory of the state as a special kind of firm, it becomes clear that firms, as working parties of the bourgeoisie, should be viewed as just as much a part of the superstructure as states. Functionally, they are almost on a par with each other, except that the state has the distinctive role of setting the generally permitted level of monopoly for other economic agents. (The gulf that separates them is legitimacy.)[4]

The effect of this interpretation is to de-emphasise those conspiratorial, Hobsonian, elements in the classical theory of capitalist imperialism which play up the manipulation of the state by financiers, and to lay stress instead upon the increasingly nationalistic and corporatist character of the bourgeoisie as a single phenomenon with largely independent manifestations in, on the one hand, imperialist and populist states, and, on the other hand, bureaucratic and oligopolistic firms. This fits very well the architecture of Lenin's essay, with its clearly analogous and simultaneous, rather than causal and sequential, relationship between states and firms.[5] It also provides a rationale for the pursuit of business history in its own right, rather than for the light it might shed upon the history of colonial acquisitions and state imperialism.[6] Within this interpretation, the book is intended as a history of one aspect of the onset of imperialism.[7]

This working of the political theme, and the new, more autonomous status it confers on firms in the analysis of imperialism, explains the central position given to a fourth theme, the rise and fall of the cosmopolitan bourgeoisie, which provides the title and main narrative thread of the book. The history of the cosmopolitan bourgeoisie is, of course, not simply a chronicle; it is also a history of their consciousness. I regarded it as a centring upon Enlightenment doctrines concerning the causal links between commerce and peace, artistocracy and war, individualism and liberty. The cultural facet of imperialism is displayed in a collapse of this bourgeois tradition and a revival of corporate values expressed in spurious medievalism, adulation of the aristocracy, racism and militant nationalism. The late nineteenth-century bourgeoisie were free to follow this path because changes in business organisation had freed them and their families by alienating them to an extent from direct participation in business. But why did they *choose* to follow it? To some extent imagination was surely guided by interest. The cultural reconciliation of bourgeoisie and aristocracy followed the patterns of interest delineated by Hobson, or by Schumpeter in his chapter on export monopolism.[8] But this only shifts the problem; it does not solve it. Why did the Edwardian generation allow pecuniary interest to get the upper hand in situations where their Victorian forebears had, on the whole, been content to drive it in tandem with their long-range political programme of cosmopolitan liberalism?[9] It was surely loss of confidence in their own liberal ideology and a growing self-consciousness and awareness of liberalism *as* ideology at the end of the century that laid the British-based bourgeoisie, at least, open to the attractions of a chivalric revival to which they had proved quite resistant earlier. This loss of confidence went hand in hand with a shift from individualistic to conspiratorial interpretation of society. Both are well chronicled in the English fiction of *circa* 1890–1930, and I have drawn on Galsworthy, Conan Doyle and Chesterton to illustrate the new cast of mind. It is paralleled by and perhaps originates in the predicament of the entrepreneur slowly losing control of his undertaking as it becomes more bureaucratic, as negotiation takes the place of market exchange, as the office comes to dominate the parlour. The best available parable might be the gradual collapse of Paul Dombey Senior and the grasping of power by his confidential clerk, Carker.[10] The publication date of this perceptive novel, 1846, provides a salutory reminder that in the very year in which the Corn Laws were repealed, a year often seen as the start of a liberal interlude, the worm was already in the bud.

The final theme is historiographic. There are a great number of reasons why the writing of business history is problematic, and some will shortly be treated in detail. The only point which need be made at this stage is that one of the most serious obstacles in the way of any improvement in the position is the attitude of businessmen to their own history. Businessmen—especially British businessmen—although sometimes pompous, do not take themselves seriously. They see history as a story about the state; their own role is historical only in so far as it appears to support the state—through war production in the past or exports today. And the reason for this, which is also the reason why the historiographic theme is essential to the argument of the book and not just an introductory grumble, is that the cosmopolitan bourgeoisie lost its sense of mission and its belief in progress when its liberal political programme foundered upon the rocks of oligopolistic competition at the turn of the century. This is to say that the historiographic problem besetting business history is an outcome of that history, and can only be unjammed through this realisation. The loss of direction is reflected in much of the amateur corporate history which has been written this century and in the patterns of business patronage of historical writing. It is stultifying, since it prevents historical analysis from making the contribution it could make to efficient production. It is ironic, since it has led to a position where only Marxists really take the bourgeoisie seriously any more, and they are wrong to do so precisely because the business class no longer believes in itself.

COBDEN'S DREAM

Just now, identifying the rise and fall of a cosmopolitan bourgeoisie as the main narrative thread of the book, I suggested that bourgeois consciousness and its collapse were central to my account. Because it is accorded this privileged position a little more had better be said about it. Richard

Cobden provides a point of entry, precisely because he is not profound and in no way transcends his class, as intellectuals are apt to do. Cobden was never overawed by tradition. In Greece,

He was amazed to find the mighty states of Attica and Sparta within an area something smaller than the two counties of Yorkshire and Lancashire. 'What famous puffers those old Greeks were! Half the educated world in Europe is now devoting more thought to the ancient affairs of these Lilliputian states . . . than they bestow upon the modern history of the South and North Americas.'[11]

In Rome he visited the Sistine Chapel, but found it:

A deplorable misapplication of the time and talent of a man of genius to devote years to the painting of the ceiling of a chapel, at which one can only look by an effort that costs too much inconvenience to the neck to leave the mind at ease to enjoy the pleasure of the painting.[12]

There is more than a hint of Pooter here, but a Pooter read by tens of thousands, a Pooter with a seat in the House of Commons, a Pooter at the head of a successful national movement.

Richard Cobden's dream was of a world of nations living in amity. This was to be achieved through free trade, and it was the campaign for free trade in England that provided the chief focus of Cobden's public activities. For a number of reasons the Radical theory of the interconnexion of commerce and peace espoused by Cobden was largely forgotten after his death. This was partly because the element of social analysis which played so important a part in classical political economy slipped gradually away as the subject became more abstract in style. Also political opponents were inclined, whether deliberately or inadvertently, to simplify Cobden's arguments almost to vanishing point.[13] Disciples also played their part. Pacifists and idealists of the early twentieth century were still inclined to stress the value of liberal international economy in assuring peace, but they seldom advanced the original supporting arguments.

An educated person in the 1960s, living in the Anglo-Saxon world, might have been forgiven for thinking that the nineteenth-century liberal political justification for inter-national commerce had been based on just two arguments:

the Ricardian theory of comparative advantage, and a less formally expressed and rather improbable functionalist hypothesis to the effect that personal contacts of all kinds—the meetings of statesmen, student exchanges, cultural delegations and, not least, the constant meetings and transactions of businessmen of different nationalities—were inclined to foster understanding in the long run and create interest groups and climates of opinion unsympathetic to war. To be sure, material interest and public opinion were important for Cobden, but there was also a third argument, which he derived from eighteenth-century thinkers, and which is the most interesting aspect of his theory, both because it is the most plausible and because it is the most historically specific. This third argument has to do with the relation between international trade and domestic forms of government. It grows directly out of the Radical theory of the state.

The clearest exponent is Tom Paine. Paine supposed that ordered civil society arose naturally among men. 'It existed prior to government and would exist if the formality of government was abolished.'[14] The state was a later development. In a quasi-historical account he reasoned that:

It could have been no difficult thing in the early and solitary ages of the world, while the chief employment of men was that of attending flocks and herds, for a banditti of ruffians to over-run a country, and lay it under contributions. Their power being thus established, the chief of the band contrived to lose the name of Robber in that of Monarch; and hence the origin of Monarchy and Kings.[15]

The solution to the domestic political problem lay in the replacement of monarchy and aristocracy by democratic and republican forms of government. By analogy, the same sort of harmony, supported by natural or customary international law, would prevail in a world of many civil societies as was found in a society of many individuals. And as injustice entered into civil society through imposition of the state by coercive individuals, so war between nations was the fruit of a society of coercive states. 'War', Paine argued,

Is the common harvest of all those who participate in the division and expenditure of public money, in all countries. It is the art of *conquering at home*: the object of it is an increase of revenue; and as revenue cannot be increased without taxes, a pretence must be made for expenditures. In reviewing the history of the English Government, its wars and its taxes, a bystander, not blinded by prejudice, nor warped by interest, would declare, that taxes were not raised to carry on wars, but that wars were raised to carry on taxes.[16]

The practical implication of this line of thought was that only an end to hereditary and coercive forms of government would secure the twin objectives of Radical policy: individual freedom at home and peace between nations. The beauty of free trade was that it could be a means to both these ends. Free trade, of course, was not simply or even primarily a question of tariff reduction. Under the mercantile system states had granted trading monopolies along with delegated political and diplomatic functions to privileged groups of merchants. The call for free trade was therefore first and foremost an attack on the propriety of this form of state intervention in economic life, and an appeal for maritime trade to be opened to all who had the capital to undertake it.[17] Here, the argument concerning material interest was significant. It was believed that freedom to engage in commerce would result in an increase in aggregate national wealth. The state, which depended for its military effectiveness upon the size of its tax base relative to those of its rivals, could hardly afford to stand in the way of this, and so a virtuous spiral would develop. In these circumstances, wrote Immanuel Kant,

Civil freedom can no longer be so easily infringed without disadvantage to all trades and industries, and especially to commerce, in the event of which the state's power in its external relations will also decline. But this freedom is gradually increasing. If the citizen is deterred from seeking his personal welfare in any way he chooses which is consistent with the freedom of others, the vitality of business in general and hence also the strength of the whole are held in check. For this reason, restrictions placed upon personal activities are increasingly relaxed. And thus . . . *enlightenment* gradually arises.[18]

For Kant, therefore, the removal of legal constraints on commerce, forced upon states by their insatiable demand for funds, progressively undermined the coercive basis of government. For Cobden, perhaps rather more parochially, removal of the tariffs on imported grain encapsulated in the infamous Corn Laws became a prime objective because this, too, promised to undermine the position of the aristocracy: firstly, as landowners, benefiting directly or indirectly from high prices subsidised by the mass of consumers; and secondly, as an hereditary military and ruling caste for whom the revenue on imports was a significant source of funds for the support and equipment of the armed forces. It was reasoned that if the lost revenue were to be recouped, it could only be by direct taxation. But this, too, had political implications.

The essence of the Radical position was that free trade promised not only to benefit those who participated in it and yield an increase in aggregate communal wealth, as Smith and Ricardo had suggested, but that it promised to strengthen the bourgeoisie as a class, relative to the aristocracy. The bourgeoisie would now be better able to take part in public life, enter the House of Commons, and participate in government. In so doing they would represent their own direct material interests in peace, as merchants or manufacturers reliant on overseas markets or sources of supply, and they would also represent the interest in peace of working men who shared their dependence on the smooth operation of international markets and had come, through the shift from indirect to direct taxation, to a fuller awareness of the potential cost of warlike preparation and other redundant activities of the state.[19]

The realisation of this programme depended upon a progressive and universal strengthening of the bourgeoisie. But a number of serious obstacles stood in the way of this. Firstly, the bourgeoisie lacked confidence. Old habits of deference died hard. Secondly, as Joseph Schumpeter was later to explain, important sections of the bourgeoisie in many countries had risen to wealth and prominence as the privileged beneficiaries of state policy, often providing monarchs with an essential counterweight to landed classes.[20] Their interests, narrowly conceived, as well as the nationalist ideologies they had developed to justify themselves, stood in the way of the full realisation of free trade and capitalism.[21] And they were easily offended; Cobden and the English free traders of the 1840s found it wiser not to push for the introduction of free trade overseas, since this could so easily be interpreted as an attempt to suppress nascent European and North American manufacturing industries. The free traders laid themselves wide open to this by their charge that the Corn Laws, by preventing the United States and Germany from exchanging their corn for British merchandise, forced them into manufacturing.[22] Thirdly, it was already apparent that imperfect competition posed a threat. By the 1850s, Cobden, like Marx, 'could see quite clearly that concentrations of capital in the industrial sector had produced a new oligarchy as powerful as the old'.[23] This could easily drive the wedge of conflicting interest between manufacturer and consumer, employer and labour, and split the emerging anti-aristocratic alliance.

These obstacles to the achievement of Cobden's dream readily yield the outline of a history of the bourgeoisie in the nineteenth century. A confident class ready to play an independent role in government could only emerge from a history of economic and administrative success. The management of large aggregations of capital and labour together with the businesslike conduct of municipal affairs were an essential political apprenticeship.[24] The spread of free trade and democratic government to other lands depended, ultimately, on the replication of this pattern in country after country. Yet it was plain that the British commercial bourgeoisie, standing at the interstices of a host of semi-autonomous national or regional economies, was in a position peculiarly convenient for the promotion and advocacy of Radical ideology abroad. They were the mercurial, *déraciné*, light cavalry of capitalism. Again, the ability of capitalists to operate in relative autonomy, free from undue dependence on the state, would be a function of the sorts of activity in which they engaged—how large they became, how public, how directly relevant to the common wealth and the security of the state. Finally, the scale of enterprise had implications not only for the direct relationship between the bourgeoisie and the state, but also for relations with the workforce and consumers, and for the character of competition between firms and the prevalence of collusion. The essential features of mercantilism—its privileged groups, its transfer of resources from one section of the population to another, and its creation of real sectional interests in internal repression, imperialism and war—could creep back into society through the back door and ally with residual aristocratic elements to regain control of the state if a majority of the bourgeoisie did not succeed in maintaining its class alliance with the proletariat, operating an aggressively cost-cutting, atomistic economy, developing a property-owning democracy, and stubbornly resisting assimilation into the culture of the old ruling class.

Cobden's dream of a progressive bourgeoisie pursuing universal free trade as the means to democracy and peace became a nightmare towards the end of the century as new attitudes to colonial empire, enthusiasm for tariff reform, mounting expenditure on armaments and, finally, a great European war coincided with a wave of amalgamations, concentration of capital, the enoblement of leading businessmen, their extraordinary prevalence among the companions of Edward VII, their increasing hostility towards labour, and their steady movement into the Liberal Unionist Party and so, finally, to Conservatism. This cultural disaster, I shall argue, is only fully intelligible in the context of the economic history of the cosmopolitan bourgeoisie. Cobden had been precisely accurate in his identification of concentration of capital as the great threat to a liberal future.

THE TROUBLE WITH BUSINESS HISTORY

I have already suggested that the cultural and political collapse of the cosmopolitan bourgeoisie produced residual national bourgeoisies which were, in most instances, so captivated by local emblems of national authenticity and intimidated by the overwhelming legitimacy of the state that they became incapable of recognising or formulating their own history as anything but a derivative of state history.

The practical working out of this theme may be seen in several interconnected issues.

To begin with, it should be clear that this book represents a move into relatively unoccupied territory. Social historians working in the tradition pioneered by E. P. Thompson, have rightly been concerned to develop the neglected history of the common people and the labour movement. In much the same way, historical writing about newly independent states in

Africa and Asia, and even about the longer established Latin American republics, has for some years been inclined to concentrate on indigenous populations and movements. As Tony Hopkins put it ten years ago: 'a balance sheet, especially an expatriate one, was an inadequate passport for an academic world which had [by 1960] become preoccupied with radio-carbon dates, king lists, sickle cells and *jihads*.'[25] Both of these tendencies were part of a reaction against national and imperial historiographic traditions which were unashamedly Eurocentric, saw the records of the state as the paramount source for scholarly work, and took the rise and fall of nations and empires as the only legitimate themes.

But the enthusiasm for neglected classes and downtrodden nationalities coupled with an irrational disdain for the bourgeoisie tended to draw the attention of the Left away from a third area which had also been neglected by traditional historiography. The commercial middle classes, shunned by social historians and historians of today's Third World, were of interest to British political, cultural and economic historians only in so far as they contributed to national political, cultural and economic life; and their activities were studied all too often in isolation from one another and accorded a merely instrumental value. This was partly a consequence of the very different methodological assumptions of different schools of historians. It was also, however, a result of the failure of business history to perform an integrative role by developing an eclectic attitude to sources, to abandon corporate history in favour of a more thematic market or industrial history, or to develop a new relationship with its patrons.

The chief obstacles in the way of any improvement in the condition of business history have been two. The first of these is subservience to mainstream economics. Business history has generally been viewed, and has viewed itself, as a poor cousin of economic history, which in turn has been a beggar at the economists' feast. This might have mattered less if economists had taken more interest in firms. Economic historians, of course, could never entirely do without firms, but have tended in recent years to emulate economists of a generation ago by devising strategies for evading the central issues of class, nationality, the pattern of authority within the firm, and relations with states. Once upon a time those whose fundamental disciplinary allegiance was to economics could plead that these problems were not their concern. Their field was the analysis of market relations and the evolution over time of national economies. The firm was, in essence, a special kind of utility-maximising individual. If it failed to employ its resources in such a way as to maximise the return on capital in the long run it would surely perish. Even though firms replaced or substituted for markets where transaction costs were relatively high, they were ultimately constrained by competition in markets.[26] One could therefore safely ignore those firms that took a broader view of their function in society, whether because of the balance of internal forces, the predilections of individual entrepreneurs, or especially close relations with the state. These were non-economic matters, the concern of other specialists; and, in any case, firms carrying this sort of lumber could not win in the end, because they would be driven out by more devoted maximisers.

It is more than a generation since anyone believed all this. The notions of constrained rationality and satisficing, the theory of collective goods, theories of rent-seeking behaviour and the modern theory of the firm have all emerged from economics to enrich contemporary understanding of firms and, indeed, of all large organisations.[27] In spite of these advances in microeconomic theory, the history of business firms has continued to be valued by economic historians chiefly for the light it may shed on macroeconomic questions. Do the histories of British firms towards the end of the nineteenth century provide evidence for a damaging general failure of entrepreneurship? Did City firms starve manufacturing industry of capital by their tendency to direct funds overseas? I would contend that this preoccupation with the *national* economy stems from the same bourgeois crisis of confidence that gave rise to the emphasis on *national* history. The deleterious effect of the inherent nationalism of the neo-classical tradition upon business history is to be seen, perhaps, as the issue of an incestuous union of intellectual siblings.

And, in spite of encouraging developments within microeconomics, at least one major vice of the empiricist neo-classical tradition still permeates the contribution of economists to debate in business history. This is the continuing desire for a universal descriptive language, and it is illustrated nowhere better—or in a way more relevant to the themes of this book—that in the debate of the past decade over the criteria for distinguishing direct from portfolio foreign investment.

Until about ten years ago, economists counted as direct only those investments which involved managerial control and did not employ the medium of the stock exchange. This worked very well for the middle years of the twentieth century as a way of distinguishing investment by parent corporations in overseas subsidiaries over which they retained strategic control from portfolio investments undertaken by rentiers through the stock exchange where no control was exercised. The practical effects of employing this criterion, based as it was on twentieth-century practices and organisational forms, was to yield statistics which showed direct foreign investment to have grown rapidly since the turn of the century from a low base, to be a tactic more often employed in the past by manufacturing and extractive firms than by banks or commercial corporations.[28]

Then a succession of papers upset the paradigm.[29] It was realised that in the very different legal environment of the nineteenth-century corporations formed under British or European law had often been able to do business overseas through unincorporated branches. In addition, companies operating in this way were often effectively parts of larger groupings of capital, even though their shares were widely dispersed. Many limited companies were recognised by contemporaries to be the creatures of small groups of entrepreneurs, commonly organised in unincorporated partnerships or loose syndicates, who sustained their controlling position by the weight of personal reputation and patronage, the prestige of their central financial or mercantile firms, the creation of webs of interlocking directorships, or the exaction of long-term agency or management contracts, rather than by large holdings of shares.

Some scholars reacted to this discovery by dropping the second of the two criteria which had previously been used to distinguish direct from portfolio investment, so that control alone became the hallmark of direct foreign investment. A slightly distinctive line was taken by John Stopford, who posited a third, intermediate category, which he called expatriate investment, to cover the troublesome middle ground.[30] Either way, the revision was large. Instead of 10 per cent, more than 30 per cent of British foreign investment in 1914 was now characterised as direct, with proportionate consequences for interpretation of the relative importance of British and United States direct foreign investment, for the rate of growth of direct foreign investment in the long run, and for the distinctiveness of political responses to post-war direct foreign investment.

All of this provides a great temptation for the historian of nineteenth-century international business history, for it rescues his subject from oblivion and makes it seem of greater contemporary relevance. In so far as the argument is an empirical one, I am inclined to fall for the temptation and back the new criterion and the new interpretations. But it is not *simply* an empirical argument. What is at stake is not just whether one criterion or another is valid, but why it is that one replaced the other, and whether *any* single arrangement of descriptive terms and criteria can cover all the data in this case, and perhaps in many other cases.

Let us take replacement first. It is clear that the old criteria for distinguishing between direct and portfolio investment were devised, largely for national accounting purposes, by economists for whom the paradigm of direct foreign investment was the wholly-owned overseas subsidiary of a corporation such as IBM or Coca Cola. It is less evident, but, I believe, equally true, that the revised distinction, allowing control alone to be the deciding factor, has coincided with a shift since the 1970s towards joint ventures and other less monolithic structures of ownership, and that the revision has been carried out by people interested at least as much in the management of resources once an investment has taken place as in its effects on national accounts.

The first element in the social conditioning of the revision therefore stems from the environment and objectives of the researchers. The second has to do with the culturally derived character of the terms in which both the old and the new distinctions must perforce be couched. The most important of these are nationality and control.

Any distinction between domestic and foreign investment requires unambiguous definition of the nationality of investors. Both the old and the new criteria for distinguishing between direct, portfolio and expatriate investment require unambiguous definitions of the nationality of the controllers of a business. But how is this to be achieved in other than a spuriously legalistic manner over a period of years when not only did the place of residence of very large numbers of mercantile families change, but, in addition, the concept of nationality itself and the importance attaching to it were in flux? The point will not be laboured here, but in later chapters the reader should bear in mind that the controllers of the British-based international corporations of the last third of the nineteenth century included a great many men, like the Günthers, Frederick Dalgety, Thomas Russell or Cecil Rhodes, whose nationality was ambiguous. The character of that ambiguity is outlined in Chapters 2 and 3. It is a problem which cannot be defined out of existence without doing violence to the genuine doubt which existed in the mid-nineteenth-century bourgeois mind about the future of the state system.

Many objections to the new distinction between direct and portfolio investment have centred upon the problem of managerial control. Writing of the Rangoon Oil Company in 1871, T. A. B. Corley claimed that it represented a *direct* investment because directors in Britian 'exercised a degree of control through the telegraph, denied to their predecessors'.[32] The implication is that any case where there is less than close supervision will not count as direct investment: mere responsibility without effective control is not enough. A related point is raised by P. J. Buckley and B. R. Roberts. British-registered land companies operating in the United States in the late nineteenth century were not really instances of direct foreign investment, they contend, even when control was exercised from Britain. The reason for this was that the investment was held by individuals and syndicates, not by companies. It was therefore 'akin to a portfolio flow'.[33] Here the implication is that control, other than by a parent company, is unlikely to prove effective. This is, of course, to confuse the development of management structures with the parallel history of legal forms of enterprise. Effective management does not require corporate form; the law does. Equally, there have been many properly constituted corporations which have lacked adequate systems of managerial control. But the serious points at issue are that it is not the effectiveness of control but the intention to control that must surely be the criterion for distinguishing direct from portfolio investment, and that the possibilities of management at a distance (and so the plausibility of such an intention) have been in a constant state of flux, making the attainment of objective criteria here, as with nationality, a fool's errand.

My charge, in short, is that successive interpretations of the direct–portfolio distinction, and even the basic concepts in terms of which any such distinction must be couched, are culturally derived and, as such, are unstable in the long run. Economists in this small area have been characteristically unwilling to realise and exploit this fact. Historians can avoid it only be sheltering under the skirts of a positivistic social science.

There has, of course, been a dissenting tradition in economic history. Indeed the subject originated, in England, as a dissenting group challenging the increasing abstraction and claims to universality of economics.[34] Historians writing in this tradition, from Ashley onwards, have examined the archives of firm after firm paying close attention to motive, to organisation, and to public affairs. Without their work, much of it published in the 1950s and 1960s and now no longer fashionable, this book could certainly not have been written.[35] However, this tradition, originating in public conflict over methodology, lost its nerve in the post-war era, accepted its status subordinate to economics in the universities, and declared itself not merely empirical but dogmatically empiricist. It fell into the positivist trap, regarding the history it was producing as value-free, factual, and in no sense *engagé*. Honest men and women, the practitioners regarded themselves as quite free from the influence of the firms they wrote about, and which were frequently their patrons. They reflected little, in print at least, on the social circumstances which had brought them and their patrons together. This is not surprising. Virtually the whole of the Anglo-Saxon intelligentsia had fallen under the spell of Karl Popper. Economics reigned supreme among the social sciences.[36] People took it very seriously. Economic historians, relieved to be on the right side in the battle between scientific and traditional history, counted more and more things without troubling too much about the methodological questions of why the surviving documentary record made some things so much more countable than others; or why, of those things which were countable, some apppeared so very much more interesting than others. This book, for example, is full of hypotheses which are quantifiable in principle. In virtually no case can anything be done about this in what is essentially an illustrated essay, because raw data in the primary sources, where they exist, have not been gathered and processed in even the most rudimentary way.[37] Doubtless, the spasmodic and fragmentary survival of business records has much to do with this; yet there are other cases where the ingenious use of surviving public records might have been attempted, but has not.[38] The only plausible reason for this is that the questions on which these data would shed light have not been considered important by the new economic historians.

The heavy hand of neo-classical economics with its positivist methodology has been only part of the problem. The second substantial reason for the current disarray of business history has been the failure of businessmen to realise their own historical significance or to reflect such recognition in their patronage of history. This problem is undoubtedly more marked in Britain than in the United States. There, business history has a place in the business schools, and businessmen tend to have a keener sense of strategic development over time. In Britain, businessmen may be divided into two camps on the question of the importance of history. The old guard value history and have commissioned many corporate histories of varying quality. A more recent generation, educated in the business schools, have come to look to quantitative and analytical management techniques to rescue them from history. History appears to be against them, so they try to turn their backs on it.

Reverting, briefly, to the old guard, it is true that many of the histories they have commissioned have been extremely slight.

Economic historians, especially the very few who specialise in the history of firms themselves, have tended to be very scathing and dismissive.[39] They appear in a better light when viewed, not as failed attempts at some scholarly ideal of the ultimate corporate history, but as primary sources of evidence on the self-image of the business community at the date of publication, and as sources—sometimes secondary, sometimes primary—for the social rather than the economic history of business. There is great variety in this literature, as might be expected, but the prevailing themes are a nostalgic preoccupation with the role of the individual—all those lists of branch managers and directors, all those photographs of indistinguishable besuited men—and most of all a universal conviction that the firm is a *private* enterprise which enters into public history only vicariously. This is shown in the extraordinary—even disfiguring—prominence given to participation in both world wars, and to any contact with royalty, no matter how irrelevant to the main business of the firm, in one after another of the second- and third-rate histories.

I recall a visit to one prominent manufacturer of fire-fighting equipment. I was introduced to an employee of many years' service. Together we descended into the cellars of the factory, to a small vaulted room almost like a chapel, the walls hung with memorabilia and photographs. 'Those servants of the Company who fell in the two World Wars . . .', of course; but my companion drew me on to a corner where the photographs were most faded. Here was the history of the firm: the nobility of England pictured outside their country houses with their male household and outdoor staff grouped formally around fire engines of the 1880s and 1890s, sometimes in elaborate uniforms into which they could hardly have had time to change before dealing with a fire. And here, like an icon, the supreme treasure: an oriental despot suspended against the wall of his palace in an elaborate sling, his serenity marvellously undisturbed by the ludicrous inelegance of his posture. This, I was told, was the last Sultan of Turkey trying out the escape equipment supplied for his palace by the firm.

For a great many businessmen, then, history has been the history of government, of states, of the aristocracy, of wars; not of labour, certainly, but not of their own class either. This inability to see themselves at the centre of the drama naturally had its effect on the disposition of the bourgeoisie to produce and retain records. They moved from one house to another more frequently than the landed classes, and this must have taken its toll of what documentation they did produce. In addition, they allowed themselves, in general, less leisure. All these factors limited their output of diaries and letters and the survival of what they did produce. I can think of no quasi-public diary of a business hostess to compare with the stream of journals and correspondence, written with half an eye on publication, by the political and intellectual hostesses of the nineteenth century.[40] But the root cause of this dearth was a lack of self-regard.

There are exceptions. Among the very largest firms—industrial giants like ICI or Unilever, major banks, or extractive companies such as British Petroleum or Rio Tinto-Zinc—there has been a much clearer recognition of the value of the history of a business organisation in its own right. This recognition by the directors has been reflected in appropriate and distinguished histories.[41] Yet even these valuable works create a problem for the historian of business in general and of international business especially. In effect, the system of private commissioning of corporate histories ensures that the literature reflects the distribution of business power at the time of writing, and so insidiously misrepresents that past. Through no fault of any individual author, the scholarly literature on British business history is now by and large devoted to how the firms which have dominated the British economy over the past thirty years first came into being and rose to prominence.[42] But history is not just about how things came to be as they are. It is also about how things once were. And a history which simply traces to their origins current styles of management, current legal forms, currently dominant industries, and currently successful firms must almost certainly fail through its inability to encounter the context within which institutions first emerged in anything like a balanced and detached manner. It must also prove ephemeral because of its attachment to the present.

The scholarly corporate histories raise a second problem. The companies that have commissioned them have clearly been exceptional in their success and maturity, so that the heavy volumes are apt to stand like tombstones at the dignified end of a long life. But they have been exceptional in another way too. They have, by and large, been public and bureaucratic in style. They have, in short, been the corporations most closely resembling states.[43] This is only to be expected. If my argument about bourgeois loss of confidence is correct, then it is precisely those firms which are most like states that will feel most entitled to have their histories written. Moreover, it is these firms that will have kept the most state-like archives and will therefore seem the most suitable candidates for scholarly treatment to historians whose judgement of the practicability of a research project will be formed by setting the primary sources against the paradigm of European public records.[44]

By bringing forward social arguments to account for the poor condition into which neo-classical economics and the business establishment have, between them, brought business history, I invite the classical riposte to all sociology of knowledge. What makes *me* immune from social influences? But can *I* stand outside the game and comment on it when there is clearly nowhere outside society for me to stand?

First of all, it should be said that the firms chosen to illustrate the themes of this book in subsequent chapters are not to be regarded as a representative sample of all firms active in international business. They have been chosen, within the constraints of a very patchy and eccentric literature and a necessarily limited acquaintance with primary materials, to illustrate my own interpretation. In addition, though it may not always seem so, they have been selected for their ability to provide lines of continuity from one chapter to another and cut down the number of names and individuals with which the reader has to cope. But this does not make my selection arbitrary. It is in fact quite unclear by what criteria a *representative* group of nineteenth-century international firms could be assembled. Representative of what? Plainly the criteria for selection would constitute an interpretation of the history of the period. An interpretation must precede and inform any selection of cases. In admitting this, I am placing myself at no disadvantage against those who might contest my interpretation.

I am less happy about geographical selection. Here it would have been better to have said more about the United States as well as India and Latin America in the early chapters. North America loomed large as a destination for capital and mercantile migration. I have no better excuse here than to say that the secondary literature proved unyielding, while that on India and the East did not.

It should also be said that what follows is at times very descriptive, even anecdotal. This is not because I believe there is no place for the analytical techniques of empiricist economic history. It is because, for reasons I have already explained, the literature and sources, the basic taxonomy of the subject, and the interpretative literature just are not in the kind of shape at present that would permit the successful application of sophisticated techniques.

But preliminaries and apologies aside, I would respond to the challenge of the apparently reflexive character of criticisms emphasising the social origins of knowledge in the following way. First, sociology of knowledge is not simply an explanation of error, but also of truth.[45] And I would claim truth for my own interpretation of the past because it is not merely consistent with the facts as we know them, but also provides a plausible explanation of why its major rival exists and is false. This will work so long as the social explanation of my own interpretation does not also imply its falsity.

What is this explanation? My view of international business history is that of the son of a Liverpool bourgeois family born in the middle years of the twentieth century to parents old enough to possess and transmit childhood memories of the city in its Edwardian heyday but young enough to ride high as entrepreneurs in the 1960s on what may prove to have been, for Liverpool, the very last long boom. My parents tried, by long-established methods, to translate me from their provincial elite into a national elite. But, as sometimes happens, public school and Cambridge distanced me in some degree both from my origins and from the destination my parents had intended for me. In short, the explanation of my interpretation is also the authority for it. It is that I stand both inside and outside the bourgeois experience of one of the great nineteenth-century trading cities. My interpretation is in the broadest sense autobiographical. Even the patterns of diversification and migration which I have used to make sense of nineteenth-century business history are akin to those which my parents characteristically used to place people socially and explain their circumstances. So my escape route from the apparent dilemma of the sociologist of knowledge is that of Karl Mannheim. It relies upon self-consciousness and perspective. I take the realist view that in the study of society as much as in natural sciences the ultimate criteria of truth and falsity lie in an external, objective world. But I also accept that:

Only as we succeed in bringing into the area of conscious and explicit observation the various points of departure and of approach to the facts which are current in scientific as well as popular discussion, can we hope, in the course of time, to *control* the unconscious motivations and presuppositions which, in the last analysis, have brought these modes of thought into existence. A new type of objectivity in the social sciences *is* attainable not through the exclusion of evaluations but through the critical awareness and control of them.[46]

And, again with Mannheim, I take the view that to be in such a position of control is in part a matter of good fortune. 'It is one of the fundamental insights of the sociology of knowledge—he wrote—that the process by which collective-unconscious motives become conscious cannot operate in every epoch, but only in a quite specific situation.'[47] I am lucky to have been in a position to tell this story in what I believe is an illuminating way.

2 The Pattern of International Commerce

One of the clearest lessons of the debate about direct and portfolio investment is that the concept of nationality and the importance attached to it have changed quite profoundly over time and that this cannot be ignored with impunity by the historian. In this chapter and the next, the elasticity of nationality will be explored as the image of a cosmopolitan bourgeoisie is gradually developed and explored. The mid-twentieth century has been a time of strong and competing nationalisms. By contrast, the middle years of the nineteenth century saw a world of international trade and finance which was in many respects highly integrated and cosmopolitan. It had not always been so. During the mercantilist era the states of Europe placed substantial restrictions on trade and attempted to reserve certain trades and manufactures to privileged groups of their own nationals. This was either done by direct state action or by delegation of political functions along with economic privileges to some form of regulated corporation. Long-distance trade in particular was subject to these methods because of the important function it was believed to play in assuring the strength of the state, whether by training mariners, securing strategic materials, or obtaining bullion.

During the late eighteenth and early nineteenth centuries the mercantilist empires broke down. At the same time profound changes took place not only in the location, techniques and costs of manufacture, but also in the geographical pattern and composition of international trade in manufactured goods. The broad effect of these changes was to drive out of business many of the established merchants of the eighteenth century and, at first, to encourage manufacturers to market their goods directly to new markets overseas. Yet before long, new and innovative intermediaries developed: wholesale warehouses to serve the export trade, and a new kind of international firm, the commission agency, comprising partners of limited capital but extensive resourcefulness, backed by the financial strength of London acceptance houses or merchant bankers.

All this required migration. Continental merchants and bankers settled in London and the textile regions of the North of England. Sons of British and European manufacturers and merchants travelled the world in search of export markets, and often settled in some foreign trading port only to develop a business quite tangential to the original family concern. The mercantile diaspora embraced all the trading and manufacturing nations: Catalans, Basques, Germans, Danes, Chinese, Parsees, Jews, Armenians, Portuguese, Greeks, Dutch, North Americans, Scots and English. The outcome was a cosmopolitan trading community centred on London in which nationality was often very blurred. It was a community in which partnerships between men of differing distinct nationalities were not uncommon. English was widely used as a common language. Miscegenation also played its part. It was a dispersed community, spread out across the trading cities of the world, in any one of which a man of middling origins might make his way among acquaintances and friends of friends on the basis of little more than a letter of introduction and a clean record, and perhaps not even that. Finally, while it was substantially, though by no means entirely, a Protestant world, its most fundamental legitimising ideology was a secular one— economic liberalism: a profound faith in the collective virtue of aggregated individual self-interest and the moral validity of market sanctions.

It was this community and its ideology that were to collapse in the years after 1890, sending firms and individuals racing from the apron strings of newly assertive states. Nationalism and regulation, imperialism and racism were the hallmarks of the *fin de siècle*. The catastrophe of cosmopolitan liberalism is at the heart of this story, for it did much to shape the multinational corporations of the twentieth century and mark them off from their predecessors; but its significance cannot be grasped without a sense of the social order that preceded it.

Three examples will be enough. In Buenos Aires, Spanish mercantilism gave way to British-dominated but extremely cosmopolitan mercantile culture, well integrated with the local landed and governmental elites. In the East, British mercantilism, in the shape of the East India Company, was gradually replaced by a new generation of private traders, while administration passed to the British Raj and land remained in local hands. In Britain, merchants and bankers from all over Europe redesigned or adapted eighteenth-century metropolitan institutions to meet new needs, while, to the North, the marketing arrangements of industrial Britain were revolutionised.

BUENOS AIRES

The Argentine example is especially instructive since it shows a number of conflicting movements all contributing to a single outcome in an elegant liberal parable. Initially, in the sixteenth and seventeenth centuries, Buenos Aires had played a peripheral role in the Spanish imperial system, essentially a strategic outpost to check Portuguese southward expansion. Gradually, however, its economic advantages as a base for the supply of the leading South American mining centre of Potosí in Upper Peru became apparent. Illicit Dutch and British ships called in defiance of Spanish restrictions to trade cloth, slaves and hardware for silver and vicuña wool.[1] In an effort to hold the empire together and reconquer markets for its reviving metropolitan manufacturing industries the Spanish Crown was eventually driven in 1778 to legitimise use of the River Plate route for the supply of Upper Peru, even though this offended entrenched interests along the old official trade route by way of Callao, on the Pacific coast.[2] One result of this reform was a threefold increase in legitimate trade between Buenos Aries and Spain between 1748–53 and 1796.[3] Indeed, legitimate trade with the Empire as a whole increased by about 400 per cent in the years after 1778.[4] It also contributed to a fivefold increase in the average level of migration from Spain to

America between 1710–30 and 1780–90. To Buenos Aires came remnants of the old Irish gentry, in flight from British rule by way of Spain, Sephardic Jews from Portugal, but, most of all, Galicians, Basques and Catalans, men from the peripheral regions of Spain, intent on mercantile careers.[5]

The most successful of all these immigrants was Juan Esteban de Anchorena y Zundueta, who was born in 1730 and left Spain in 1765. Starting in a small way of business as a Buenos Aires shopkeeper, he was soon concerned in trade with the interior. Importing slaves and European manufactured goods, at first on consignment and later for his own account, he travelled up country to sell in Tucuman and beyond. The collection of local produce for export was a logical extension of this trade, a function of the growing difficulty of finding sufficient specie to cover Upper Peruvian import requirements. Business prospered, and before long Anchorena became a member of the *cabildo* or council of Buenos Aires, and also of the *real consulado* or chamber of commerce, and the militia.[6]

On the death of Juan Esteban in 1808 control of the business passed to his sons, of whom the eldest, Juan José Cristobal de Anchorena, was the most active. The family responded to the uncertainties of the revolutionary period by diversification. Like so many others at this time, they dabbled in the arms trade. Faced with competition in their general trade from British firms after 1806 they opened a branch in Rio de Janeiro and established connexions with firms in Liverpool and London.[7] Increasingly, however, as the new century advanced, the family directed its attention to the acquisition of land, political influence and office. Tomás Manuel de Anchorena, third son of Juan Esteban, was most conspicuous in this sphere, with estates of about 1200 square miles in the Province of Buenos Aires (an area comparable to Barbados or Luxembourg) by the middle of the nineteenth century. Some forty years later Juan Anchorena (1829–95), a son of Tomas Manuel, owned one of the largest fortunes in Agrentina, while, in the present century, Juan Oddone found the Anchorenas still among the ten biggest landowning families in Buenos Aires Province.[8]

The Anchorenas were exceptional only in the degree of their success. The Azcuenagas and the Basavilbasos, both from the

Basque country, had experienced a comparable if less spectacular rise under less favourable circumstances a generation before. Subsequently, the bankers José de Carabassa and Carlos Casado de Alisal, the first of Basque origin and the second from Palencia in León, would be among many who would follow a similar path. It is the familiar rags to riches story. And as is so often the way, though they may have struck contemporary society in their country of adoption as 'hard, ruthless and parsimonious men', vulgar or quaint by reason of their class and regional origins, these men almost without exception began with some capital, albeit meagre, and a sound commercial training.[9]

This influx of immigrant merchants to Buenos Aires and their subsequent absorption into the existing landed oligarchy should not be viewed as a once and for all occurrence. It was simply the first wave in a continuing process of mercantile migration which would continue well into the nineteenth century. Next came the Yankees; after them, the British and the Germans.

United States merchants and mariners had been obliged to search out new areas of trade to compensate for the loss of their once extensive intercourse with British Caribbean dependencies in the aftermath of the War of Independence. One contemporary, describing a common pattern of trade between 1798 and 1806, explained how North American ships would call first at southern ports to pick up raw cotton for sale in Europe. The proceeds would then be invested in a miscellany of goods, usually including textiles, for the South American and West African markets. Next they would go south to Africa to barter for slaves who, when necessary, could provide the pretext for an officially illegal but tolerated trade in contraband goods at Buenos Aires. Loaded with hides and tallow, the Americans would then set sail once again for Europe— Amsterdam or Hamburg according to the political climate— before taking on a final general cargo. Though all the intermediate journeys might offend in one way or another against current United States regulations, the first and last legs were irreproachable, and the silver earned by the trade served the growing Far East trade of the New England ports which has already been mentioned.[10] By contrast, many sailed directly south from the 1780s to hunt whales in the Antarctic Ocean or seals on the coasts of Patagonia and southern Chile. Typically, they would take on salt at the Cape Verde Islands before turning south-west to catch, dry and cure sealskins in Patagonia, where they traded in a small way with local Indian and Spanish communities for silver. Carrying skins and silver, they next crossed the Pacific, returning to Boston or New Haven after voyages of two or three years, laden with tea and silks from China. In this way the North Americans came to rival the British in the scale of their China trade within a few years.[11]

These sealers and petty smugglers were ideally qualified to take advantage of the Spanish wartime order of November 1797 which permitted neutral vessels to participate freely in the carrying trade of the empire, finally abandoning the intra-imperial free trading experiment that had begun in 1778. Though this concession was formally revoked two years later, the Americans had by this time established personal contacts which would enable them to come and go more or less regardless of Madrid in future.

Among the sealers-turned-merchant was David Curtis DeForest, a New Englander whose travels brought him to Buenos Aires by way of the Patagonian seal coast in 1802, there to learn the local conventions and procedures governing illicit trade. Not until 1806, however, did DeForest manage to find the backing he needed to establish himself in the River Plate. Initially lacking capital of his own, he appears to have acted as a commission agent, selling goods consigned to him by East Coast United States houses, buying nutria furs on behalf of John Jacob Astor and receiving commission on these transactions. During the British invasions and their aftermath he was protected by Bernardino Rivadavia, future leader of the United Provinces of the River Plate and advocate of the Enlightenment. Then came DeForest's great opportunity as the Argentines declared their independence in 1810 and commenced a war with Spain. At the start of hostilities DeForest found himself well placed to supply Baltimore-built ships to the patriots for use against Spanish merchantmen.

During these years of widespread warfare the East Coast United States ports performed a second function which helped shape the nineteenth-century Buenos Aires commercial community. It was estimated that they took about half the annual output of the Silesian linen industry, of which an unknown but substantial proportion was shipped south to Latin America for sale.[12] Baltimore, in particular, became an entrepôt for German goods destined for South America, which had formerly passed through Spain.[13] Much of this enterprise was in the hands of German Americans, some of whom, by specialising in the River Plate trade, would eventually settle in Argentina. In this way the Tornquists, later to become leaders in Argentine business affairs, reached Buenos Aires by way of Baltimore, Mecklenburg and Hamburg, from more remote late seventeenth-century origins in Switzerland.[14] Georg Tornquist, the first of the family to leave Europe, was a merchant in Baltimore until he returned to Hamburg in 1803. His eldest son, Georg Peter Ernst, who set up as an importer in Buenos Aires in 1823, may have been influenced and assisted by connexions established by his father while at Baltimore.

New York also had its part to play. There, German-born John C. Zimmermann arrived in 1808 to work as a clerk in the export-import house of Frederick and Franz Diederichs & Co. There he met his future wife, Helena Halbach, the niece of his employers and daughter of an ironmaster of Remscheid in Zimmermann's native Duchy of Berg. Halbach exported to France and Spain. It is not known whether he was selling, through the Diederichs, to an established Spanish American clientele before 1812, but this much is clear: when the firm of Diederich & Co. reconstituted itself after a bankruptcy brought on by the Anglo-American War of 1812, Zimmermann was still associated with the brothers and their partners, Señor Vasquez; a year later he sailed from Baltimore on board a schooner bound for Buenos Aires, its cargo consigned to DeForest. To complete the picture, Halbach's son Francisco came to Buenos Aires in 1818, where he joined his brother-in-law's firm, Lynch Zimmermann & Co., doubtless bringing a valuable Ruhr connexion.[15]

As for the British, their goods had reached Spanish America in substantial quantities since the seventeenth century by a combination of licit and illicit trade, but they themselves had seldom established a permanent presence. In 1713, by a clause in the Treaty of Utrecht, the British South Sea Company was given the *asiento*, a contract to supply African slaves to Spanish America. Similar arrangements to cover this large and lucrative trade had been made before, most recently with French merchants, but under this new treaty the British were permitted to operate through an unprecedented number of ports, to own land and build premises, to establish resident factors and, by a supplementary treaty of 1716, to store at their Buenos Aires factory any goods left over after bartering with the Africans.[16] Most important in the present context was the right of residence and *internación* by which servants of the company were allowed to travel and trade in the interior.[17] This permitted the English for the first time to gain intimate knowledge of demand in different regional markets and establish personal contact with dealers in inland centres. Even after the loss of the *asiento* and the demise of the company, intelligence gathered during these years continued to bear fruit. The erstwhile factor in Buenos Aires, Robert Mayne, continued to export goods from Britain to the River Plate for his own account through agents in Cadiz. He abandoned the slave trade and his Buenos Aires factory in 1752, but his family continued to operate one of the most notable English houses in Cadiz until nearly the end of the century.[18]

Another of the handful of Englishmen who maintained direct contact with Spain by extensive travel and residence was Antony Gibbs, who came of a West Country family widely engaged in the export of Newfoundland salt cod and English woollens to Mediterranean ports and the return trade in wine, wool and other primary products.[19] Gibbs began his mercantile career apprenticed to an Exeter house in 1774, but soon became partner in the firm of Munckley Gibbs & Richards. His business in the last quarter of the eighteenth century appears to have been based on the export of textiles, but fruit and wine provided convenient if risky means of remitting the proceeds of textile sales back home, and for this purpose Gibbs joined in a further partnership with Juan Pomar, of Malaga.[20] Gibbs and his son pursued a halting trade through the difficult wartime years with the help of Spanish and Hispanicised Irish partners in Cadiz, and in consequence they were in a position to benefit from their long experience and Lima connexions by making direct contact with South American markets in the new century.

By and large, however, the lines of personal continuity in Anglo-Hispanic commerce from the eighteenth to the nineteenth centuries were very few. This was no accident. During the reign of Charles III (1759–1788), Spain had embarked upon a last determined attempt at general reform. The paramount concern of imperial defence led the Crown to try to engineer an expansion of the fiscal base of the Empire by promoting metropolitan manufacturing industry and imperial trade at the expense of the North Europeans. In the River Plate region this new aggressive stance found expression in a blockade of the Brazilian smuggling centre at Colônia, initiated in 1762, which produced a marked diminution in bullion remittances from Rio de Janeiro, and effected a sharp reduction in apparent Portuguese demand for British goods. British exports to Portugal fell from £1.25 million per annum in the quinquennium 1757–61 to £0.85 and £0.72 million per annum in the two subsequent quinquennia. Portugal, like Spain, was pursuing mercantilist policies at home, and these must have accounted for some of the falling-off in British exports, but the extent of the decline can only be explained by a substantial reduction in the Colônia trade.[21]

This tough new Iberian mood also resulted in pressure on legitimate British trade through Spain and Portugal to the Americas. In a petition to the British government of February 1783, the London merchants trading to Spain complained at the prohibition of imports of cotton, linens and calicoes, 'in which a very extensive British trade hath been carried on in Spain not only for the consumption there, but for the exportation to South America'. They estimated the volume of trade in Manchester cottons alone to have averaged £300,000 per annum before 1767.[22] Similar prohibitions reduced the Portuguese trade.[23]

So by 1783 British merchants were very much on the defensive in their dealings with Iberia and the Americas. Contraband trade, damaged by the blockade, had been reduced to a mere trickle by the Spanish capture of Colônia in 1777. An attempt by English and Portuguese forces to recapture the settlement failed utterly.[24] Worse, the same year saw the seizure of all English shipping on the Mississippi by the Spanish Governor of Louisiana. For fourteen years, from the end of the Seven Years War, the British and Spanish empires in America had bordered upon each other with the Mississippi as frontier. Now Spanish action over navigation rights, together with the revolt of the British colonies, were to close a useful point of access to Mexican markets.[25] Aside from a restricted legal trade, only the Caribbean contraband routes were left to British goods seeking entry to Latin America. All this is reflected in the figures for British exports during the later eighteenth century, which peaked, respectively, to Portugal in 1731–60 at £1.14 million per annum, to Spain in 1751–80 at £1.01 per annum, and to the West Indies in 1771–1800, at £2.02 million per annum.[26]

On top of this squeeze on British trade with Iberia and Latin America came exclusion from North European markets and disruption of the North Atlantic trade as a result of Napoleon's Continental System and the retaliatory British Orders in Council. In 1793, war had broken out between France and Spain. A great deal of legitimate French trade with the Indies had hitherto passed through Spanish ports, where there were strong contingents of French merchants.[27] Together with their capital these now withdrew, as did the many French craftsmen working in Spain. The French blockaded the ports of north-west, Spain, and French armies occupied Catalonia and the Basque Provinces. Orders were given by the French for the foundries and armaments factories in occupied Spain to be destroyed. In the midst of this destruction of the achievements of a generation of reform, one port, already second (though by a long way) to Cadiz in the American trade, experienced increased prosperity. Corunna, in the extreme north-west of the country, was relatively secure, and rapidly became the entrepôt for a good part of the remaining legitimate trade between Northern Europe and the Americas, especially the trade in German manufactures.[28]

In Germany itself, a corresponding prosperity was experienced by Hamburg. Wealthy refugees from France and the French-inspired Batavian Republic brought with them to the German port of great deal of business formerly done in Le Havre, Antwerp and Amsterdam. Hamburg thrived on the importation of British and French goods bound for Germany and Russia.[29] In addition it developed close links with Corunna in the 1790s, exporting Silesian linens for redistribution throughout Spain and Spanish America. Silesia benefited by wartime disruption of the Spanish textile industry and the inadmissibility of French goods. John Quincy Adams, visiting Silesia in 1800, found, for example, that goods were being finished and packed in deliberate imitation of French textiles. Some were 'rolled up à la Morlaix; because the Spaniards were, formerly, furnished with those articles from manufactures established at Morlaix, in the Province of Brittany'.[30]

The Hamburg–Corunna axis was shortlived. Hamburg was occupied by the French during the War of the Third Coalition: an occupation with an element of retribution for the part played by the city in undermining earlier French attempts to exclude British manufactures from Europe.[31] Significantly, the capture of Hamburg took place in November 1806, only a month before the Berlin Decrees instituting the Continental System, which aimed to keep British goods out of Europe. For the first time Napoleon was confident of his ability to control the Atlantic coast, and his power was soon strengthened by the closing of Russian ports to Britain in November 1807 following the Treaty of Tilsit, and by the occupation of Spain and the evacuation of Corunna in 1809.

Although never watertight, the Continental System undoubtedly exerted great pressure on British exporters between 1807 and 1814.[32] In addition it led to friction between Britain and the United States of America, from whose ports the principal neutral mercantile marine in the Atlantic did much to reduce the effectiveness of the British counter-blockade. The Americans retaliated against the British Orders in Council of 1807 by placing an embargo on their formerly very considerable imports of British goods in 1808. Kindred difficulties arising from Anglo-French economic warfare led to war between Britain and her former American colonies in 1812.

These events represented the culmination of a half-century of resistance to British expansion by her Atlantic rivals. Imagine the British, excluded from many of their customary overseas markets and deprived of raw materials by French American action, now suddenly hearing of the capture of

Buenos Aires by Sir Home Popham in 1806. Memories and rumours abounded of the wealth of South America. Here, surely, was the very thing that was needed: an outlet for stockpiled manufactures and a source of hides and tallow, both important strategic materials, and both in short supply.[33] Then came the capture of Montevideo (a temporary affair, like that of Buenos Aires) and, in 1808, the removal of the Portuguese court, lock, stock and barrel, to Brazil, carried by the British navy and attended by an eager retinue of British merchants and adventurers. Would the recapture of Latin American markets save manufacturers cut off from their traditional northern markets? Would it, less spectacularly, allow middlemen of an earlier generation to re-establish themselves?

There is evidence that both of these happened. The firm of Antony Gibbs, which had formerly sold in Spain, now made direct contact with Latin American markets. Frederick Huth, a young Hanoverian who had been a junior partner in the Corunna and Hamburg firm of Brentano Vobara & Urbieta, exporting Silesian linens to South America until the evacuation of 1809, now settled in London. There he developed a direct trade with the West Coast of South America, which he had visited as a young supercargo in 1800.[34] DeForest represents a third line of personal continuity from the colonial to the independence period. Although he returned to the United States in 1818, his firm, Lynch & Co., survived as Lynch Zimmermann & Co., with Patricio Lynch, locally born in spite of his name, and John C. Zimmermann as partners.[35]

But if there were continuities there were also great changes.[36] First of all, the market for European goods turned out to have changed quite dramatically over the period, since the mid-eighteenth century, during which direct British contact had gradually been cut back. In 1824 the British merchants in Buenos Aires estimated that of the total population of 1.65 million reckoned to have received imported goods through Buenos Aires before the Wars of Independence, only 450,000 remained in full trading contact with the port.[37] Another indicator of the relative decline in overland trade from Buenoes Aires to Potosí is the decline in specie, obtainable only from Upper Peru, as a proportion of Buenoes Aires exports, from 79 per cent in 1796 to 27 per cent in 1837.[38] Secondly, many of those who came from Britain after 1806 were not merchants in the proper sense, nor even agents of merchants, but the emissaries of manufacturers, desperate for markets, cut off from their traditional outlets, and poorly served by established networks of intermediaries. Christopher Platt presents such men as further evidence of continuity on the ground that their goods had long found a market in Latin America. But it is one thing to make goods which are consumed abroad, and quite another to take on the task of marketing them directly. Some continuity in trade there may have been, but a vital discontinuity in business organisation.[39]

This may most easily be appreciated by looking at the Revolutionary and Napoleonic years from the point of view of the British manufacturer. R. G. Wilson does this for one major industry, woollens.[40] He finds a history of growth in the late eighteenth century brought almost to a halt by the multiple crises of the new century. The closing of German and Dutch markets in 1803 forced the manufacturers into a heavy reliance on army contracts and the North American market. Then came the Berlin Decrees and the Orders in Council, bringing the failure of three Leeds merchant houses in 1807 and of several more not long afterwards, as the United States market, too, was cut. South America briefly provided an outlet for surplus stocks, but that boom collapsed in the mid-1820s leaving the Yorkshire industry facing high tariffs in the United States and much of Continental Europe.

Wilson argues that one effect of these vicissitudes was to drive the dominant non-manufacturing Leeds merchant houses of the eighteenth century out of business. It was not simply a matter of bankruptcies and deaths, but of deliberate withdrawals from trade, of unwillingness to adapt to adverse circumstances. Instead, the trade passed into the hands of direct representatives of the manufacturers. There were several reasons for this. Firstly, the old merchants had been accustomed to trade through established and trusted correspondent houses in the major ports of destination. When old markets closed and new ones had to be developed, the merchant's connexion, his knowledge of the men with whom he was used to trade, was gone. In a new market he was on equal terms with pushy amateurs. Moreover, few established merchants were willing to commit sons or nephews, raised to a genteel life, to the uncomfortable and unhealthy ports of Spanish America or India; yet without doing so they could hardly risk competing with the new traders in the keenness of the credit terms offered to consignees of their goods. Finally, there was no compulsion on merchants to continue in trade. They could easily curtail the volume of business they handled in bad times; but manufacturers, because of their substantial fixed investment in buildings and plant, and fixed interest obligations on this account, could not. Not only could merchants run down their business; they could withdraw entirely and invest in land and government stocks. And this was no mere possibility, but rather a traditional pattern of upward mobility that had been followed over several generations in Britain, and elsewhere.

Writing of Glasgow, T. M. Devine provides further support for the thesis of a general merchant withdrawal at the turn of the century.[41] Merchants of that city had gradually moved into land throughout the eighteenth century, much like their contemporaries in South America. Often, indeed, they had been recruited from minor gentry, and were using trade as a means of re-establishing family fortunes. But in the war years the traditional symbiosis of land and trade turned sour. To maintain a position in wartime trade required constant flexibility in the amount of capital committed, for prices, insurance, wages and freights all fluctuated wildly. Merchants who had invested their surplus in land were not sufficiently liquid to meet the challenge. The leading Glasgow West India house of the eighteenth century, Alexander Houston & Co., failed during the Napoleonic Wars. Though partners' landed assets far exceeded their commercial liabilities, they simply could not be realised quickly enough in such adverse times.[42] Nor was this an isolated case. Many of the biggest Glasgow merchant landowners became insolvent in the last quarter of the eighteenth century.[43] More fortunate, or perhaps more prescient, was the Ulsterman, Robert Oliver. Faced with Jefferson's embargo, Oliver moved the fortune he had made over the past two decades as a Baltimore merchant progressively into real estate, long-term personal loans and securities until, by 1819, his firm was so illiquid that it could no longer safely respond to commercial opportunities, withdrew entirely from trade, and became in essence a family investment bank.[44]

If the Yorkshire and Glasgow manufacturers, deserted by their established intermediaries, were left to find their own way to market, there is evidence of similar abdications elsewhere. Sometimes a direct link can be established between individual traders in overseas centres and manufacturers in Britain; sometimes there is evidence of the failure of diversification of traditional middlemen; elsewhere, reliance on local capitalists or British acceptance houses for financial support sometimes provides a negative indication of the lack of any solid mercantile base at home. So, returning to Buenos Aires, we find among the most prominent British arrivals of the Independence period James Brittain, Edward Lumb and Thomas Fair. The first came to Buenos Aires as representative of a firm of Sheffield knife manufacturers, Brittain Wilkson & Brownell, in which his family was interested. He was certainly in Buenos Aires by 1810 and among the leading traders in the city by 1817.[45] By this time he was in a position to make a personal investment of $30,200 in the first Argentine bank, the Caja Nacional de Fondos de Sud-America, and a further investment of $34,829 through his firm, Winter Brittain & Co.[46] Lumb arrived in Buenos Aires in 1818 as witness to an uncle's last attempts to resuscitate the wholesale and export business of Poynton & Co., of Holborn and Sheffield, hardwaremen and merchants, which had failed in 1815, but had been exporting to Havana shortly before.[47] The speculation appears to have been successful, for Lumb and his uncle, Charles Poynton, set up a Buenos Aires house. But there is no sign that they acted as agents for any Sheffield or London firm; their trade appears to have been largely coastal, and Poynton soon returned to England leaving Lumb to build up a business which was based firmly in Argentine produce. Thomas Fair, by contrast, appears to have had no substantial base in Britain. Arriving about 1810, he set up as an importer with financial backing from the Anchorenas before diversifying into land from the 1820s.

One great difficulty in categorising the early post-independence British houses in Buenos Aries stems from the fact that many did not survive the general downturn in trade after 1825, while several of those that endured did so only by diversifications which obscured the nature of their original business in the city. Thus Duncan Wright, born near Paisley, who went to Buenos Aires after an apprenticeship with a Glasgow manufacturer, soon set up with two other clerks the import-export house of Parlane McAlister & Wright, which appears to have had strong connexions with the Manchester textiles industry. But towards the end of the 1820s the firm changed course. A cargo which they had sent up river was seized by one or other faction in the civil wars that were raging in the interior. The government—presumably the provincial government—compensated the young Scots with a grant of about 100,000 acres in Entre Rios, fronting the River Uruguay.[48] This land, the Yeruá estancia as it became, was operated on their behalf by a resident agent. Wright withdrew to Britain, dividing his time between an estate in Wigtownshire and a house in Bowdon, Cheshire, and managing a branch house, Wright Parlane & Co., which sold piece goods, mainly to India and Australia, as well as acting as agent for the Buenos Aires house.[49] Parlane McAlister & Co. continued in business, at least to the 1850s. Their business, however, bore the marks of their early mischance, for they were distinguished from many other houses of the 1840s by the fact that they generally remitted payment for imported goods from Britain in the form of local produce, and were said to have 'large shipping interests in this [produce] trade'.[50] Indeed, a distinctive feature of the Yeruá estancia in the 1840s was the facility to load produce at the riverside straight on to ocean-going vessels.[51] They seemed not to have had any capital to start with, and to have been little better off a quarter of a century later, continuing to rely mainly on credits from Liverpool and Manchester banks in the 1840s, though by 1852 they were admitted, in a generally over-sanguine report, to be 'in good credit'.[52]

INDIA

In India, as in Spanish America, the earliest British adventurers encountered a flourishing empire. While remaining predominantly Hindu in culture, the sub-continent had long been dominated by a Moslem military aristocracy of Turkish origin and Persian culture. After a period of dislocation in the fifteenth century, the Moslem ascendancy was reasserted by the Mughal emperors. The Moguls were not unequivocal sovereigns of a discrete territorial empire. There was no nation-state, nor was there absolute dynastic authority. Instead, the Emperors ruled, taxed, adjudicated and compromised in a world of semi-autonomous communities and corporations where military, fiscal, contractual and family obligations interacted to produce an elaborate political culture, not dissimilar from that of late medieval Europe.

In the sixteenth and seventeenth centuries this was not only an ordered empire but a wealthy one. Considerable economic specialisation had developed, producing large manufacturing areas linked to domestic and overseas markets by exchange relations every bit as elaborate as those current in Europe.[53] The British role in this economy was peripheral at first. A Mogul decree of 1717 allowed the British East India Company to trade in Bengal and granted freedom from customs duties for its goods and a right of settlement to its servants comparable to the privilege of *internación* given four years earlier by the Spanish authorities to the South Sea Company.[54] Elsewhere, at Bombay and Madras, bridgeheads were established and maintained by agreement with successsor or subordinate states in an empire which was beginning to drift towards a disordered anarchy.

The Moguls were willing to treat the British as allies and allow them commercial privileges because British naval strength had broken the Portuguese hold over Indian seaborne trade and restored the safety of the pilgrim route to Mecca. Use of a delegative, corporatist structure to formalise the new relationship made just as good sense to the Indian as to the European mind in the early eighteenth century. The British newcomers posed no apparent threat to Mogul power; rather the reverse. For their part, the British initially saw trade concessions in India as a poor second-best, to be settled for only when denial of Dutch control over the lucrative spice trade of the East Indian islands proved beyond them. Yet a number of profitable Indian export trades did develop. Cotton and silk textiles, indigo and saltpetre all found a market in Europe. Later, an immense trade in China tea grew up, and this, too, lay within the monopoly of the Company.

This corporation, the United East India Company of 1709, was to become the most powerful and anomalous of the British chartered companies. It was anomalous in that, unlike most of its predecessors, it had a permanent joint stock. Instead of providing a protective and regulatory framework for a multiplicity of economically autonomous shortlived partnerships and sole proprietorships, the East India Company acted as an economic agent, participating directly through its collective management and salaried staff in oriental trade. But such was the power of tradition that a complicated system of privileged private trade came into existence, more or less legitimately, alongside the collective venture. Ships' captains, civil and military servants of the Company: all were allowed to engage in trade for their own account within certain limits. Since the monopoly of the Company extended only to trade between Britain and the East, and even then imperfectly, Company servants were free to engage in a local trade, which became known as the country trade, extending to the Red Sea, the Persian Gulf, the Dutch East Indies and the South China Sea. In addition, the factories of the Company itself had to be provisioned and its troops supplied. As the number of Company servants grew, contracts of this sort became extremely profitable. As a reward for his military service against the French, Robert Clive was made commissary and steward of the British settlement of Madras in 1749. Over the next four years he accumulated a substantial fortune, estimated at £40,000, from these offices.[55]

It might appear that a corporation allowing such freedom to its executives could hardly hope for more than the leavings of trade; and to make matters worse, the Company seemed to push its servants towards private ventures by paying inadequate salaries. Yet the system was not without logic, and was well in line with the conventions of public office-holding prevalent in Britain at the time, where, as in India, perquisites compensated for low stipends.[56] What sometimes escapes the modern mind is that appointment and promotion depended upon patronage. No one became a servant of the Company whose name had not been pressed on one or other of the London merchants and shipowners who directed it by some cousin or client. Unspoken constraints were placed on the balance of corporate and individual interest by the threat of disfavour and the need for preferment. This was so in India, as in Britain, up to the middle of the eighteenth century, but thereafter the perquisites of Company service blossomed to the point where they conferred an unprecedented financial independence on returning nabobs, enabling them to challenge the traditional power of Londoners on the board of directors. This came about because of a combination of circumstance which were quite unrelated to the traditional trade of the Company. In the first place there was a breakdown of the convention that European wars, as matters of state, need not poison relations between the rival European trading communities in the East. The totalitarian mercantilism of Colbert and his successors, with its cosmic view of French welfare, made imperial conflict unavoidable. Secondly, growing political disorder in the hinterlands of the European factories provided opportunities for intrigue and king-making and, at the same time, gave rise to economic incentives for intervention to protect the quality and supply of exportable commodities.

The first clear breach in the established order came in 1757, when the British deposed Siraj-ud-daula, the Nawab of Bengal. Subsequent interventions in 1760 and 1763 diminished the authority of the office of the Nawab, which, since the early years of the century, had been tantamount to sovereignty.[57] War in India against the French had provided the initial justification for an expansion of the military establishment of the Company, but such an establishment was expensive, and could only be paid for by the sale of European goods, by borrowing, or by taxation. The first of these alternatives was out of the question. The Company had never been able to sell enough British goods in the East to finance its investment in homebound oriental goods, let alone subsidise an army. The second alternative was resorted to on a large scale. Company servants and private merchants deprived of adequate means to remit their priviate profits to Britain by the monopoly of London trade were grudgingly content to hold Company bonds. But accumulating interest payments in India simply added to their frustration, increased the gross infraction of the monopoly through clandestine trade, and contributed more voices to the mounting appeals for free trade between Britain and India as the century drew to a close. The remaining solution was for the Company, by its intervention in local politics, to become a territorial power in India with an independent fiscal base. So, guided by its need for funds, the Company acquired one petty state after another. The whole process could be publicly justified in Britain, in spite of the doubts of government and the opposition of leading directors of the Company, by appealing to a broader national interest, increasingly plausible at home, though less and less so in the East: the French must be checked.

Yet alongside these public motives, as Pamela Nightingale has observed, there ran a streak of private interest and advantage which represented so gross a corruption of the old system of patronage and perquisites as to prompt a strong moralistic reaction in which conservative paternalist outrage and the new materialist economic liberalism worked together towards a new conceptualisation of the proper relation between public and private, society and the individual. The first element in this corruption came in the form of gifts from Indian princes to their British backers.[58] The second element arose from the confusion of private and public roles which the Company had taken on. Once their own candidate was installed as Nawab, the Company servants in Calcutta slipped into the habit of interpreting the old imperial decree as applying not only to Company goods, but also to their private trade goods. It was an easy step from this to the use of coercion against producers of primary commodities, customs officers and Indian dealers, as the British sought to enforce what they presumptuously regarded as their rights to unimpeded trade in the interior.[59]

This confusion persisted and came increasingly to confuse the purpose of the Company until the withdrawal of private trading privileges from civil and military servants between 1788 and 1806. It was aggravated by the emergence, during the second half of the eighteenth century, of British private traders, sometimes holding no office under the Company, yet still able to influence its policy. Nightingale, writing of Bombay, interprets the territorial expansion of the Company after 1790, southwards to the Malabar coast and north to Gujarat, as a product of the intermingling of private and Company interests. Here she joins Tripathi, whose concern is Bengal, in identifying an important transition in the third quarter of the eighteenth century, which set the scene for the dramatic events at the end of the century. The dominant entrepreneurs had formerly been ships' captains, glorified pedlars, engaged in the country trade. The connexions or agents of such men in the major Indian ports, who had often started out as Company servants, gradually grew stronger relative to their peripatetic principals. This followed from the greatly enlarged capital resources accumulating in the hands of Company servants in Bengal for whom the agents acted as bankers, the volume of trade in bonds of the public debt which they engrossed, and the development, especially in Bombay, of more fixed patterns of trade, bringing the possibility of tighter control over producers. At the same time, the resident agents or partners became detached from the Company by the Cornwallis reforms. In this way equal partnerships developed.

These firms, which became known as agency houses, developed a varied business often organised in a loose federation of joint-ventures, partnerships and corporations around a central firm, and embracing international trade, the finance of plantation agriculture, marine insurance and shipowning. The major agency houses of the 1790s were Francis Latour & Co. and Arbuthnot & Co. in Madras, Bruce Fawcett & Co., Forbes & Co., and Alexander Adamson in Bombay and, in Calcutta, Fairlie Fergusson & Co., Paxton Cockerell & Delisle, Colvins & Bazett, Joseph Barretto, and Lambert & Ross.[60] In Bombay, they continued to be closely linked to Company servants and to manipulate policy into the early nineteenth century. In Bengal, the heart of the East India Company's sphere of influence, the growing hold of the agency houses led to an eclipse of official trade on a scale analogous to British penetration of the Spanish American commercial monopoly in the mid-eighteenth century. Tripathi cites figures given by David Scott, one of the leading private traders of the 1770s and 1780s and later a director of the East India

Company, in his campaign for free trade.[61] These indicate that during the 1780s more than four-fifths of the outward trade from Europe by value, and three-quarters of the much more valuable Indian export trade to Europe was being handled either by non-British East India Companies or by British and other private traders acting in breach of the Company monopoly.[62] The foreign East India companies were often little more than devices to legitimise a trade conducted by British subjects, who were frequently in cahoots with the agency houses. In the same way much of the clandestine trade, which, Scott averred, had been negligible before 1777, consisted of the movement of British goods in British ships, financed by the agency houses.

The issue between the Company and the agency houses now reduced to the single question of capital movements. Company control of trade and shipping first inhibited the remittance of private fortunes in the late eighteenth century and then threatened to choke off investment in plantation investment, in which the agency houses had become deeply interested in the early years of the nineteenth century. Further afield, in Canton, where British merchants had been active since the 1750s, the sale of Company bills had made possible remittance to London or India of the proceeds of private exports of raw cotton from Bombay, while, at the same time, providing the Company with about a third of the resources it required to invest in homebound cargoes of tea and silks. But this mechanism proved inadequate to support the growing trade in Bengal opium for China in the early nineteenth century, and, in Canton as in India, British private merchants were driven into illegality, buying American bills drawn on London or New York.[63] So agency house partners, anxious to be rid of inconvenient and costly subterfuges, campaigned for free trade in Parliament and within the Company hierarchy itself. They could point to the threat posed by illicit trade to the status of London as an entrepôt for Indian goods destined for the Continent. They could play on the loss of revenue to the British state arising from smuggling of tea and other East India goods. They could harp on the new themes of the political economists—the need for a separation of public and private interests, and the public benefits to be had from free trade, both in India and at home—which had already influenced the Cornwallis reforms that excluded Company servants from trade in Bengal and Madras. And they could find allies among British manufacturers and outport merchants and shipowners, desperate for easier access to assured markets in the difficult wartime years when first one and then another of their traditional outlets was blocked off.

So, after long debate, the East India Company was deprived of its monopoly of the India trade in 1813, and finally ceased trading altogether after 1833, when its much abused monopoly of the China trade was also revoked. For another quarter century, up to the assumption of direct imperial control in 1858, the Company would continue to rule British India; but the commercial power had passed into different hands.

There is a sting in the tail. The Calcutta agency houses, which might be thought the natural successors to the Company and leading beneficiaries of the Charter Act of 1833, had vanished within months of their seeming victory. During the 1820s the leading firms had expanded and diversified on the strength of a growing equity base and the availability of plentiful, cheap loan capital. Much of the new business was more industrial than mercantile, and involved the sinking of capital in fixed assets, or, what was little better in a rather immature capital market, loans secured against fixed assets. Shipowning, brewing, distilling, mining, milling, real estate and plantation agriculture—indigo above all—were the darlings of the market.[65] But in the second half of the decade the boom faltered. Local interest rates rose. There was no prospect of help from London, where a collapse in the post-independence Spanish American boom had destroyed enthusiasm for overseas landing and commodity prices were depressed. To make matters worse, the equity of some of the leading houses was reduced at this critical time by the retirement of partners. In 1832 came the failure of Scott & Co., London house of the firm established almost seventy years before by David Scott. By 1834 almost all the major Calcutta agency houses had followed.[66]

Who, then, were the residuary legatees of British mercantilism in India? As in South America, the turbulent decades leading up to the final British victory of 1815 had brought considerable fluctuations and displacements. Arabs, long excluded from the country trade by Europeans, recovered in the later eighteenth century to the point where they rivalled British tonnage calling at Surat. In the closing years of the century this had much to do with the immunity of Arab vessels from French privateers and British warships alike. War produced a further boost as the French sold off prize vessels at advantageous prices. Moreover, the Arabs were not treated as foreigners in law by the British, and so escaped discriminatory duties and embargoes.[67]

Bombay, the chief port for the Arab trade, provided a base for one of the most successful and anglophile client groups in British India, the Parsees. Distinguished by their Zoroastrian religion and Persian origin, this community produced innumerable shipbuilders, shipowners and merchants, doing a big business in opium, dominating the export of raw cotton from Bombay to China, and later diversifying into the manufacture of cotton textiles, besides playing an important part in the development of banking and other services in the city.[68] Few could rival Jamshedji Jeejibhoy, whose central role in the opium trade earned him a fortune, and whose philanthropy, estimated at about £90,000, brought him a baronetcy. Few could match Khurshedjee Rustomjee Cama, whose firm became the first Indian house with a branch in London 1855. Yet many enjoyed wealth comparable to their European competitors and operated in much the same way.

Other Asiatic groups also found profitable niches under the new regime. Moslems from the Bombay region spread throughout the Middle East, and were especially numerous in Muscat, the chief port of the 'Umani Arabs, and at the pearl fisheries of Bahrain.[69] Bombay also provided, along with Karachi, headquarters for the many Indian factors who settled on the 'Umani-controlled coast of East Africa, dealing in slaves and ivory; and this, in turn, made Bombay a natural locale for specialist European merchants like Meyer & Company of Hamburg, major ivory dealers.[70] Jews from Syria reached China by way of Bombay, finally displacing the Parsees and the Scots in the opium trade. The most powerful of these, the Sassoons, arriving in Bombay in 1825, were able to use Hong Kong as a springboard to the heart of the world economy, founding a London merchant bank, and gaining the favour of the King Emperor, Edward VII.[71] In Calcutta, where many Bengali merchants had done well in the later eighteenth century as middlemen for the British, it used always to be alleged that indigenous capital was diverted into real estate by the unprecedented rights conferred on individual landowners in the Permanent Settlement of 1793.[72] But recent research has cast doubt on this, and Rungta makes clear that Bengali merchants, Dwarkanath Tagore chief amongst them, continued to be a force to be reckoned with at least up to the 1840s.[73]

More isolated figures appear from time to time. Paul Chater, who rose to prominence in Hong Kong towards the end of the nineteenth century, was grandson of a prominent Calcutta merchant of Armenian origin, Agah Catchik Arnkiel. At the end of the eighteenth century, one firm, Johannes Sarkis & Co., is said to have 'monopolised the Armenian market'.[74] But the great period of Armenian trade in the East had passed.[75] More exotic still was C. E. Schoene, who founded an import-export house in Calcutta in 1842, and was 'probably a Russian, who is said to have spoken five languages'.[76]

Europeans and North Americans also found their place. Scots predominated, as they had done throughout the eighteenth century. Jardine, Matheson in Hong Kong, James Finlay & Co., or Mackinnon Mackenzie & Co. in India, Robert Campbell or Frederick Dalgety (the son of a Scot, though Canadian born) in New South Wales: the list could be continued almost indefinitely. Some came as private individuals to take up clerkships in the firms of their kin. Others, like William Jardine, began as East India Company servants, and accumulated capital from privileged trade before going independent.[77] The lesser ranks of the Scottish gentry, fortified by an education system better adapted to commerce than that of England, provided an endless stream of recruits.[78] Scottish, too, though often with strong bases in London or Liverpool, were some of the late eighteenth-century agency houses which survived outside Calcutta, such as Arbuthnots and Binnys of Madras. Even in Calcutta, the discontinuity was in part merely apparent. It is true enough that the principal Calcutta agencies failed in the 1830s, leaving deficits of more than £14 million.[79] Yet W. E. Cheong has observed lines of continuity between one of the biggest of these firms, whose net deficit in the 1840s exceeded £3 million, and the leading Hong Kong house, to this day, of Jardine Matheson & Co. Cheong's account is worth quoting at length because it so perfectly captures the way in which continual changes of partner tend to obscure the essential continuity of undertakings in this pre-corporate world.

William Fairlie and John Fergusson were in China in the eighties—Cheong explains. By the end of the decade the firm of Fairlie, Fergusson & Co. had been established in Calcutta but was trading in China. During the same period, John Reid had been in China, trading as Reid & Gildart. Early in the decade Andrew and David Reid appeared in China and soon the fortunes of the elder Reid was (*sic*) joined with that of the Fairlies and the Fergussons to produce Fairlie, Reid & Co. of Calcutta. This house was to become Fairlie & Gilmore in 1796. The house then became Fergusson, Gilmore & Co. when Fairlie went back to set up a house in London. When both the London and the Calcutta houses fell in 1832, the London house was called Fairlie, Clark & Innes and the Calcutta branch, Fergusson, Gilmore & Clarke. During the period after 1800, the China connections of these two houses were built up through Reid. He joined the Beale brothers, David and Thomas, and Alexander Shanks to form the China agency of Reid & Beale. The house soon became Beale & Magniac and finally emerged in 1832 as Jardine, Matheson & Co.[80]

But if there was some measure of continuity, liberalisation of the India trade also offered opportunities to groups which had been excluded under the old regime. Many of these, of course, were also Scots. In their campaign to achieve free trade with India, the agency houses and their London affiliates had found competitive allies in the merchants of the outports. Liverpool, for one, had been active in the campaign for free trade, trying to buy its ways into the Company's privileges in 1768 and viewing the East as its salvation following the decision in 1792 to abolish the slave trade on which the prosperity of the city was believed to depend.[81] This pressure on Whitehall and Leadenhall Street continued into the new century, especially between 1816 and 1820, when George Canning, Member of Parliament for Liverpool, was President of the Board of Control for India, and culminated in the 1830s.[82] It was accompanied by a modest diversion of Liverpool capital from the West Indies into Indian ventures.[83] The most prominent example of this eastward shift was John Gladstone, a wealthy Liverpool merchant of Scottish extraction who had built up strong interests in West Indies trade, shipping and plantations. After 1815, Gladstone moved some of his ships from the Atlantic to the East India trade. He formed a new partnership, separate from his West India interests, to deal with India, and one of the partners in this firm was sent out to represent Gladstone in Calcutta in 1818. Supercargoes were also used, and F. M. Gillanders, a cousin of Gladstone's wife, went out twice in this capacity, in 1818 and 1820, receiving one per cent on all transactions and an eighth of the net profit of the voyage. Later, Gillanders set up partnerships in Calcutta and Liverpool with a nephew of John Gladstone. Gladstone financed the new firms and employed the Calcutta house as his agent in India, so delaying the need to enter formally into an Indian partnership until after Gillanders retired in 1837.[84]

A second source of new blood derived from the odd courses taken by trade, in the East as in the Atlantic world, during the war years. It has already been shown how Anglo-French conflict drew New Englanders into a long-distance trade linking their home ports to China by way of Europe, Africa and Spanish America. These connexions clearly account not only for the brief presence in Calcutta of New Englanders in the first decade of the nineteenth century, but also for the more enduring Yankee presence in Canton, where Stewart & McCall of Massachusetts was established by the 1820s and, by 1818, the more enduring Boston-based firm of Russell & Co., which was to continue with at least one New Englander among its partners until it fell at last, in 1891, to a Scot.[85]

Evasion of the Company monopoly and the exigencies of war with France and Spain had brought others into oriental trade besides the North Americans. One of the principal functions of the agency houses in the late eighteenth century had been to provide a channel for the remittance of private capital to Britain. This was generally achieved by the clandestine export of diamonds and other goods in French, Dutch, Portuguese, United States or Scandinavian vessels. The goods were sold in Lisbon, Amsterdam, Hamburg, or some other centre, and the proceeds remitted to the London branch of a British agency house by its European correspondent. To facilitate this business, each of the agency houses developed its own set of connexions: Fairlie Fergusson & Co. with the French; Paxton Cockerell & Delisle with Dutch merchants; and so on.[86] Another device was the bogus East India company. English mariners and merchants including the notorious Murdock Brown were dominant in the affairs of the Imperial East India Company of Ostend. In the same way, Scots colonised Gothenburg and used their family connexions with the agency houses to develop a Swedish East India Company that was little more than a legal cover for clandestine trade. Colin Campbell of Edinburgh, whose marriage in a Scottish Episcopal church implied Jacobite affiliations such as had driven so many of the Scottish gentry into exile and trade, served in the Imperial East India Company before taking Swedish nationality and sailing as supercargo to China in 1731 on the first vessel despatched by the Swedish Company.[87]

Last, came a group already familiar from South America: the agents of British manufacturers and wholesalers, sent out to buy and sell in an effort to compensate for the wartime loss of traditional markets and the inadequacy and conservatism of established intermediaries. As in Latin America, so in the East, the difficulties of remittance and the opportunities of developing markets generally seduced these men, for good or ill, into a wider business. Andrew Melrose, a wealthy Edinburgh tea importer, found that: 'in order to benefit from his vastly superior knowledge of the domestic market, [he] needed as a complement to his own activities in Britain a personal agent in China who was both well-trained and attentive to the requirements of his principals.' He sent out a former partner to represent him as soon as the East India Company monopoly expired, and established close links with Jardine Matheson to complement his long-standing contacts with the leading London tea brokers. But these were interim measures. By 1842 his son William had arrived in Canton after a long training in his father's house and with the London brokers, Ewart MacCaughey & Co., to round off his commercial apprenticeship with a three-year spell as tea taster to Jamieson How & Co. Finally, after a furlough in Scotland, he returned to Canton as buying agent for his father's firm in 1848, remaining in that capacity for five years.[88] Melrose stuck firmly to tea, but W. R. Adamson, who arrived in Shanghai in the 1840s to buy silk for a syndicate of Macclesfield manufacturers, soon branched out into general trade and, in partnership with George Dodwell, into shipping agencies, including the Hong Kong agency of Canadian Pacific.[89] James Finlay & Co., one of the biggest of the managing agencies, originated in eighteenth-century Glasgow as a firm of merchants trading primarily to North America and diversified towards the end of the century into manufacture of cotton yarn for sale to continental Europe. Disruption of their traditional markets may have been behind the decision of Finlay & Co. in 1816 to send a trial shipment of yarn to Bombay in charge of a supercargo, whose job it was to see to the sale of the cargo and the remittance of funds. But the supercargo, whether by accident or design, settled in Bombay, starting the firm of Ritchie Steuart & Co., in which James Finlay, of the Glasgow house, was also a partner. This connexion, later in the century, would be developed into a fully-fledged branch house, providing a base for diversification into jute spinning, tea gardens and a wide range of other activities.[90]

BRITAIN

To add a third area in illustration might seem superfluous. After all, the main themes of this chapter are now clear: the migration of merchants along trade routes, the stimulus of political upheavals, and the great variety of nations actively involved in long-distance trade. Yet Britain was a major centre of trade, of manufacture and of finance. Largely in consequence of this, it was also a centre of innovation and adaptation in marketing and the finance of trade, prefiguring later developments elsewhere. Moreover, the predicament of merchants on the periphery of the world economy, as it developed during the nineteenth century, was to be in large measure the reciprocal of institutional change at the centre.

Stanley Chapman has drawn attention to the very substantial number of international houses which opened branches in London or transferred their headquarters there from the mid-eighteenth century onward. Jews from

Amsterdam, 'international Huguenots', Orthodox Greeks, Irish Presbyterians, all congregated in the City. At the same time, Jews and other merchants from Hamburg, Frankfurt, and elsewhere in Germany, with interests in the textile trades, settled in the northern industrial cities. The attractions of complex and rapidly developing markets go far to account for this concentration, but Chapman also stresses the decline of Frankfurt and the Leipzig fairs and the catalytic role of the European wars. He lays special emphasis on French control of Hamburg and Frankfurt after 1806, which led several houses to move to London. Frederick Huth, whose part in the Silesian linen trade has already been noted, was one. Schröders, E. H. Brandt, and Fruhling & Göschen also transferred to London at about this time.[91]

The wars had other, more subtle, effects. Many customary routes were disrupted; many established intermediaries displaced. Examples of this have been provided from Spanish America and the East, but a single European case may bring the point home. During the 1790s, James Finlay & Co. expanded sales of cotton yarns to Continental Europe and established a branch house in Germany. In 1789 the firm ceased to be pure merchants when they brought mills at Ballindalloch and, three years later, Catrine. At some point in the first decade of the nineteenth century the firm began to buy raw cotton direct at New Orleans and Charleston through an affiliated house. During the War of the Third Coalition, which commenced in 1805, and through subsequent conflicts up to the eventual British victory over Napoleon ten years later, Finlay & Co. and other manufacturers who had adopted the factory system were in a novel position. Unlike pure merchants they could not simply pull out and wait for better days, letting independent small manufacturers survive as best they could. Now, irreducible fixed costs and the need to keep together a skilled workforce (Finlays employed between 2000 and 3000 mill workers at this time) made it imperative to break through to traditional markets or else find new ones. Consequently these years saw Finlays conducting a determined clandestine trade on several fronts: to Spanish America by way of Nassau, to North Germany through Heligoland, and by way of Malta and Gibraltar to Southern Europe. The same pressures led

Kirkman Finlay to load the first ship to leave the Clyde for India after the expiry of the Company's monopoly.[92]

The degree of vertical integration exhibited by Finlays was exceptional. A more common experience of the period was of an entrepreneur at some point or another in a long chain of market transactions being forced or induced to bypass a single group of middlemen. Evidence is fragmentary and ambiguous. Distribution was not always uppermost in the minds of the pioneers of business history who produced the classic works on British manufacturers of this period a generation ago and more. Secondly, it is clear that the bypassing of middlemen to reach ultimate clients and sources of supply is a perennial tactic; it is part of the history of nearly every successful firm in every period. The chief economic purpose of the modern firm, after all, is to provide a substitute for market relations. Young firms are constantly on the look out for opportunities to go past established ones; established firms grumble incessantly about the uncertainty and disruption brought into their trade by newer, smaller operators. So to collect together from the secondary literature examples depicting the replacement of one marketing system by another at some specific point in history may be to do no more than record the last disgruntled flicks of the tail from *that* year's dinosaurs. Could not the same exercise equally well be carried out for the next decade, and the one after that? And for which specific trades would the generalisation hold, if at all? There were obviously a series of different marketing systems, each for its own product or group of products, some dating back many decades, others just coming into being, and each proceeding at a different pace in each national, or even regional, market.

Accordingly, the hypothesis advanced here is limited to a handful of leading firms, in textiles most of all, which loomed large in the British manufacturing sector during the late eighteenth century and were characterised by a typically high levels of fixed costs, whether arising from investment in plant or from the need to retain a skilled workforce and make constant use of integrated sources of raw materials.[93] The argument, from Wilson, is that traditional merchants faced with new products on the one hand and disrupted markets on the other, were inclined to withdraw from trade.[94]

Manufacturers, especially the new manufacturers with their high fixed costs, could not follow them without loss, and were consequently forced into overseas adventures. It may be extended to wholesalers in a handful of trades where the need to maintain a reputation for consistent quality with a clientele of retailers acted analogously to the need to keep together a skilled workforce. Here, the movement of some tea wholesalers into direct buying after the East India Company monopoly was rescinded is suggestive.[95] An alternative, or complementary, formulation would argue that it was economies of scale that enabled larger manufacturers to engage in direct marketing.[96] But this is not much of an explanation. It shows why some larger firms were likely to be successful in their foreign ventures, but not why so many smaller manufacturers, evidently not able to support an international marketing organisation, nevertheless tried their hand.

Sydney Chapman, in his pioneering work on the Lancashire textiles industry, found Manchester finishers starting to sell direct to the Continent through peripatetic agents or partners after 1770. Earlier, Lancashire cloth had generally reached foreign markets through specialist export houses in London.[97] Stanley Chapman has provided support for this assertion in his work on the Peels, an integrated firm engaged in spinning, weaving and printing, who were 'amongst the handful of London and Manchester merchants who sold direct to American markets and also employed salesmen travelling in Germany and the Low Countries in the 1790s'.[98] Another Manchester firm which followed a similar path a decade or so later was M'Connel & Kennedy, cotton spinners, which began to bypass Glasgow and Manchester exporters within ten years of its establishment in 1795 by selling through a Hamburg merchant, Alexander Barclay.[99]

Further corroboration of the fixed assets thesis comes from the work of Unwin on S. & W. Salte, one of the great London 'linen houses' or wholesale drapers of the later eighteenth century. Saltes carried on a varied trade, buying Irish linens, Indian calicoes and muslins, and the new Lancashire muslins produced by Samuel Oldknow and others from the early 1780s, as well as carrying out some finishing to catch the changing fashions of the metropolitan market.[100] Saltes were a major outlet for Oldknow. Together with another London house, Parker Topham & Sowden, they took about two-thirds of the output of this foremost British muslin producer, the rest being sold through the manufacturer's own Manchester warehouse in St. Ann's Square. Yet the two firms, merchant and manufacturer, were not perfectly complementary. Indeed, conflicts of interest soon became apparent. Significantly, these centred on the capital requirements of manufacture and on marketing strategy. In 1783, strained by the costs of innovatory machinery as he moved from fustians to muslins, Oldknow appears to have sought capital from Saltes. They refused, pleading that their funds were already fully engaged. The money came instead from Arkwright, and Saltes lost an opportunity to commit themselves to a rising star.[101] An additional reason for their reluctance may have been a desire to avoid participation in the losses that were bound to result to British muslin manufacturers as, from time to time, the market was flooded by the arrival of East India Company shipments. So long as they remained pure merchants, Saltes were in a position to play off different sources of muslins against each other. Thus, in 1786, Saltes used the threat of new firms in London selling Lancashire muslins on commission to encourage Oldknow to keep his costs down.[102] This new development in the trade proved to be the first sign of an over-trading crisis which built up in 1787 and reached a peak the following year as greatly increased East India supplies flooded a market already heavily overstocked.[103] Saltes did what they could to unload existing stocks in France and St. Petersburg, but it was left to Oldknow to look for new outlets if he were to maintain production and keep down unit costs. And this he could only do by circumventing Saltes, selling to new middlemen in Manchester and London, and beginning to deal directly with the more important customers formerly supplied through Saltes and Parker, Topham & Sowden.[104]

Strutts of Derbyshire, another of the pioneering northern textiles firms, showed a similar tendency to direct marketing some fifteen years later, going past the Manchester and London houses to take charge of their own exports, at first through commission agents in Messina, Palermo, Gibraltar, New York and Charleston, and, later, by direct sales of yarn to

Continental weavers.[105] These latter sales passed through Hull, where Strutts must have employed a local house as forwarding agent, handling the mechanics of storage, shipment and insurance. Gordon Jackson confirms this marginalisation of the export business of Hull firms, and their consequent specialisation in the import of raw materials, noting that 'in the case of manufactured goods it was becoming common in the second half of the century for the manufacturer to have his own correspondents or travellers abroad, and to negotiate directly with his customers'.[106]

This trend was not limited to the new textiles areas, but was exhibited also by at least a handful of manufacturers of pottery and metal goods. The later eighteenth century saw 'a market increase in the number of firms combining the functions of production and distribution' in industrial South Wales, where the brass and copper manufacturers had set up warehouses and agencies in major English cities, or sent travellers to get orders there. But these developments, attributed to improved communications and an increase in the average size of the firm, had not yet affected export marketing.[107] Josiah Wedgwood had a partner, Thomas Bentley, who travelled in Germany, arranging sales to Hamburg houses; Matthew Boulton of Birmingham also had a travelling partner, Fothergill, on the Continent.[108] In the extensive transatlantic trade in iron rails which grew up from the 1830s marketing practices varied. A few of the largest ironmasters kept London houses to market their goods. Others, like Guest's Dowlais Iron Company, sent members of the owning family on selling trips abroad. American importers, for their part, while generally sending orders through Liverpool or London merchants, sometimes visited the ironworks. Gerald Ralston, who began as a United States importer, set up his own London buying house in the 1830s, engaging in merchant banking on the side. He also visited South Wales ironworks, including Dowlais, buying with the aid of letters of credit from Anglo-American merchant bankers and leaving shipping and insurance to older established merchants at the ports. By the 1840s, in response, British ironmasters were integrating down towards the market. Many more had opened London or Liverpool houses, and some, like Naylor & Co., had established American branches.[109] Peter Stubbs, a file-maker who set up in Warrington in the 1770s, began by selling to factors, or wholesale ironmongers, in Ashton-in-Makerfield and Sheffield, but was bypassing them to sell direct to retailers by the 1790s, employing out-riders, or travelling salesmen, by the turn of the century. The domestic pattern was soon repeated for the American export trade. This first developed in the 1790s through Jackson & Barlow of Stockport. Later, some time after 1806, Stubbs went past them to sell direct to the United States.[110] Stubbs may well have sold to firms like Nathan Trotter & Co., wholesale ironmongers of Philadelphia, whose records reveal the other side of the transaction. Elva Tooker, historian of the firm, notes that Trotter, who had formerly bought through London export houses, shifted in the early 1820s to buying through cheaper Liverpool houses, or direct from the manufacturers. This is, of course, somewhat later than the cases cited earlier, but Tooker clearly sees Trotter as something of a conservative: 'He persisted in doing business with the commission merchants of London', she grumbles, 'even though these . . . were gradually being bypassed in the flow of goods from England's factories to its ever-growing markets.'[111]

Taken together with the cases of James Finlay & Co., the Brittains of Sheffield, or the Ashworths in Brazil, these changes in marketing practices appear to point towards the systematic emergence of vertically integrated international manufacturing concerns in response to the failure of traditional marketing institutions to measure up to the dual challenge of wartime disruption of markets and changes in the location and capital-intensivity of manufacturing at home. Yet the shift towards textiles and metalware multinationals stalled and went into reverse during the second quarter of the nineteenth century in response to the extreme difficulties of management which it raised and to the competitive pressure of four new groups of intermediaries who, between them, proved better able to handle the job than the manufacturers themselves: general commission houses, often British, in the major export markets; buying firms, mostly Continental, in the British manufacturing areas; a new generation of wholesale warehousemen devoted, by contrast with their eighteenth-century counterparts, to rapid turnover at low margins of profit; and acceptance houses in the City of London, able and willing to finance the whole process. The first of these have already been glimpsed, burrowing, worm-like, into the hulls of Spanish-American and British-Indian mercantilism. Their later development will provide a central theme of the next chapter. Here, it should simply be observed that the existence of strong commission agencies in the East, backed by British acceptance houses, enabled British textiles manufacturers to test out the China market when the Company monopoly came to an end without going to the trouble and expense of sending out their own representatives: a sharp contrast with the opening of Latin American markets a generation before.[112] The remaining three categories, briefly surveyed here, complete a picture of early Victorian British international business.

That foreign firms should send agents or partners to buy British manufacturers was nothing new. Buck, writing of the North Atlantic trade, found it to have been common practice before 1812, but much less so between 1812 and 1830. Thereafter, however, the system revived as American and Continental houses sent resident agents to northern manufacturing cities, including Manchester and Bradford:[113] the middle decades of the century saw the arrival of Philip Goldschmidt in Bradford, Jacob Phillips in Birmingham, the Behrends in Liverpool, and the Freuds, half-brothers of Sigmund, in Manchester.[114]

A second factor reducing the need for vigorous marketing by manufacturers was a change in the trading practices of the London wholesalers. James Morrison, who played a leading part in building up the Fore Street warehouse established by Joseph Todd in the 1790s, is credited with a number of innovations in wholesale haberdashery which helped raise the turnover of the business from £64,449 in 1813 to £650,570 four years later. To begin with, he placed much greater emphasis on seeking out new sources of goods, employing travelling buyers; secondly, he courted the business of London hawkers and small provincial drapers, whose accounts had been considered too troublesome by the leading houses; thirdly, he aimed at a large turnover with small margins.[115] Of these techniques, the first reduced the need for the thrusting new manufacturer to find a path round staid intermediaries, the second reduced the unsatisfied market to which such a manufacturer could appeal, while the third cut back the gains to be made from bypassing the wholesaler. Furthermore, the assault on direct selling in the domestic market provided a clear disincentive to foreign ventures, since direct marketing overseas so often grew out of a manufacturer's experience of direct selling at home.

One final group of firms, perhaps the decisive one, enabled new small firms of commission agents to develop, be they Scotsmen in Calcutta, Yorkshiremen in Buenos Aires, or Germans in the North of England. The traditional role of the merchant, as performed by Saltes, for example, had been to own goods during the crucial period between manufacture and final sale, providing credit in both directions, to manufacturer and wholesalers or retailer. Now the credit function became separated from the handling of goods and knowledge of markets, as specialist merchant bankers or acceptance houses developed in London and Liverpool. Though, like many merchant bankers, they combined a public finance business with their commercial role, Barings provide the perfect example of acceptance business, with a web of clients and connexions centring on the United States, but spreading also to the East and, later, to Latin America.

The heart of the business was the finance of international trade in raw materials. A local house, whether in Charleston or Rio, which was authorised to do so by a firm like Barings, could make an advance on crops or materials in the form of bills of exchange payable at some future date in London. Because of the prestige of the acceptor and the massive amount of international trade moving through London, such bills were easily negotiable. That is, they could be sold at a discount reflecting current interest rates and the usance or term of the bill, by importers of manufactured goods, say, who might need to make payments in Britain. They would then be remitted to London. There, if all went well, the crops or materials on which the transaction had originally been based would have been received and sold by the due date, and the proceeds used to settle the bill without the acceptor having to put up a penny. But if the original and safest basis for a bill of exchange on Barings lay in a physical shipment of goods, it soon became apparent that since such bills represented a most eligible means of payment of debts in Britain by debtors overseas, they could just as easily be created by agents or houses overseas specifically to satisfy this demand, the exposure of the London firm being met, not by goods, but by the remittance of specie, negotiable securities, or bills of exchange drawn on other British houses. This worked just so long as the transaction left a margin of profit to the protagonist and a commission for the acceptor. In this way, Barings and similar houses came to finance a mixed business in which trade and exchange or other financial operations were inextricably intertwined, as the merchant bankers' clienteles slipped gradually from trade into finance, creaming off speculative profits from their new business, but presenting to their respectable benefactors the twin threats of redundancy in the long run and exposure in the short run.

In such circumstances only superb credit information and fine anticipatory judgement could save a firm from disastrous losses in the periodic financial crises that punctuated the nineteenth century.[116] Longstanding relations with trusted houses in foreign ports could go some way towards achieving such fine intelligence, as could the despatch of trusted representatives from time to time to report on current conditions. But the tenor of a corresponding firm or agency could change quickly as some new partner became dominant; agents could all too often go off the rails, seduced by the opportunities of a fast-growing economy. So family continued to be much resorted to. Houses which had only recently set up in Britain and still maintained strong connexions overseas bolstered by kinship were therefore peculiarly well able to operate in this hazardous environment, and contributed disproportionately to the merchant banking community which grew up in England during the nineteenth century.

In the middle years of the eighteenth century the British, French, Spanish, Dutch and Portuguese mercantile systems had provided a series of mutually exclusive political frameworks for the conduct of international trade. They were already under pressure, partly because European wars tended increasingly to spill over into hostility in the Americas and the East, partly because of vigorous burrowing by merchants from the more buoyant economies of north-west Europe into the timbers of their less progressive southern competitors, and partly because in all of them, even the strongest, privilege and real economic strength were no longer synchronised. Though Spain and France attempted to save the situation both by reform and by war, it was Britain, rather surprisingly, that came out ahead in 1815. But there could be no question of her creating a unified and exclusive mercantile system to embrace her new spheres of influence and conquests. Even her traditional mercantile system was under tremendous pressure from within, made worse by the commercial gymnastics which British merchants and manufacturers had been forced to perform during the long wars.

Quite intentionally, this process has been presented here through a multitude of case studies. Although this may have been confusing, even irritating, it has the advantage of setting out, like chessmen on a board, some of the actors who will figure in subsequent chapters and of illustrating characteristic patterns of migration and adaptation which were to dominate the next half-century before being swept away on a tide of technological and institutional innovations. Above all, it has demonstrated in a way that no state-oriented account could, the mixing of nationalities that had occurred in the world's major ports during the generation before the outbreak of the long *Pax Britannica*.

3 A Cosmopolitan Bourgeoisie

The actors are now in position. In the major ports there are merchants of very varied ethnic origins engaged in international trade. It is evident that these different communities interacted through the market, but this could not provide any basis for claims that a cosmopolitan bourgeoisie existed, that a new class was in process of formation. Did members of the different communities combine together in firms of mixed nationality? Did the communities mix socially? Did their members intermarry and lose their distinctiveness? How far did merchants, of whatever community, relate to established governing groups? Did they develop any unifying ideology?

A merchant travels abroad in his youth, first as a supercargo, perhaps, or to a clerkship in a friendly house. He prospers and establishes an independent partnership, perhaps affiliated to and supported by a firm in his home port. He grows wealthy. The time comes to marry, to educate children, to retire. Will he go home for a bride? Will children be packed off to the old country for education? Or will the local community be thought able to provide suitable brides and schools? Retirement approaches. Is going back any longer attractive? Or is the merchant now so bound up in the public life of his new country, and his family so much at home there, that they have ceased to be foreigners and made the place their own? Take another case. For two or three generations a family has lived abroad. Sons have been sent home and educated in the Scottish academies or the English public schools, one, at least, always returning to continue management of the counting house, the mine, or the ranch which is the root of the family wealth. Are these people still British? Are they Anglo-this or Anglo-that? Or are they simply South Africans, or Swedes, or Argentines with pretensions?

The answers to these questions matter because classifications depend on them. What shall count as foreign capital and what as native? Is this a distinction that makes sense, other than for public accounting purposes? More subtly, how unified in culture can the national bourgeoisie of a recipient country be if the loyalties and experience of its leading residents remain foreign? Setting aside differences arising out of crude material interest (for these may be overcome by forces of shared ideology and legitimacy), what unanimity can be anticipated from a bourgeoisie that is neither properly national nor fully cosmopolitan, but multinational and divided in its perceptions?

Like the questions of diversification and integration which have already been touched upon, these issues of settlement and return crop up again and again over the long history of capitalist international trade. But during the nineteenth century the ways in which they were dealt with changed fundamentally and irrevocably. In general, poor communications and devotion to business had tended to overcome centripetal forces of original patriotism. Even where distances were not overwhelming, as in nineteenth-century European Russia, foreign merchants, whether Germans, Frenchmen, Poles or Jews, integrated and Russified. British houses of the eighteenth century, like Thorley Bolton Ouchterloney & Co. of Narva or Thornton Cayley & Co. of St. Petersburg, appear to have merged into the local business community and broken loose from their original moorings in Hull by the nineteenth century, though observers of a later period were to note the British as exceptionally resistant to naturalisation.[1] In the same way, the Scottish mercantile community in Gothenburg, no great distance from home, gradually blended with their surroundings. The British factory there still existed in the 1950s as a kind of club, but the remaining members were all Swedes. Some Swedes of Scottish descent were still being sent to Scotland for education in the early twentieth century; but then so too were some unimpeachably Swedish Swedes, for Scottish schools were generally held in high esteem.[2] Similar patterns may be seen in the Luso-Hispanic world where eighteenth-century Basque and Catalan merchants became nineteenth-century landowners in Buenos Aires with scarcely a glance over the shoulder, and the Portuguese merchant houses of the Brazilian empire continued to act as a conduit for new waves of ambitious *peninsulares* who found their way to permanent places in American society through clerkships.[3] London absorbed Greeks, Jews, Germans, Huguenots, Spaniards and North Americans. The highest levels of English society were extremely cosmopolitan by the later nineteenth century. Anglo-American marriages had become quite the fashion. By the middle of the nineteenth century, in the eyes of a historian reacting to the suggestion that British financiers were taken for a ride by their cunning United States competitors after the 1837 crisis, 'the interpenetration and indeed community of interests of English and American financiers was too intimate to allow so sharp a distinction'.[4]

The process of integration was not without strain. Did a Baring seem more English than a Rothschild because the family had been in Britain longer, because no important collateral branches of the family remained in Germany, or because he was a gentile? Anti-Semitism abounded, especially on the Left.[5] Its portrayal in literature proved immensely popular.[6] The Indian prince at Greyfriars is a figure of fun, but he is there none the less, and is redeemed by his prowess at cricket.[7] United States populism revived deep-seated republican sentiments, xenophobic, anti-aristocratic, anti-British.

And if integration, however imperfect, was the rule, there were too many exceptions for comfort. Those British merchants who survived the rigours of the climate had always looked to return from the tropics, but many returned also from eligible lands of settlement with temperate climates and liberal institutions—from the South American republics, even from New Zealand—while retaining interests in local companies and continuing to invest in mortgage loans.[8] In Spain, the British-owned Rio Tinto Company had started life in the 1870s with a staff of young and open-minded bachelors. Perhaps a third of the senior staff were Spanish; one or two were German, as might be expected in a mining enterprise; but no marked differences in salaries or terms of employment divided the national groups. But by the turn of the century the community had developed into a staid group of families clustered in their bungalows around the *club ingles*. There were far fewer Spanish managers. Junior staff from Britian no longer lodged with Spanish families, but lived, as they did over much of the world in the later nineteenth century, in what were known as chummeries, where the hearty culture of the new public schools was prolonged in team games, hunting and raucous sing-songs around the ubiquitous piano.[9] A British employee of Rio Tinto who married a Spanish woman could expect to be ostracised. He would have to live down the road in the Spanish community. He would be invited to company social functions, and doubtless expected to attend, but without his wife and children.[10]

ARGENTINA

Some sense of chronology and of cultural distinctions is required if this welter of anecdotal material is to be reduced to order. Let us consider first the extent to which merchants of differing nationalities collaborated in joint ventures in a newly independent Argentina. Here, we find a great variety of more or less permanent relationships. It appears that established firms often financed or employed newcomers. The Anchorenas financed the import trade of Thomas Fair and others.[11] Sebastian Lezica y hnos, a Buenos Aires house with connexions or branches in Brazil and on the West Coast, specialised in the import of German goods and employed a number of Germans including one member of the Rhenish Kreglinger family, soon to become major importers of Argentine wool through Antwerp.[12] Zimmermann Fair & Co., Anglo-German successors to the undertakings of David Curtis DeForest, Johann Zimmermann and the Lynch brothers, provided a clerkship for the young Frederic Wanklyn in the 1850s, though to call the firm Anglo-German seems a little strained; after all, the Zimmermanns already spoke English at home in the 1820s. Johann marked letters, even letters from Hamburg, 'received' and 'answered', and had educated all but one of his sons in the United States; and the only one he did send to Germany for schooling finally settled in Ealing, a director of several impeccably British River Plate companies.[13]

If employment and exchange crossed narrowly conceived national boundaries, so too did partnership and collaboration in the direction of joint stock companies. The boom years of the early 1820s provide many examples, as do the years following the fall of Juan Manuel de Rosas in 1852. The Discount Bank of Buenos Aires, established in 1822, numbered among its founder directors Juan José Cristobal de Anchorena, Thomas Fair, William Cartwright, Robert Montgomery, James Brittain, Juan Pedro Aquirre and Sebastian Lezica.[14] Of the two disastrous Argentine mining companies of this period, one, the Rio de la Plata Mining Association, was British, but its rival was formed by a group including William Parish Robertson, Juan José Cristobal de Anchorena and Felix Alzaga.[15] In the world of international trade, the German-American connexions first established by men like DeForest, Tornquist, Zimmermann and Lynch in the pre-independence period continued to flourish in a series of transnational partnerships. Originally arising from the export of German textiles, this cousinhood survived to become a conduit for Argentine wool, which proved more suited to Continental than to British requirements. Lynch Zimmermann & Co., 1818–22, gave way to Juan C. Zimmermann & Co., 1822–24, Zimmermann Frazier & Co., 1824–58, and Zimmermann Fair & Co. The partners, in 1836, included Zimmermann, Antonio Lynch and Franz Halbach in Buenos Aires, Benjamin W. Frazier of Philadelphia and a German, Charles Rodewald, at Montevideo. The firm also employed a permanent representative or agent in Bremen, one Wilhelm Haas. Sebastian Lezica y hnos, with its largely German staff, acted as consignee for goods sent by the Rhenische-Westindische Kompanie, and continued to rival the Zimmermann connexion up to its failure in 1835, at which point many of its employees passed to the rather grandly named Carlos Augusto Bunge von Reinessend y von Rausenbusch, the Remscheid-born son of a Lutheran pastor, who had married a widowed first cousin of

Sebastian and Faustino Lezica the year before. His firm, Bunge Heretz y cía, was succeeded in 1849 by Bunge Bornefeld y cía, under the direction of a younger brother or nephew, Hugo Bunge, also or Remscheid. Finally, three Argentines, Braulio Costa, Felix Castro and Marcelino Carranza, were in partnership during the 1820s with William Parish Robertson, Scottish scion of the Hamburg Parish family, to distribute North American wheat imported by William Ford & Co., an American house.[16] By the 1840s the nationality of such firms was unclear. Baring Brothers' representative, Francis Falconnet, in a report dated June 1844, listed Bunge Heretz y cía, 'a highly respectable import-export house . . . possessed of extensive means, with unlimited credit', as German, and Zimmermann Frazier & Co., 'a very large, connected commercial house . . . in good credit, not very wealthy', as American; but such distinctions were neither easy nor important.[17]

Certain aspects of this cosmopolitan tradition were further developed during the dictatorship of Juan Manuel de Rosas. In the wake of an unsuccessful rebellion of 1840, as Rosas launched a campaign of terror against his political opponents, a number of wealthy Argentines transferred their properties to British citizens.[18] In May 1842, as the *mazorca*, Rosas' internal security force, ran loose in Buenos Aires, many *unitarios* sought shelter in the houses of British and other foreign merchants. There they 'were stored away for days, weeks, even months, . . . until they could be smuggled off to sea in disguise'.[19]

Two houses, one North American and the other British, were clearly implicated. The first, S. B. Hale & Co., had been founded in the 1830s by a Bostonian, Samuel Hale, who operated a fleet of 'Portland coffins', carrying Maine pine south to exchange for South American hides which he sold to the New England footwear and saddlery industries. Introducing the firm to Rathbones of Liverpool in 1856, Brownells Grey & Co. guardedly declared that it was 'considered reputable, and said to have property'.[20] A more fullsome report reached Baring Brothers the following year, in which the firm was described as 'in very good credit', and Hale himself as 'rich, prudent and clear-headed'.[21] Prudent or not, Hale aligned himself firmly with the *unitario* faction. A firm friend of politician, publicist and future president, Domingo Faustino Sarmiento, Hale is said to have assisted in the escape of many enemies of Rosas.

The second case is of the Buenos Aires merchant, Edward Lumb.[22] Among Lumb's close friends was Alvaro de la Riestra, a captain in the bodyguard of Fernando VII of Spain, who had been forced to leave Spain and had settled in Argentina. The two families were clearly intimate by 1840, the year of the *unitario* revolt, when Lumb's eighth child was christened Elizabeth Riestra Lumb. It was natural, therefore, that Alvaro's son, Norberto de la Riestra, should look to Lumb for assistance when the family estates were seized and he became a fugitive. De la Riestra took refuge in Liverpool, where he became a partner in Joseph Green & Co., the Liverpool affiliate of Nicholson Green & Co. of Buenos Aires and Montevideo and Green Nicholson & Co. of Valparaiso.[23] But the Buenos Aires managing partner of Nicholson Green & Co. in 1844 was none other than Edward Lumb, and the alliance was to be made still more sure when Henry Applin Green, who had arrived from Liverpool to take up a junior partnership in 1839, married Mary Ann Lumb, eldest daughter of his partner, in 1846.[24]

Britons, Germans, Yankees and Argentines, the last generally with little more than a generation's lead in local residence over the others: they did business together, they formed partnerships. But were these simply cordial and lucrative engagements between distinct communities, or was a single cosmopolitan class coming into being? Intermarriage, the attainment of public office, the acquisition of land, and failure to return to the country of origin are the key variables. Less tangible, but no less important, is the existence of a shared ideology.

Vera Reber succeeded in finding data on 68 of the 148 men who joined the Buenos Aires foreigners' club in 1841, the year it was founded. Of these, 56 per cent married Argentine women, while 25 per cent married women of other nationalities, not necessarily their own.[25] Even allowing for the fact that those traceable in Argentine sources are more likely to have married than those who disappear from the record, these figures hardly support Reber's earlier suggestion that marriages between British merchants and Argentine women were unusual. Occasionally a marriage encountered opposition from the ecclesiastical authorities. That of Samuel Lafone to Maria Quevado y Alsina in 1832 was denounced, and a fine extracted from Lafone by the ecclesiastical court before a further wedding was permitted the following year, the Roman ceremony preceding the Anglican.[26] But this apparently isolated case may be put down to the general mood of reaction against liberalism which followed the downfall of Bernardino Rivadavia. Writing at the peak of post-independence liberalism, one English observer noted that several Englishmen had recently married Argentines, submitting to the Roman ceremony, and that this had caused no great difficulties.[27]

Though he himself married an Englishwoman, Elizabeth Yates, in 1825, Edward Lumb provides, through his offspring, an indication of the sort of cousinhood which developed in mid-nineteenth century Buenos Aires.[28] The eldest child, we know, married the Liverpool merchant and partner of her father, Henry Green. From this marriage were born some eleven children, of whom six married. Their issue, by the 1940s, had intermarried with the Bunge, Casares, Casal, Vedoya, Devota, Bullrich and Sanchez Elia families, among others: an eminent selection from the Argentine social register. Green's third child, Lucia, forged an especially useful alliance with a merchant and *estanciero* of Liverpool-Scottish origins by her marriage to John C. Bell. By other marriages the Lumbs linked themselves with the leading Anglo-Argentine landowning clans: the Thompsons, Napps and Goads. Edward Lumb's second child and eldest son married a Keen, daughter of one of the earliest and most successful of the Irish Catholic families who came to Argentina and developed sheep farming in the south of Buenos Aires province. The sixth child, next to marry, took an Argentine bride, Rosita Miers y Buxo, and the issue of this marriage led, over the next two generations, to links with the Casares, Lynch and Ocampo families. The eighth, Elizabeth Riestra Lumb, married Frederic Wanklyn, a second-generation Buenos Aires merchant whose roots, in spite of the Welsh name, lay in Manchester.[29] This, like the marriage of the eldest daughter, reinforced a business partnership between the two families. One son married in England, while the two youngest daughters also married away from the River Plate, to the diplomat, Sir Hugh Guion Macdonell, and to William Napier, later tenth Baron Napier and Ettrick.[30] Only seven of the twelve children of Edward Lumb married, therefore, and, of these, only one married an Argentine. Yet with such large families even a minority of marriages across ethnic boundaries in each generation would suffice, in a favourable political environment, to develop an integrated landowning and mercantile class with a shared culture over two or three generations because of the complex networks of cousins they created.

But the political environment was not consistently favourable to this cosmopolitan tendency. In the early 1820s and again after 1852 the country enjoyed bursts of internationalist liberal sentiment. The intervening years were dominated by Rosas, who had very different ideas of the proper development of Argentine society, harking back to an earlier, corporatist tradition. The result of events and policies of this period was to divide the German and British communities from each other and to set barriers between them and native society. Foreigners ceased to play a prominent role in public affairs. Rosas encouraged the creation of foreign communities with their own schools, welfare provision and cultural associations, and went to great lengths to emphasise the exemption from military service and arbitrary seizure of foreigners and their property.[31] This punctiliousness of Rosas is usually ascribed to his desire to avoid affording any pretext for intervention to the French and British forces which intermittently blockaded Buenos Aires during the 1840s and early 1850s. Doubtless, this was one motive, perhaps the main one, but the policy also emphasised the distinction between foreigner and Argentine in a way that served Rosas' broader strategic aim of avoiding any stealthy denationalisation of the state. William MacCann, an English traveller who spoke with Rosas in 1842, found the apparent ambiguity of the dictator's attitude to the British to be easily resolved. He reports Rosas' observation that:

All that these infant Republics required was commercial intercourse with some strong and powerful nation like Great Britain; which, in return for the benefit she would derive from trade, would afford them the benefit of her moral influence. They wanted this and no more: they wanted nothing which would savour of a protectorate, nor detract one iota from their liberty and national independence.[32]

It happened that this policy coincided with two unrelated tendencies. A decline in business activity and the collapse of the many joint-stock ventures of the early 1820s led many merchants, foreign and native, to shift resources into land during the 1830s and 1840s, a policy facilitated by Rosas' huge land grants of these years. While much of the land was stocked with wild cattle in the traditional manner, some was by now more intensively used for systematic sheep-breeding or agriculture. This brought into the country, sometimes at the instigation of foreign merchants, new groups of European immigrants, generally of considerably inferior social status to the merchants themselves. Irish Catholics formed a quite separate group from the English and the Scots from the start. South German Catholics seem to have had the effect of drawing anglicised North German Protestants like the Zimmermanns into a specifically German community.[33] It appears that these settlers and, to a lesser extent, those merchants who had diversified into landownership, were sympathetic to Rosas, and opposed to the hostile stance taken by the British government towards him.[34] In this they were out of tune with the more liberal and internationalist views of the principal merchants, men like Edward Lumb or Samuel Hale.

Policy, economic recession and blockade, together with lower-class immigration, led to the creation of distinct foreign communities with ties of gratitude and loyalty to their protector, Rosas. They also kept foreigners out of public office. Hence social integration, which continued even during the Rosas years, could not lead on to political integration. This process, which might so easily have developed on foundations laid in the 1820s, was interrupted, not to be resumed until the 1850s.

As for land, there has never been any doubt that the British—and most of all the leading merchants of the early independence period—were major landowners in Buenos Aires and the other littoral provinces, as they were to a lesser degree elsewhere in Latin America.[35] Recent research has indicated that Britons may have been responsible for as much as 10 per cent of total investment in the rural sector by 1910.[36] By and large, there had been little transfer of capital to Argentina; rather, capital accumulated through commercial activity by Britons resident in Argentina was diverted to land. Why should such assets be regarded as foreign at all? Only hindsight permits this, and indeed Míguez has to justify the classification of this massive sum as foreign investment on the ground that many Britons, or their descendants, eventually returned to Britain, drawing income out of the country or repatriating their capital.[37] But this is a retrospective judgement. The first generations of British landowners in Argentina appear to have been fully committed to the country. Reber, writing of the period up to 1880, reaches the more reasonable view that an *estancia* company registered in London and owned by Anglo-Argentines who had retired to Britain ought none the less to be regarded as *Argentine* capital, since it had been accumulated in Argentina and, in most cases, continued to be effectively managed there by one of the Buenos Aires mercantile houses.[38] Without further evidence, those who 'returned' might just as easily be regarded as *emigré* Argentines, rather than aborted immigrants. In any case, the numbers returning to Britain was quite low. Of the 98 founder members of the Buenos Aires foreigners' club for whom information is available, only 25 per cent returned finally to Britain.[39] Some of these, doubtless, left siblings or descendants in Argentina. Reber concludes that 'probably not more than thirty per cent of the British merchants in Buenos Aires returned themselves and their capital to the United Kingdom'.[40]

The balance of the somewhat fragmentary evidence on marriage, landownership, and continued residence indicates the smooth progress of a British mercantile elite into the Argentine governing class up to the 1870s. The only exception to this pattern was their relative absence from public office, and even this began to give way in Buenos Aires province after the fall of Rosas in 1852. Thomas Gowland, for example, who had arrived from London as a child, developed an import-export business, and married a Catholic, served in the provincial army in 1853 and was given citizenship. The following year he sat in the provincial Chamber of Deputies.[41] He was also a director of the Buenos Aires Stock Exchange, whose presidency was held by five foreigners—four Britons and Edward Zimmermann—at various dates in the 1850s and 1860s.[42] One of those four British presidents, George Drabble, also held elective office in local government in the 1860s. Michael Mulhall, writing in 1878, felt with some justification that:

... we may reasonably anticipate that English relations will progress as steadily in the future as in the past; and the beginning of the next century will perhaps see a preponderance of English ideas, as well as the elevation of men of English descent to some of the highest posts in the public service.[43]

The final cement bonding the heterogeneous Argentine mercantile and landowning elites was liberal ideology. The rhetoric of Argentine politics during the half-century following the War of Independence centred upon two clearly differentiated and opposed factions. By the 1820s:

The ruling group, professionals and intellectuals of the revolution together with some business allies, came to form an incipient oligarchy; they were unitarians [*unitarios*] with a relatively liberal ideology, looking abroad for ideas, foreign capital, and overseas trade. The second group turned inwards to develop land, cattle, and saladeros, extending the frontier, improving their investment by commercialising the livestock industry for export. These major economic intersts, the merchant-landowners, were represented by the federalists.[44]

The distinction between these two groups was not social, nor was it a rift between capitalist modernisers and a pre-capitalist landed class. As John Lynch makes clear in his biography of Rosas, the *estancieros* represented by Rosas were a market-oriented, entrepreneurial and innovative group. The essential distinction lay between *estancieros* whose power-base lay in land, livestock and the rural population of gauchos, and the career politicians and office-holders of the city, who lacked a solid economic base, but had found some support for their economic schemes amongst recently arrived European and North American merchants.[45] In these circumstances, rival publicists could not build on notions of social class, ethnicity or fundamental principles of economic organisation, and were obliged to fall back instead on the competing rhetorics of nationalism and cosmopolitanism. Federalists and their political heirs stressed the denationalisation of the *porteño*, city-dwelling elites, and contrasted this with their own authentic familiarity with rural life. *Unitario* intellectuals attested to the barbarism of rural life and adopted from the British political economists a historicist view of the development of capitalism in which unobstructed international trade and investment coupled with European immigration would develop a civilised society while arbitrary authority was disarmed by the anonymous force of material interest.[46]

To the *unitarios*, then, the foreign merchants of Buenos Aires were not merely practical allies who had assisted their ill-fated schemes in the 1820s, helped them flee from Rosas, or protected their property. They had also a symbolic function, through their participation in international trade, in the struggle for liberation, first against Spain and then against Rosas. Bartolomé Mitre, first president of the United Argentine Republic in 1862, looked back in his history of the independence struggle to the part played by the illicit trade of the eighteenth century in which British goods had figured so largely and discovered it to be 'a normal function of the economic organism, a circumstance superior to the power of the King of Spain'. He went on to conclude, of the same events, that 'in the struggle of vital interests, natural law is bound to prevail, as did in fact happen'.[47] Here Mitre echoed, whether knowingly or not, the declarations of British free traders of the early nineteenth century who had entertained the same vision of authority broken on the wheel of natural law and attached the same providential significance to the clandestine trade. Samuel Wilcocke, in his *History of the Viceroyalty of Buenos Aires*, had asserted that

. . . necessity, more powerful than any statute, defeated its operations [those of the Spanish mercantile system], and constrained the Spaniards themselves to concur in eluding it.[48]

To political radicals of all nations, smuggling was less a criminal act than a gesture of liberation, calculated to undermine arbitrary authority; the imposition of barriers to trade less an act of policy than an unnatural and ultimately futile restraint upon the irresistible growth of civil liberty.[49]

Even Palmerston found that smuggling 'conjured up a picture not so much of rogues criminally defying authority, as of authority criminally denying the benefits of legitimate trade to its subjects'.[50]

Cosmopolitan merchants in Argentina had become, by the middle years of the century, a powerful force providing symbolic as well as practical support for an indigenous governing elite with which they were already closely linked by marriage and joint ventures. Yet the Rosas dictatorship had already provided a warning. Cosmopolitan liberalism was only one strand in the local political culture. It would require only the right combination of circumstances for reserves of xenophobic nationalism to be mobilised.

INDIA

For a time it seemed that a breakdown of the traditional system of separate communities was under way in the East, as in Latin America. Collaboration between merchants from different communities in eighteenth-century Asia was of three principal kinds. The first of these was quite the reverse of integrative, being designed rather to isolate Europeans and minimise their disruptive influence on local society. In Madras, during the middle years of the century, each East India Company servant had a *dubash* or secretary who conducted his private trade. But the effect of this was to cut the British off from markets and to obviate any need to learn Tamil.[51] In Bengal, too, Company servants delegated their trading rights to *banians* who, in turn, subcontracted the collection of produce for export to other natives.[52] *Banians*, far from being creatures of the Europeans, had often been wealthy independent merchants in their own right, and retained considerable autonomy in their conduct of what amounted to a joint venture.[53] Initially, foreign merchants in Canton had to deal with a small exclusive group of Chinese merchants, the Cohong, but after the abolition of this system in 1842 linguistic incompetence, the need for guarantees of the creditworthiness of Chinese staff and merchants, and a continuing official ban on travel outside the treaty ports led Europeans to rely on Chinese compradors as intermediaries.

A second sphere of commercial collaboration was between the various European groups, who had traditionally kept their distance from each other in the East. Accumulation of capital in India arising from the immense private trade of the British Company's servants and their prerequisites of office pushed them more and more in the last quarter of the eighteenth century into the hands of Danes, Frenchmen, New Englanders and Netherlanders, all of whom, at one time or another, provided facilities for the remittance of funds to Europe. These linkages were reflected in the cosmopolitan character of some of the agency houses. Pelling & DeFries of Madras illustrates this. John DeFries had been born in Madras, though of Portuguese descent. He financed Portuguese and Armenian country traders. Partnership with an Englishman opened up a wider range of business to DeFries and a channel of remittance to Pelling's English connections. The firm also had strong Danish links.[54] At Bombay, another Anglo-Portuguese partnership, between Daniel Seton and Miguel de Lima e Souza, was active in the trade in raw cotton to China.[55] De Lima e Souza, though Portuguese, was a subject of the British East India Company at Bombay, and engaged there in partnerships with other Britons, including P. C. Bruce, Henry Fawcett, and the firm of Tate & Adamson.[56] In Calcutta three of the leading agency houses of the 1790s had marked foreign links: Fairlie Fergusson & Co. with the French, Paxton Cockerell & DeLisle with the Dutch, and Joseph Barretto with the Portuguese.[57] At the European end, too, clandestine trade fostered connexions between London and Continental houses with East India connexions. But many of these relationships were swept away by the French wars, and those that remained were finally made redundant by the advent of free trade.

In their place came closer relations between British and local merchants, the third category of mercantile collaboration. Though the comprador system in China grew out of a kind of commercial apartheid, it very soon developed into a more intimate and integrative arrangement. The compradors bought produce for European and American houses. They recruited and managed the Chinese staff. Frequently, they were also treasurers, even bankers, to their nominal employers. Indeed they were far more than mere salaried executives, and often did business for their own account, or for joint account with their employers, as well as acting as their agents. In this way they became something close to local partners in the foreign houses, their wealth not inferior to that of the European partners, and their connexions vital to the well-being of a firm. Many compradors later went into business entirely for their own account. They were notable among the new houses that challenged established names in the 1860s with the assistance of bank credit and the telegraph. Even as independent merchants, however, they sometimes retained trading connexions with former employers, cooperating in commercial ventures and more novel schemes.[58] Comprador capital and business skill grew rapidly. By the 1860s compradors were already providing substantial percentages of the capital needed for local shipping and industrial ventures. In joint-stock companies where comprador capital predominated or where the Chinese state was interested, a comprador merchant would act as managing director.[59]

Collaboration of this kind came earlier in India, where local imperial control was far less secure. In the late eighteenth century it became common for Indians to buy shares in European ships.[60] More intimate and enduring commercial relationships were common. In 1812, 'there was hardly any European agency house in Bombay which did not associate a Parsee merchant in "most of its foreign speculations" '.[61] Commercial apprenticeship in a European agency house, leading to an appointment as broker, was a common route to fortune for aspiring Parsees, who would then proceed to set up independently, perhaps in partnership with a European.[62] Sometimes this process was reversed, a reminder that British economic supremacy should by no means be assumed. William Jardine, later of Jardine Matheson, first travelled East as a ship's surgeon with the East India Company in 1802, and gained experience through participation in the country trade between Bombay and Canton before leaving Company service in 1819 to act as agent for two Parsees: first Franjee Cowasjee, and subsequently Jamsitjee Jeejeebhoy. His future partner, William Matheson, had a spell in a Spanish firm at Canton, Yrissari & Co.[63]

There was also collaboration between native communities,

Company servants, and private European merchants in the creation of public corporations. Rungta notes that Indians, mostly Parsees, supplied about a third of the capital of the Bank of Bombay when it was set up in 1840, and collaborative ventures, particularly in banking, appear to have continued in Bombay up to the 1860s, when the Asiatic Bank and the Financial Association of India and China were set up, both drawing on the capital and direction of Cowasji Jehangir, as well as agency houses of British and, in the later case, Asiatic Jewish origin.[64] Similarly, the Hong Kong and Shanghai Bank was established in 1865 with British, Parsee, American, German and Jewish support. Its first manager, who may have been French or German, was poached from the Comptoire d'Escompte.[65] Indigenous groups were far less prominent in the early corporations established in Madras, and after some early participation in local ventures the strength of the Bengali merchants appears to have been broken by the commercial crisis of the mid-1840s in Calcutta.[66] Yet up to the failure of Carr Tagore in 1851 a cosmopolitan business world still seemed possible. Tripathi, who clearly hankered after this lost opportunity, applauded the early signs of cooperation between East and West before concluding ruefully that:

> ... unfortunately, free trade imperialism would frustrate the industrial development, based on Indian and European collaboration, of which Dwarkanath [Tagore] and his European partners dreamt in the 1830s and the 1840s.[67]

Part of the reason why this dream was only a dream lay in the fact that commercial partnerships between Europeans and Asians were not and could not be underwritten by absorption into a landed aristocracy of mercantile origin through settlement and intermarriage in the way that they were in Latin America. In the mid-eighteenth century there were signs of social integration. British merchants of the 1750s emulated the Mogul aristocratic style in their dress and in the architecture and decoration of their homes.[68] Holden Furber is anxious to impress upon his readers that in the later eighteenth century:

> We are dealing with a period long before the advent of European women in large numbers brought about a great racial cleavage between the rulers and

the ruled. In these years, Company servants exchanged hospitalities with their Indian friends.[69]

He sees the British settling into Indian society as a superior caste, cohabiting openly with Luso-Indian women and providing amply for them and their children.[70] To V. G. Kiernan, a hostile observer of the British after Plessey: 'this first and . . . worst chapter of British rule was also the time when Englishmen were most fully immersed in Indian life.'[71]

In China, social integration was less substantial, and involved imitation of European styles by a handful of Chinese, rather than the reverse. Some compradors adopted western dress and furnishings. Some took to Christianity or horse racing. But just as many, while happy enough to operate in pidgin, or business, English and to work alongside foreigners, continued to measure their status in traditional terms, buying offices and titles from the state, engaging in philanthropy in the style of the landed gentry, and retaining their own religion.[72] In the middle years of the nineteenth century, before European women arrived in any numbers, there were liaisons between foreign merchants and Chinese women, usually mission-educated. There is a tradition that one comprador of Jardine Matheson, Ho Tung (later Sir Robert Ho Tung), was the son of a Belgian merchant. Ho Tung's wife, Margaret Mak San Ying, was certainly the daughter of Hector MacLean, who was with Jardines from 1855 to 1894. There may have been other occasions on which miscegenation provided recruits for the comprador class.[73] But the arrival of European women brought respectability and racism here too. 'Hong Kong left its raffish days behind and, as far as expatriates were concerned, rapidly assumed a respectable, somewhat philistine way of life.'[74] Symptomatic of this closing up of society was the history of amateur dramatics in the Colony. A group had been set up by the military officers stationed at Hong Kong. It was an all-male affair, evidently rumbustious and jolly, and it was open to civilians. The first signs of exclusiveness came in 1859, when a group of Parsee merchants were refused admission. European women were allowed to take part in productions from 1879. By the turn of the century the list of players for each production was being vetted for social acceptability.[75]

Social integration of any substance in a society with quite alien religious and cultural traditions and a strong communitarian habit was going to be a quite different proposition from integration in a young, open society such as Argentina, with a largely European population, recently arrived. Integration by marriage was in an important sense unnecessary, since Indian public life, at least, allowed for participation—though hardly on equal terms—of a multiplicity of endogamous groups. Fuller social integration with merchants, however achieved, would also have been in some measure counter productive, especially in China, for the status of merchants in local society was much lower than it was in the European settler communities of Latin America and the British Dominions: lower, even, than in Europe. In India there was a further major constraint stemming from the evolution of the Company into a territorial power. Nightingale observes that after the civil and military servants of the Company were excluded from trade formality and separation soon replaced 'the easy relations which came from partnership in trade'. The public keeping of Maratha mistresses ceased, because it was felt to undermine the prestige and authority of the British as governors.[76] More and more the social inferiors of those who ruled India, British merchants were none the less relied upon to support this small and increasingly beleaguered group.

If there were glimmerings of social integration there were also, in the early days, strong resonances of the same variety of liberal ideology that was to help unite *porteño* politicians and British merchants in Argentina. Holden Furber is very much alive to this element in the clandestine trade of the late eighteenth century. He tells how:

In one form or another . . . capitalistic forces, which disregarded the laws by which the great maritime powers attempted to regulate the India trade, built, manned, and freighted the ships which brought India goods to Copenhagen, Ostend, and Lisbon.[77]

He brings as witness Robert Charnock, a free trader who ran foul of the Dutch authorities for sailing what was evidently an English ship under Dutch colours in 1788. Called upon to justify himself, Charnock, who evidently had taken learned counsel, produced a submission well grounded in the works of

Adam Smith and other figures of the Enlightenment. He declared roundly that he was:

A merchant, that is to say a man whose operations are not confined within any region, but spread over the whole globe, and who constantly behaves as if he regarded himself as a burgher of the whole world.[78]

For another prominent East India merchant, David Scott, British mercantilism appeared criminally obstructive since:

There is not a proposition in Euclid more certain than that trade will ever find its way to that country, where, with equal advantages, it enjoys most freedom.[79]

But while free traders and a free trading ideology were victorious on the economic front in India as in South America, Manchester School economic liberalism never became the ideology of state in India, and, in consequence, it never became the ideology of those indigenous elites who aspired to participation in or control of the state. India got Bentham, not Smith; London, not Manchester. Eric Stokes observed that 'it was India which most clearly exposed the paradox in utilitarianism between the principle of liberty and the principle of authority'.[80] The Radical argument in favour of free trade as an instrument of social regeneration and political reform rested on the assumption that people—all peoples—would respond as rational maximisers to opportunities for material gain given half a chance. The state need do no more than provide law and order and the market would do the rest. By contrast, for the utilitarians, led by John Stuart Mill, who gained control of the Company administration in the second quarter of the nineteenth century, the route to improvement lay through government and law. Good government was a necessary condition of individual wealth. Only when a population had attained certain minimum conditions of material wealth did it become receptive to education. In its present circumstance, India could not respond to the market as the free trades predicted it would, and the only agency capable of overcoming the barriers to development was the state.[81]

In this way, Company rule and the British imperial

government which followed evolved an autocratic, paternalistic style far removed from the economic liberalism which swept Argentina after 1852. And this had effects which bear strongly on this narrative. For it presented indigenous collaborating groups with a statist world-view quite inimical to that of the expatriate mercantile bourgeoisie, while at the same time encouraging them to enter the public service or practise law rather than engage in trade. In this way the main thrust of Indian nationalism came to be constitutional and anti-capitalist. In China, by contrast, though something of the same ambiguity existed, the absence of permanent and extensive British rule may have made it a little easier for compradors to identify the capitalist entrepreneurial values of their employers with their own brand of positivistic nationalism. Most favoured political and economic reform. Many took part in Sun Yat-sen's revolution, and when his first uprising failed in 1895, some of his lieutenants found temporary refuge as compradors to foreign firms, a status which provided partial immunity against the legal proceedings of the imperial government, in a manoeuvre reminiscent of Buenos Aires in the era of Rosas, half a century before.[82]

BRITAIN

In Argentina the creation of a cosmopolitan bourgeoisie was well under way in 1870. In India, tentative efforts in this direction had been all but defeated by a local British state which required the social isolation and unquestioned political supremacy of Europeans to be constantly emphasised, regardless of cost to material interests and social life. In Britain, integration was well advanced. In many parts of the country partnerships between foreign merchants and Britons were no longer unusual. Houses directed from overseas—those of Baron Mauá and Khurshedjee Rustomjee Cama were mentioned earlier—constituted a significant minority in all commercial centres, as did houses managed by foreigners who had settled in Britain. Foreigners also held senior salaried positions in many commercial firms. At a lower social level, itinerant hawkers, many of them Jews, moved back and forth freely between the British ports and manufacturing centres and Continental markets.

Many of these patterns, not least the southward movement of young Scots, dated back to the eighteenth century; but by the 1830s they were more readily accepted and tolerated than ever before. Anti-Jewish popular sentiment was common up to the late eighteenth century.[83] During the French wars this was exacerbated by a more general suspicion of foreigners. Fear of industrial espionage, strong in the North during the late eighteenth century, faded thereafter.[84] In 1806 there were fifteen German merchants trading in Manchester. Twenty years later this figure had tripled.[85] What is more, they now 'played as conspicuous a part as their English counterparts in civic, philanthropic and cultural ventures'.[86] The same was true in Bradford, where the commercial quarter became known as 'Little Germany'. Many of these Germans were Jews, though some of them had converted, but this did not materially inhibit their assimilation into English society. Endogamy did not prevent full participation in business and municipal affairs. Organised anti-Jewish feeling, though it survived locally on the extreme evangelical wing of the Church of England, lacked force in a provincial society whose native leaders were mostly nonconformists.[87]

Legal barriers to participation in public life were falling. Full political rights were granted to non-conformists in 1828 and to Roman Catholics in 1829. Participation in municipal government was opened to Jews by the Jewish Disabilities Removal Act in 1845; the House of Commons in 1858.[88] A prohibition on alien ownership of land, though not removed until 1870, had not prevented British subjects of foreign birth from acquiring country estates and undertaking the public duties which went with them, as justices of the peace or officers in the militia.[89] This was no trivial matter, for the Whig faction, still dominant in English liberalism during the middle years of the century, took land very seriously, firmly believing that:

The possession of Land in this Country is directly or indirectly the source of political Influence and Power, and that Influence and Power ought to be exercised exclusively by British subjects and not to pass in any degree into the Hands of Foeigners.[90]

Education in the small private schools of the North of England which catered to the commercial classes moulded men eager to snatch the opportunities provided by permissive legislation. Alfred Horn recalled in old age his education at St. Edward's College, Liverpool, in the 1860s, where he had rubbed shoulders with youths from Venezuela, Colombia, Haiti, Brazil and Spain. 'We were, I think, without a doubt, the most cosmopolitan group of youngsters ever gathered together for commercial education,' he declared. 'I believe the old Idea in mixing the young Britisher with his brothers of every clime was to make him cosmopolitan and naturally we soon learned each other's language.'[91] Liverpool, in the same period, offered the only slightly less cosmopolitan alternative of the Unitarian school run by John Brunner's German-born father, where Brunner and others of foreign descent, such as Bernard Samuelson, mixed with sons of the native bourgeoisie—William Rathbone, Henry Mitchell, James Stansfeld and Charles Tennant—with whom they would later sit, as Liberals, in the House of Commons.[92]

After school came commercial apprenticeship. Customarily, families concerned in foreign trade places their sons in the houses of their overseas correspondents to learn office routine, languages and accounting, and to get some sense of the trade. George Behrend, son of a German who had developed a shipbroking business in Liverpool, served an apprenticeship in the early 1830s in the offices of a Hamburg shipbroker, Robert J. Sloman Junior. His son, in turn, spent some months in Bremen to learn German before sailing for Texas, where he worked as a clerk in the offices of Adoue & Lobit, merchant bankers, of Galveston. Later, a son of Adoue came to Bahr Behrend & Co. in Liverpool to train.[93] In much the same way the Liverpool house of Wm. & Jno. Lockett, which acted as agents for the sale of cognac supplied by Martell & Co., received Theodore Martell's sons Edouard and Gabriel as apprentices in the 1830s and, a generation later, their nephew, René Firino.[94]

Education and apprenticeship not only conveyed a cosmopolitan liberal ideology from generation to generation and from country to country, they also created social contacts that would lead on to intermarriage, welding the immigrant bourgeoisie firmly to indigenous nonconformist cousinhoods. If Anglo-Jewry remained, by and large, an endogamous community, the same was by no means true of Protestant newcomers. Brunner, for example, by his second marriage, to Ethel Wyman, acquired connexions with the Nettlefolds, the Harmers, the Kenricks and the Chamberlains.[95]

This cosmopolitan strain in British liberalism, deriving in large measure from international commercial connexions and migration, had broader political implications. It gave rise to a persistent faction, as much opposed to a narrow Manchester School economic liberalism as to Palmerston's Whiggish aloofness, which advocated active intervention on behalf of liberal nationalists in Europe and gave practical assistance to Continental refugees in Britain. These, indeed, were the central objectives of the People's International League of 1847, in which James Stansfeld, a graduate of Brunner's school, and his father-in-law, the solicitor William Ashurst, were both prominent.[96] Ashurst's son and namesake, W. H. Ashurst, together with Stansfeld, was once again to the fore in 1858 in a successful attempt to defeat Palmerston's Bill 'to call foreigners to account who in this country conspired against a friendly government abroad', drafted hurriedly in the wake of Orsini's attempted assassination of Napoleon III of France.[97] Members of the same group were in close touch with Continental republicans including Kossuth, Ledru Rollin and Mazzini. William Ashurst Jr., for example, was Garibaldi's treasurer in Britain in the 1860s and was one of the organisers of the British Legion which travelled, posing as tourists, to fight alongside him in southern Italy. The Ashursts were also frequent hosts to Mazzini during his years in London.[98]

The problem in England, then, was not social integration or participation in public life, both of which were relatively smooth processes. It was rather the incipient fragmentation and loss of identity of the indigenous bourgeoisie itself, which meant that newcomers, while appearing to join a single, gently progressing mass, soon found themselves becoming separated from one another by ever-deepening crevasses. A successful immigrant might pass through manufacturing or commerce into provincial society in Manchester or Liverpool, or into the London Radical *demi-monde*; he might gain access to London society through merchant banking and finance; but whichever path he took would carry him off into a culture which retained only the most tangential links with its rivals. In the first he would find himself wealthy and, within a limited sphere of municipal politics, powerful, but always mindful of the silken cord which, as late as 1870, separated aristocracy and commoners at a municipal reception in Birmingham town hall.[99] In the second, there was not even the satisfaction of lording it in their own city, for London was above all the imperial capital and home of a court which still dominated a primarily aristocratic society. Here he could only follow his English companions into a tradition of comfortable though generally ineffectual protest. Only the third, in which the aristocracy of capital merged imperceptibly into an increasingly embourgeoised aristocracy, combined social confidence and a measure of control over the state.[100]

But in 1870, these divisions, though apparent, did not seem unbridgeable. The lines were still open from the free-thinking Ashursts to their immensely wealthy clients, the Morrisons, and to the redoubts of provincial nonconformism. James Morrison, indeed, had conceived of himself as a Radical, in touch with Francis Place in 1824 over the production of tracts on political economy for the working classes, assisting the cause of Greek independence, and urging railway nationalisation in the 1840s.[101] His son, Walter, was a Liberal, and shared the Ashursts' sympathy for European republicans, though demonstrating it in less practical ways:

In middle age he could never bring himself to drink or to offer any guest of his anything that came from a country of whose national policies he disapproved. An unwarned guest at Malham could thus be somewhat surprised to find himself offered at dinner only Chianti; and this would be followed by some very moderate brandy that came from Jerusalem.[102]

Mazzini could half-seriously plead with Emile Ashurst in 1857:

Is there not a benevolent young lady who would flirt a little for my sake with the son of Morrison, who does nothing with his money, and who would give some £2,000 to me with the same inconvenience I have from giving away two shillings.[103]

Walter still retained enough of his father's Radicalism to

regard limited liability as a vital means to the creation of a property-owning democracy, while John Morris, who followed Ashurst Jr. as senior partner in what became Ashurst Morris Crisp & Co., and acted as a lieutenant of the Morrison brothers on the boards of many public companies, identified the aim of their business ventures in Argentina as 'the application of capital to the development of the natural resources of the country', and contrasted this in a public address with 'the abuse of capital [by] those that deal in government loans, concessions, etc. [and] go to make pots of money'.[104] Morrison and Morris both linked the very nature of capitalist enterprise with reform. Others, still within the Radical tradition, saw commerce more crudely as a means to wealth, and only indirectly an instrument of reform. The sixth William Rathbone (1819–1902), a thoroughgoing if somewhat simplistic utilitarian, began by giving up a tenth of his annual income to philanthropy.

He increased the percentage as his income rose because he argued that, as his income increased, it would not increase his own family's business 'in proportion to what it would do if expended for the benefit of others who were not so well off'.[105]

But the rot had set in. In 1886, Walter Morrison split with Gladstone, becoming a Liberal Unionist. The slide had begun which would bring the family, in less than a century, to a condition which would have puzzled James Morrison: one a peer, another deputy chairman of the Conservative Party, a third, Lady in Waiting to the Queen of England.

This chapter has brought the narrative of international business history approximately to 1870, the date which, for Lenin, would later mark the beginning of a period of proto-imperialism leading up to the advent of fully-fledged monopoly capitalism at the end of the century. Corporations, already important within the industrialised economies of the North Atlantic seaboard, were as yet subordinate to traditional partnerships in international dealings. Those traditional firms were operated by families with Liberal inclinations and a relaxed attitude to nationality. Many of them had moved from one state to another within the past few decades. Now, as far as local cultural and political circumstances would permit, they inclined to mix freely with families of their own sort, regardless of origin. The system of mercantile apprenticeship in friendly houses overseas fostered this tendency, and it was further reinforced by adoption of a self-consciously progressive and cosmopolitan ideology. Attitudes of local states to this incipient class varied considerably, from feverish enthusiasm in Argentina to blank hostility in China.

The remainder of this book examines the disappearance of the institutions and ideology of cosmopolitan liberalism. There are many familiar elements in the story, which is, of course, a chapter in the development of imperialism. The rise of bureaucracy, the divorce of family from undertaking, the increasing power of metropolitan finance capital and, subsequently, international industrial capital, increasing levels of concentration of capital, the emergence of new strategies of oligopolistic competition, the rise of jingoism and the survival of aristocratic influence: these have been the stock in trade of historians and sociologists for nearly a century. What is attempted here is a version of the story which gives due prominence to the extent to which the interplay of technological innovation and business organisation in international markets produced many of the features of imperialism in relative autonomy from the state. There will be an element of pretence in this account (abstraction is just a fancy word for pretence) for it is obvious that states cannot be ignored in a history of imperialism, indeed, are central to it. But the attempt to tell the story in terms of market relations, management organisation, collusive relations between firms, and the personal and social aspirations of businessmen will justify itself by setting in a new light the complexities of relations between firms and states.

The procedure adopted is to take merchant firms—many of them already familiar from these early chapters—and examine their adaptive responses to the challenge of technological, legal and organisational innovation during the second half of the nineteenth century. The tactics of merchants in extra-European centres are contrasted with and superimposed upon those based in the major British ports. Then the development of metropolitan finance capital and its effect upon the spatial distribution of power within the world of international capitalism is examined. In the final chapter the predicament of the remnants of the mid-century cosmopolitan merchant families in the early twentieth century is reviewed.

4 Adaptation on the Periphery

CHRONIC PROBLEMS OF PARTNERSHIP

My argument has been that the conjuncture of wartime disruption, a move to more capital-intensive manufacturing techniques, and the breakdown of long-established systems of regulated trade produced a more than usually high mortality rate among international merchant houses over the half-century or so following American independence, accelerated and redirected the traditional processes of international mercantile apprenticeship and migration, and fostered to an unprecedented extent an intermingling of merchants of different nationalities. The degree to which this intermingling spilt over into more complete social integration; how far newcomers diversified out of international trade into landownership in their adoptive countries; and the ways in which such tendencies interacted with relations between indigenous bourgeoisies and local states: all were matters of contingency, depending upon a wide range of cultural and legal influences. The outcome was in no sense neat and tidy, but at a broad level of generalisation it may be said that there had come into being, by the middle of the nineteenth century, a cosmopolitan commercial bourgeoisie in which ethnicity and nationality were not the primary determinants of status and where authority over enterprise remained quite decentralised without any apparent sacrifice of the growing economies to be derived from a centralised system of credit and information based upon the London capital market.

There were a number of inherent difficulties in the new

system. Indeed, while it was new or innovatory in some aspects of its social and managerial organisation and aspirations, the system still relied on legal structures that were centuries old. Unlimited liability made construction of international houses from series of interlocking partnerships a risky business. One could bring down the rest. Authority, if dispersed, could fail to produce decisions with sufficient speed and, if concentrated, could easily miss lucrative opportunities or, equally risky, could simply be ignored by enterprising subordinates on the spot. In the successful firm, capital tended to accumulate beyond the requirements of the original undertaking. Yet the failure of the Calcutta agency houses in the 1830s had demonstrated clearly the dangers of diversification on the basis of short-term debt capital, which was the only practical source of large-scale external funds available to mercantile partnerships at the time and hence the only means of achieving a profitable ratio of equity to fixed interest obligations. Diversification might spread risks, but in a world of unlimited liability it did not insulate them from each other. Moreover, a firm could be pulled apart as its branch house drifted into new businesses which no longer complemented the network of skills and connexions originally established by the parent firm. In a certain sense this was not a problem, for partnerships had traditionally been transitory, intended to be abandoned as partners drifted away from each other into new ventures. But to men trying to employ this legal form to build up a group of interrelated commercial interests over a lifetime, and then to pass them on to the next generation, the centrifugal tendencies of partnership were a problem as, too, were periodic withdrawals of equity by partners on retirement.

These difficulties in the partnership system had existed for many years. The middle years of the nineteenth century saw ingenious attempts to overcome them. The device of partnership with unlimited liability was being pushed to its limits in these years much as the technology of sail was, and with commensurate results.[1] But as sail was finally overtaken by steam, so partnership rather more gradually beat a retreat in the face of the joint-stock corporation with limited liability.

This transition was made with some reluctance. Many merchants of the 1850s and 1860s, sons of pioneering free traders, attached great moral and political weight to the question of business organisation. Partnership stood for individual responsibility; corporations were part of the Old Corruption that had only recently been swept away. If this generation adopted the corporate form when it became more readily and cheaply available, it was not simply on the basis of relaxed calculations of material interest, but because there was a very strong pressure on them to do so. The sources of this pressure were multiple. First of all, a marked acceleration in the rate of improvement of transport and communications had lowered barriers to entry in international trade, bringing in a host of new entrants and instigating an unstable period of experimental bypassing of traditional intermediaries reminiscent of, but surpassing, the time of the French wars. Transport and communications were abetted by the way in which the initial adoption of joint-stock organisation in specialist sectors, most notably banking and shipping, brought competitive pressure to bear on the established merchants, either by its manipulation of the great weight of accumulated European capital in direct competition with them, or by the support that the new credit and shipping facilities provided for small men entering trade for their own account.

The resolution of this set of problems was to result in a considerable increase in the level of capital employed in international trade and commerce and a simultaneous reduction in the autonomy of this sphere of exchange as strong tides of vertical integration swept up and down the intricate channels from raw materials producers to manufacturers and from manufacturers to consumers. It would also destroy the incipient cosmopolitan bourgeoisie, driving its remnants into the arms of increasingly nationalist states. And all of this took place, after 1873, against a background of falling prices and interest rates which provided further encouragement to establish firms to defend themselves by erecting new barriers to entry: technical, legal, official, financial or collusive.

Before examining the new pressures on the partnership system that arose after 1850, we should briefly survey the chronic difficulties and constraints which it imposed. To do this we need go no further back than the European discovery of America. During the first half of the sixteenth century the

Spanish drew on legal forms developed over the past five hundred years for the conduct of long distance trade by merchants from Genoa, Pisa and Venice. The parties to these contracts of *commenda* or *societá* were the sedentary merchant and the traveller, the latter being often more navigator than trader. In the *commenda* arrangement the merchant provided the whole of the capital in the form of goods, money and ships, while the traveller simply contributed his labour. Profits were divided in agreed proportion. In a *societá* the traveller, perhaps as owner of the ship, provided part of the capital. This style of business was well adapted to new trades where the precise destination of a voyage was unclear. It did not differ materially from the arrangements prevailing between East India Company servants and ships' captains in the country trade before the development of the agency houses. And as in India, so in Spanish America, trading captains and supercargoes soon gave way to a more settled system. By the middle of the sixteenth century, goods were being consigned to resident agents in America for sale on commission. These agents, in their turn, became or were replaced by full partners (*compañeros*) of the Spanish principals.[2] This ideal progression was not universally followed. In some firms, overseas representation remained in the hands of an agent or factor, a salaried employee who might also be allowed a share in the profits.[3] Each of these arrangements had its strengths and its shortcomings. A factor was exclusively committed to the firm which employed him, but his limited interest in the profits could make him indolent or irresponsible.[4] Partners had greater incentive, but might be less single-minded; *compañeros* in American ports appear frequently to have entered upon partnerships with a number of Spanish merchants concurrently, a course which naturally gave rise to serious conflicts of interest.[5]

These difficulties of management continued to plague international firms well into the nineteenth century, and to be dealt with, in general, by pragmatic methods. John Owens, who diversified from manufacture into the export of Manchester goods in the early nineteenth century, began by selling for his own account through commission agents in Boston and Baltimore. Finding this arrangement unsatisfactory, Owens first went to America himself, leaving a son in charge at home, and recruited an agent, George Wragg, who was to take over the sale of Owens' exports and, in addition, to consign raw cotton to Owens for him to sell in Manchester on commission. But this experiment failed because Wragg allowed remittances to lag up to eighteen months behind shipments of goods to New York, leaving the Manchester house dangerously exposed. So Owens switched to another method and another port, entering into partnership with Thomas Owen, a Manchester man living in Philadelphia. Owens supplied the capital for the new venture and charged interest on that capital plus a share of Manchester head office and warehouse expenses proportionate to Philadelphia sales. Owen received 'reasonable living expenses'. The profits were shared. But remittances continued to be a problem, the difficulty now being not so much delay as unsuitability. Owen sent not only raw cotton and sterling bills of exchange, which his principal well knew how to handle, but apples, flax seed, rice and other goods which had to be entrusted for sale to expert brokers, and could easily result in loss. But Owen died before serious damage was done, and Owens reverted to a New York agency, while gradually diversifying into new export markets elsewhere.[6]

A more spectacular demonstration of the difficulties of international trade at this time is supplied by the Leeds cloth merchant, Abraham Rhodes. With his brother, Rhodes had risen by the end of the eighteenth century to the middle rank of Leeds merchants, exporting principally to Southern Europe and the United States through commission agents. When the European trade was threatened by the growth of French power Abraham decided to hedge his bets by moving into the newly opened Brazilian market. A junior partner, Henry Glover, was sent out from Leeds. But to justify the expense of a full-time partner the firm had to enhance its basic trade in woollens with a general commission trade in Birmingham and Sheffield goods, Leeds pottery and miscellaneous manufactures. In 1810, the firm stepped in deeper with the purchase of three ships. Like Thomas Owen in Philadelphia, Henry Glover found an inadequate supply of sterling bills and remitted instead in speculative and circuitous ways. Soon, the firm's ships were taking mixed cargoes of manufactures to Brazil, shipping jerked beef from Brazil to Cuba, sugar from Cuba to Gibraltar, and Spanish wines back to Brazil. By August 1814 the Leeds firm's advances to its Brazilian branch totalled £45,000. The Rhodes' credit in Yorkshire was compromised and their activities constrained. A stormy dissolution of the partnership ensued, but was not completed before 1820.[7]

In each of these cases part of the difficulty may have arisen from the fact that the senior partners were men with little or no direct experience of the markets to which they were selling. The major Anglo-American merchant and merchant banking houses of the nineteenth century usually grew out of the existing web of cosmopolitan family connexions. A new house would be set up by men who had served as clerks or salaried partners in the overseas markets with which they intended to deal, but had returned to Britain for reasons yet to be examined. They might bring with them some crumbs of business from the table of an established firm. They would then assure future continuity of management by taking in kinsmen as clerks. But even so, they could not entirely avoid the problems met with by intruders like Owens or the Rhodeses.

Up to 1850 the Anglo-American merchant banks, whose headquarters were in London or Liverpool, generally controlled their overseas operations through resident agents, who acted under powers of attorney granting them very extensive freedom to commit their principals, and were rewarded by salaries swollen by profit-sharing and performance bonuses. But this system was by no means proof against disaster. The optimism of his American junior partner, John Cryder, brought James Morrison close to disaster in the 1830s.[8] Later, in the 1880s, the independent action and poor judgement of a salaried agent in Buenos Aires was to bring the Barings close to ruin. To avoid such risks, the merchant banks increasingly preferred collective representation by a trusted house which would perform business for them partly on commission and partly for joint account.[9] Such arrangements could easily develop, through exchange of kin and intermarriage, into integrated international connexions with partners in common. Rathbones of Liverpool relied for representation in the United States on Henry Gair, whose sister, Lucretia, was married to William Rathbone; and this arrangement was not simply adventitious, for Gair's father, Samuel, had been a partner in Baring's Liverpool house, while William Rathbone had served his apprenticeship as a clerk with Barings in London, providing an earlier bond between the two families.[10]

In the principal West Coast houses, too, supreme executive control and the bulk of the equity generally belonged to senior partners resident in Liverpool or London who had earned their spurs by an earlier stay in Peru or Chile. By the middle of the nineteenth century, control over junior partners was exerted through judicious exercise of carrot and stick. The incentive lay in profit-sharing, which allowed salaried partners to accumulate sufficient capital to replace retiring seniors. Antony Gibbs & Sons allowed 12 per cent of local profits to its senior man in Chile, Williamson, Balfour, 15 per cent, and Huth, 14 per cent. The sanction, embodied in the deeds of partnership and sometimes supplemented by detailed written codes of conduct, was the threat of dismissal or recall in the event that an overseas partner took an interest in any other commercial undertaking, became involved in government, or, in the case of Huth & Co., married a local woman.[11] Such restrictions were rapidly becoming standard, except in those parts of the East where the more anarchic comprador system operated; even there, European partners were constrained. In Australia, for example, all but the two senior partners of the Dalgety firms bound themselves in 1861 'to devote their whole skill and attention to the co-partnership', while all but Dalgety himself gave assurance that they would enter into no other partnerships and accept no office with a government or corporation without the unanimous assent of their partners.[12]

It will be seen that in their efforts to solve the problem of control at a distance these houses were beginning to prohibit social and business intercourse between their representatives and the local population in ways which would mark out foreign houses from locally managed expatriate houses before very long. The need for discipline within the firm was starting to override natural centrifugal tendencies.

The second perennial source of difficulties in the partnership system arose from the tendency of the successful firm to accumulate more capital than could safely be employed in the original undertaking. If partners drew heavily on the profits to invest in land, support public careers or launch their families into society, then they stood in danger of drifting away from the firm and impoverishing its management. If, on the other hand, capital was allowed to accumulate within the firm, it could only be put to use by diversification into new lines of business or new markets and such innovations commonly carried high risks.

Very frequently, a merchant would be happy enough to withdraw gradually into retirement, becoming a rentier or gentleman farmer, and setting his sons up in the professions. In later years John Owens abandoned his vigorous attempts to sell Manchester goods abroad and settled for investment in shares and personal loans secured on shares.[13] Robert Oliver of Baltimore, after making a fortune in active trade between 1783 and 1799, moved steadily into land, house property, securities and personal loans.[14] This pattern, which we have already seen in eighteenth-century Leeds and Glasgow, is epitomised in Rathbones of Liverpool.

Up to the 'fifties—the firm's historian writes—they were primarily concerned with building up their resources, . . . from the 'fifties onwards, their major occupation was in finding ways of keeping their growing capital and potential capacity for credit-creation continuously and profitably employed.[15]

Here, then, was a system which had facilitated international trade for generations. It relied strongly on kinship and affinity. It was well adapted to the conduct of fluctuating trades in primary commodities. It provided rather uncertain overseas outlets for the growing output of North European manufactured goods. It was flexible and alive to opportunity. But it was not well suited to the running of permanent undertakings or to the creation of integrated groups of undertakings, and it was precisely in this direction that market forces and technological innovations were beckoning by the middle of the nineteenth century.

THE REVOLUTION IN TRANSPORT AND COMMUNICATIONS

How would this rickety and seemingly obsolescent system of

business organisation react to the changes in transport, communication and company law which took place during the middle years of the century?

Transport was an area of obvious concern to merchants, many of whom were also shipowners. Marine freight rates fell markedly over the period 1750–1913. Improved design of sailing vessels, better port facilities and the development of steamships all played their part.[16] This was complemented by the building of canals and improved roads in many countries which, once again, took place steadily over a long period, starting well before the spread of the railway. Improvements in transport helped reduce prices and broaden markets. Their impact was, in some respects, secular and continuous. But within this pattern of steady change a more revolutionary phase can be detected, spanning the central decades of the nineteenth century. There had been some more or less reliable patterns in eighteenth-century shipping. Seasonal winds, the seasonal pattern of harvests, requirements of imperial communications, and the frequent need for ships to sail in defensive convoys all contributed to this. But precise times of departure and arrival could by no means be guaranteed. This started to change from the 1830s as steampackets, leaving at predetermined intervals and following regular routes, began to be introduced first across the North Atlantic and to India, and later to South America, where a direct service from London to the West Coast was finally inaugurated in 1868.[17] In addition, the development of higher pressure marine steam engines during the 1860s, by reducing the space occupied by fuel, made steamships much more effective competitors in carrying manufactured goods and, by the 1890s, even bulk cargoes.[18] On land, railways offered the same improved reliability, spreading rapidly outwards from Europe and North America after 1850.

Predictable transport meant a good deal to those concerned in long-distance trade. If they could be sure of receiving fresh supplies promptly and regularly, overseas merchants need not hold such large stocks of manufactured goods. In this way the same turnover could be maintained with a reduced capital. Within Britain itself, the banker, George Carr Glyn, pointed out in 1848 that:

As every ten or twenty miles of railway were opened, a very large quantity of fixed capital was released by enabling shopkeepers in all the towns to hold comparative short stocks of goods.[19]

Further afield, regular North Atlantic packets, running well into the winter months, were already reducing the need for American importers to hold large inventories to see them through to the spring by the 1820s, so permitting a more even spread of payments through the year.[20] In this highly-developed overseas trade, it was evident by 1836 that major American wholesalers were bypassing commission houses in the major European ports by sending agents to buy direct from the manufacturers.[21] Doubtless, the availability of credit from Anglo-American merchant banks was necessary to this process, but it was clearly facilitated by improved personal transport and the greater availability of reliable, uncommitted shipping space for high-value goods. More than this, the very same houses which were being cut out by direct purchase were in many instances shipowners as well, and were gradually being edged out of this line as well by the growth of specialist, highly capitalised companies. The consequences of acquiescence in this growth of shipping as an autonomous activity would become clearer towards the end of the century as services were cartelised on all the major trading routes. In these circumstances it paid either to have retained strong connexions with the surviving shipping companies, perhaps as agent for one or other of them, or else to be able, individually or collectively, to pose a credible threat of re-entry into shipping to curb collusive conference rates.[22]

Dramatic improvements in communications compounded these developments in transport. The spread of telegraphy was extremely rapid. In the 1850s long-distance telegraphy was still beset by technical problems. But the third quarter of the nineteenth century saw the creation of a worldwide system of land and submarine lines. In 1865, an overland cable from Karachi to Europe reduced the message time between London to India from a month to less than a week. Direct communications between Bombay and London reduced this still further in 1870. The first successful transatlantic cable was laid in 1866. Direct communication between Buenos Aires and

London was established ten years later, in 1876.[23] Because telegraphy has now been so entirely superseded by other media it is easy to forget that its introduction brought the sharpest and most disruptive increase in message speeds ever. The lapse of time between order and receipt of goods was almost halved, producing further substantial reductions in the inventory requirements of international trade.

A final element in the transformation was the relaxation of laws governing incorporation. Throughout the first half of the century, a gradual erosion of official opposition to the principle of limited liability had been under way in Britain and Western Europe. Major railway undertakings and banks achieved limited liability one by one, through legislative acts, and at great cost, until in one country after another this form of incorporation was made available by a simple process of registration under a standard set of regulations. In Britain, this was achieved by a series of Acts of the 1850s, and extended to banks by a consolidatory Companies Act of 1862. In France, the laws of 1863 and 1867 were crucial. British Dominions generally followed the British lead. New Zealand, for example, first allowed general limited liability in 1860. The East India Company fiercely opposed the granting of charters by the British Parliament to companies intending to do business in India. Acts of incorporation had been passed very sparingly in India itself, and for the most part businessmen had relied upon extension and manipulation of the partnership system to produce forms of quasi-incorporation, until an Act of 1850 allowed for voluntary registration on rather onerous terms. The position was eased by further Acts of 1857, 1860 and 1866, the last of which effectively extended the provisions of the British Act of 1862 to India.[24] In Brazil, as in India, the change was gradual. A new commercial code of 1850 had made available the French-style *sociedade em comandite* as a halfway house between partnership with unlimited liability and incorporation with limited liability. But a position approaching that in Britain after 1862 or India after 1866 was not achieved there until 1882.[25]

The effects of these legal changes upon merchants were considerable. They offered a number of new solutions to the perennial problems of management at a distance and the safe employment of surplus capital. First, they reduced the relative advantages to British-born merchants of remaining overseas. Now that personal or family investments outside the purely mercantile business—in pastoral ventures or urban real estate for example—could be organised as joint-stock companies, it was much easier and safer for an owner to leave direct supervision in the hands of a local managing agent (his own mercantile house in all probability) while he returned home to live the life of a rentier or a City man, spreading some of his capital across the wide range of securities now on offer or picking up substantial fees for service as director of some of the new Anglo-overseas companies in the capacity of local expert.

Stephen Williamson viewed the craze for limited liability which followed the British Act of 1862 with disdain: 'It is un-English and, I think, will lead to mischief.'[26] Yet before long his firm was in the business of company promotion and management, while towards the end of his life he moved a part of his own fortune into publicly-traded government and company securities, many of them plainly portfolio investments. Excluding all Chilean, Californian, Liverpool and Peruvian securities, and others in which Williamson may have played an active role, about £15,000, or 17 per cent of his non-shipping investments outside the firm took this form in 1889.[27] By 1897 this proportion had risen to £48,714, or 27 per cent of a larger total. This figure was still dwarfed by Williamson's equity in the Liverpool and San Francisco houses, shipping property, and securities more or less closely related to the business, together amounting to £452,416, but it demonstrates new possibilities of a gradual disengagement from direct managerial responsibility without undue sacrifice of return on capital: possibilities which simply had not been available fifty years before.[28]

The second effect of incorporation was to allow merchant firms to diversify while avoiding the danger that one unsuccessful venture might bring the firm down. Each undertaking could now be insulated by the creation of a separate corporation. This solution to the diversification problem was not without consequences for the problem of management at a distance. In India, it was not until 1914 that the law required that a majority of directors of a company be elected by the shareholders independently of the managing agents.[29] Elsewhere, however, it was generally the case that shareholders could vote to remove directors when performance was unsatisfactory. To organise its undertakings in this way consequently set a puzzle for merchants. They had to weigh up the relative advantages of local and British registration and of courting local or British subscriptions (for it did not follow that British registration ruled out investment by overseas residents, or vice versa). He had then to decide where he needed to make his headquarters if he were to control the resulting structure now that not only the undertaking, but also the shareholders, could give trouble and might require careful management.

Finally, easier incorporation permitted the rapid spread of British-based banks, shipping companies and other ventures promoted by unambiguously metropolitan capital, which not only threatened to displace expatriate and local merchants on the periphery of the world economy from these activities, but also offered independent financial and transport services to new entrants seeking to break into their traditional and central trading activities. Contemporaries were quick to note that these new providers of infrastructure were permitting small, independent men to get a foothold in international trade, and allowing manufacturers for whom it had not previously been cost-effective to engage more directly in the overseas marketing of their goods or to buy raw materials in the country of origin.

Many classes of established middlemen were displaced. The transatlantic cable brought a very rapid decline in commissions paid to Liverpool cotton merchants after 1866 from about 3 per cent to 2, or even 1 per cent, because 'manufacturers in Britain and on the continent now bought their cotton by cable on samples', bypassing Liverpool.[30] In South America, merchants of British origin lost their dominant position in the import trades. With the coming of the telegraph in the 1870s, local wholesalers were able to place orders directly with manufacturers. Alternatively, manufacturers would send out travelling salesmen who could wire orders home.[31] Either way, the traditional general importer was bypassed. The São Paulo partner of a British firm which eventually moved out of general import-export business into a specialised trade in coffee noted ruefully in 1903 that:

There is no doubt ... that working in our present lines [flour, fish, and timber] we are in the position of middlemen whose intervention in the business is daily becoming less necessary to the better class of wholesale buyers.[32]

By this time the British had been losing ground steadily for a generation in textiles and hardware.[33]

Export trades witnessed the same phenomenon of bypassing. Regular shipping services and the advent of independent joint-stock banks were enough to break the hold of Buenos Aires houses over the export of Argentine wool. From the late 1860s, even before a direct telegraphic link was established, French manufacturers began to send out expert buyers to judge the quality of wools on the spot and buy on their behalf in the Buenos Aires market. At first these agents were instructed to leave the finance and shipment of their purchases to established export houses, but, increasingly, as they became more familiar with the mechanisms of the trade, these buyers took over the functions of the exporters, saving the 2–3 per cent commission which had customarily been charged.[34]

Similar patterns were observed in the East, where the British consul at Canton remarked in 1873 that 'a trade which was in the hands of the few has drifted into those of the many' because the need for a large capital had been obviated by improvements in banking facilities.[35] A later author blamed the same disruption of the China trade on the quicker and cheaper passage to the East by way of the Suez canal, which attracted smaller traders, whose influx 'brought about an artificial expansion of business in the 'seventies, much to the disadvantage of the older foreign merchants in China ... The next quarter of a century', he added, 'witnessed a steady decline in the status of the foreign merchant, especially in the import trades . . .'[36] The effect of this influx was to drive the traditional houses into relatively capital-intensive areas.[37] As Frank Forbes, of Russell & Co., noted in 1872:

The trade in tea and piece goods has also got worked down to the barest trifle of commission or expected profit. In all the old staple branches of China Commerce, the broker is taking the place of the merchant. When the period of transition is over, no doubt most of the larger firms with capital and credit will have transformed themselves from produce to industrial and financial enterprises. Those of them who, like ourselves, have the management of steam lines and insurance offices are the luckiest, and it is significant that Jardines, Heards and others are all struggling to develop this branch of business.[38]

In the absence of quantitative studies, these illustrations are far from decisive. French manufacturers who sent out wool-buyers to Argentina did so within fifteen years of their first purchase of Argentine wool. During the earliest phase of Argentine sheep farming commercial intermediaries were poorly developed and it was still not clear which was the best market for the wool. In these circumstances some of the biggest breeders exported direct to their connexions in Europe. One, with 90,000 acres near Concordia in Uruguay, loaded wool straight on to ocean-going vessels at the riverside, consigning it to his partners in Manchester.[39] Small growers, on the other hand, had no option but to deal with the local storekeeper. But as the trade grew in value, channels of intermediation became more efficient. Having initially passed through British ports, the trade was soon diverted to Antwerp and Le Havre as it became apparent that Argentine wool was better suited to French than to British needs. Direct buying was the logical next step in a business where quality was of critical importance, and it might well have developed as a natural step in the evolution of the trade even if transport, communications and banking facilities had remained constant. One must constantly beware of the tendency of contemporaries to lay hold of the nearest cause and tie it to the mast-head. Writing of New Zealand, R. C. J. Stone perceptively observed how one merchant of the immediate post-telegraph period, looking back on his career in old age, claimed:

That after 1870 the older general merchants were driven into some of their new activities as their former monopoly was challenged by the rise of local industries, the appearance of overseas manufacturers' representatives, and the development of more efficient and speedy ocean transport and telegraphic communication.

'He forgot', Stone noted, 'that Brown, Campbell & Company and the other great merchant houses had always shown wide and versatile investment interests.'[40] And elsewhere, the demise of the general merchant was delayed long beyond the coming of improved transport and communications, suggesting that it may have been the relative size and sophistication of each local market and its place in the strategies of major European and North American manufacturers that were the strongest factors in the determination of marketing structures. In Natal, for example, James Finlay & Co. found that it was not until the 1930s that 'the development of local industries and direct buying by country stores made the work of an importing and warehousing firm unnecessary.'[41]

If the notion that competition from manufacturers and wholesalers was especially ferocious after 1870 persists, then, it is partly because of the emphasis placed by contemporaries on circumstantial evidence about the scale of the changes in infrastructure which are supposed to have caused it, but mainly, one suspects, because this is known to have been a period of falling prices and fierce competition in many better known sectors, because the vertical integration of small numbers of major manufacturers into raw materials and marketing is well attested, and, most of all, because observers have been impressed by the unprecedented, in some instances dramatically successful, strategies of defensive diversification into which the handful of leading mercantile firms of the mid-century which survived into the twentieth century were supposedly pushed.[42] These must now be examined.

NICHES IN INTERNATIONAL TRADE

Throughout modern history, long-distance merchants had shown a tendency to diversify into land, into banking and insurance, into transport and physical infrastructure, and into the processing or finishing of the goods in which they dealt. The Fugger family of Augsburg, establishing themselves as merchants in the late fifteenth century, went on to control mines, land, textile manufacture and a substantial banking business through a web of branches and correspondents stretching across Europe.[43] During the seventeenth century, Vasilii Shorin of Moscow employed representatives as far apart as Archangel and Astrakhan to trade with foreign merchants, and annually despatched agents to Siberia to exchange foodstuffs, hardware and textiles for sables. His extensive business as a wholesaler dealing in domestically-produced salt, fish and grain led him into processing industries and transport as proprietor of several salt works, three weirs on the Volga, two tanneries and a fleet of barges.[44] Moving into the nineteenth century, the banking, mining and pastoral interests of the first British merchants to settle in Buenos Aires have already been remarked upon, but many of these men, including James Brittain and the Parish Robertsons, were also shipowners, working small river steamers as well as ocean-going sailing ships, while others invested in brewing, distilling, hotels and a wide range of other activities.[45] A man like Thomas Armstrong, who had originally made money in international trade and reinforced his position by a judicious local marriage, moved easily into insurance, ranching, speculation in suburban land, flour milling, and the slaughter and processing of cattle.[46]

To the North, Hidy provides a reminder that, while acceptance of bills came to be regarded as the most important function of the major Anglo-American houses of the early nineteenth century, they long retained a diversified pattern of business.[47] In the East, the interests of the Indian agency houses by the 1820s had included urban property, indigo works, coalmining, shipping and shipbuilding, breweries, tanning, distilling, plantations, saw mills, and the milling of rice and other grains.[48]

Broadly, the business strategies available up to the middle of the nineteenth century were no different from those available to the Fuggers or Shorin.[49] Assuming that he wished to remain active in business, rather than retire as rentier or landed gentleman, the merchant who was unable to employ the whole of his capital profitably in general trade could adopt one or more of five basic options. He could stand his ground, beating off the opposition by engrossing the trade in some specific commodity, whether by market or extra-market tactics, or else by trading in the same commodity in several markets simultaneously.[50] He could move into physical infrastructure, perhaps specialising in shipping, port facilities, land transport or urban utilities. He could move into commercial infrastructure: banking, marine insurance and, later, fire insurance. He could specialise in the management of liquid capital or going concern for third parties. Finally, he could move into direct local production, whether for the domestic market or for export, as owner of land, mines, plantations or factories, and perhaps also into the domestic marketing of goods produced locally by others. As he adapted to changing market conditions by shifts from one of these sectors to another, he had also to choose continually between specialisation and diversification, and between complementary integration of different activities and the looser conglomeration of unrelated activities.

Mercantile adaptation, then, was certainly nothing new, and the five basic strategies around which the remainder of this chapter is organised, were centuries old. Novelty and innovations are instead to be looked for at the level of tactics, where advances in commercial weaponry had transformed the game. The essence of the new style lay in capital-intensity. From being almost an encumbrance in the past, forcing the successful merchant either into excessive risk or the safe haven of landed retirement, a plethora of capital became the key to erecting new barriers to entry around chosen redoubts to which the merchants now withdrew as their mutually reinforcing monopolies of trade, credit, information and transport were isolated and attacked.

We shall initially take as our standpoint the counting house of an established general import-export firm in one of the newly developing producers of raw materials and foodstuffs of the later nineteenth century. What niches could be found in the rapidly changing and treacherous markets in which such a firm had to operate? Only when the options open to such a firm have been exhausted will we move on to consider concurrent changes at the centre of the world economy, and the ways in which differential responses altered the balance of power between metropolitan and provincial, British and overseas, central and peripheral, and mercantile and financial capital.

Even in the import trades, where by all accounts the pressures on established houses were greatest, there were a few toeholds for the well-heeled. Impecunious newcomers could not provide an adequate service to European or North American manufacturers whose products demanded final assembly at the point of sale, skilled installation, regular service and repair, advertising, long credits or uniform local packaging.[51] Established mercantile firms which acted as bankers and consignees to local pastoralists or agriculturalists were already in possession of a connexion which could be adapted with little or no effort to the sale of farm supplies and equipment. Furthermore, these houses were in a position to market the full range of complementary products needed by farmers at a time when individual manufacturers were often too specialised to be able to do so.[52] This meant not only that agencies for sale of sophisticated products, offering relatively high margins, fell to the older firms, but also that these firms were sometimes themselves drawn directly into production, albeit sometimes of an ancillary character, enabling them to obtain further protection—this time behind tariff barriers or specific product variations to suit local farming conditions.

There is a sense in which the beginnings of the Continental textile industries fit this pattern. The firm of Voronin Leutschg & Cheshire, established by J. A. Voronin, continued to the end of the century to be the leading Russian textile merchants but, in addition, diversified after 1868 into local weaving of imported yarns, which led it, later, back into spinning and sideways into rubber for the manufacture of that characteristically Russian product, galoshes.[53] Agricultural machinery provides further examples. The Russian merchant house of Gel'ferick-Sade, took on the partly competitive, partly complementary agencies of a number of British manufacturers including Marshalls, Ransomes, and Clayton and Shuttleworth from the 1850s. In 1879, the firm began to manufacture for its own account at Kharkov, while continuing to hold the British agencies, and this was a common pattern in Russia at the time.[54] In East Africa, Smith Mackenzie & Co. diversified during the 1960s into the assembly and distribution of motor vehicles: once again, a trade where the marketing advantages of an integrated product range, the economy of local assembly, the need for after-sales service, and the importance of long-term credit combined to offer competitive advantage to a relatively wealthy local firm.[55]

Yet in the long run, this strategy was to prove vulnerable to the forward integration of manufacturers. While there were specialist importers in late nineteenth-century Brazil offering a range of technical advice, they appear mostly to have served the smaller manufacturers. Larger mills sent their own engineers to North American or Europe to buy machinery, while the installation of this plant seems generally to have been handled by skilled labour sent out specially and employed by the makers.[56]

The example is a telling one because so many of the British merchants in Brazil had origins and kin in the textile regions of Britain, and might have been expected to make more of a bid for the supply and servicing of a major new textiles industry in their backyard. Instead, for most merchants on the periphery of the world economy, it turned out that the primary commodity trades were more defensible than specialised import trades. It is perfectly true that here, too, merchants were sometimes bypassed. Many manufacturers and wholesalers found it advantageous to integrate back, past the traditional middlemen, to the ultimate sources of supply. Shaw Wallace & Co. of Calcutta were driven out of the tea trade by wholesalers integrating back.

Constituents had a way of starting separate Calcutta offices of their own as soon as their trade grew sufficiently large, and this was notably so in the case of the Russians, when once Indian tea became firmly established in Russia.[57]

In the silk trade, also, general merchants in China were increasingly displaced by specialist branch houses of Lyons, Macclesfield and American manufacturers. By 1900 some major retailers had taken to direct buying in this trade, where nuances of quality and fashion were of such vital importance.[58] In the raw cotton trade between Alexandria and Liverpool, the lack of an agreed grading system encouraged direct and continuous contact between Lancashire spinners and Alexandria export houses right up to the end of the nineteenth century, because the exporters became the only possible guarantors of consistent quality. But while this situation appeared at first to provide a *raison d'être* for the Alexandria houses, it finally exposed them to attack. Control of Carver Brothers, one of the major exporters, passed in the early years of the twentieth century to its major clients, the Fine Cotton

Spinners' and Doublers' Association and J. & P. Coats.[59] By contrast, the North Atlantic cotton trade grew to such a size, so early, that adoption of the saw-gin, coupled with improvements in selection and packing, made it possible to offer imports 'in even running lots by sample' from the beginning of the nineteenth century. Standardisation of quality, coupled with efficient brokers handling large quantities on narrow commissions made this a relatively anonymous trade in which sporadic attempts by spinners to go past intermediary dealers and brokers were less necessary and seldom brought them face to face with Liverpool importers, let alone United States exporters.[60]

But these instances of the failure of local merchants to maintain a grip on commodity trades already point the way to the reasons why other similarly placed firms would succeed. What drew manufacturers into backward integration was, firstly, concern about continuity of supply, secondly, the need to defend against monopolistic or collusive pricing, and thirdly, concern about consistent quality. Of these, only the third drove manufacturers towards *total* self-sufficiency. The capacity to provide a small percentage of its principal raw materials internally would usually be sufficient to plug gaps in independent supply, take the edge off early season prices for organic materials, and deter attempts at cornering. To produce any more was to risk heavy loss should market prices fall below in-house production costs.

Thomas Borthwick & Sons, wholesale butchers in Liverpool and London, who acquired a string of meat-freezing works in Australia and New Zealand after 1902 and bought their first cattle station in Queensland in 1914, could accept such losses philosophically, because they were kept small in relation to the firm's total trade. In-house cattle provided only part of the supply needed by the Queensland freezing works.

They help to secure an economic balance; if the works pays too much for stock and so lose money on the meat at least the cattle station will have profited by the mistake, and *vice versa*. They can guarantee a certain supply at any time the works wants it.[61]

In Uruguay, Liebig's Extract of Meat Company, which had formerly been happy to rely on independent producers and dealers, moved into ranching in the 1880s, and was soon supplying about one eighth of its total needs from company-owned or leased *estancias*. The policy was justified to shareholders on the grounds that it gave the company independence from *estancieros* and middlemen, especially at the start of the killing season. There were further advantages. Direct control allowed the company to experiment with selective breeding to produce cattle perfectly suited to its needs. *Estancias* well placed for fattening and holding stock or for agistment (feeding cattle on the move) had the additional advantage of enabling management to secure an even flow of cattle into the factories.[62] Yet all this could have been secured by a far smaller commitment to direct production than was in fact entered into after 1909, and the problem of balancing *estancia* and production interests became a time-consuming bone of contention within the company which was not even adequately defined, let alone resolved, until administrative reform in the 1930s segregated the two aspects of the business as independent profit centres.[63] And even the inflated landholdings of Liebig's still left them buying in the greater part of their beef, some direct from big *estancias*, it is true, but much from dealers, who were by no means totally cut out of the trade.[64]

In all trades where refinement of quality control was not of the essence, or where it could most economically be achieved by independent local houses, backward integration by wholesalers and manufacturers was therefore generally no more than a negotiating tactic, designed to deter attempts by suppliers to extract monopoly rents. In trades where some backward integration took place, substantial market shares often remained for local merchants, and it was open to exceptionally powerful merchants to meet the challenge by the counter-tactic of forward integration into processing. In other trades, merchants fought successful defensive actions by developing capital-intensive processes of storage, processing and transport, or by binding producers to them through the provision of credit. In cereal production, for example, there were three means by which merchants could gain control. One was the provision of credit to needy farmers from harvest to harvest. A second was the construction of grain elevators for storage at the rail heads, without which the quality of the crop would suffer. Finally, flour milling, especially the Hungarian reduction milling required for hard wheat, was an increasingly capital-intensive process which attracted a number of erstwhile general merchants.[65]

It is not hard to think of other similar innovations in the closing years of the century which favoured concentration at some point in the chain of production and were consequently seized upon by well-placed mercantile firms. The adoption of cyanidation in South African gold mining and the supply of coolie labour to out-of-the-way tropical mines and plantations, the provision of tankers, above-ground storage, and metal cans for petroleum products, the organisation at full capacity of production line slaughterhouses and packing plants and the provision of refrigerated shipping all offered opportunities which monied local houses were, on the whole, well able to take.

Another tactic, even more secure from insurgency than capital-intensive storage and processing, was the use of advances to bind producers to the firm. A manufacturer who preferred to buy from the grower in principle might yet shrink from providing substantial advances several months ahead of the harvest, and could seldom match the expert knowledge of a local house. It is perfectly true that the newer smaller houses could play this game if their bankers would finance it, but they generally could not match the major firms in the range of ancillary services they provided or in the provision of the kinds of storage and processing facilities which have already been described. Often, too, credit relations and the attempt to compete on quality interacted. Advances not only secured consignments, but also gave the consignee a moral claim, occasionally even a legal claim, to interfere in management and so exert a direct influence on the quality of the goods he dealt in.

W. Steel Strang & Co. of Rangoon, which had originated as an importer of piece goods on commission, soon diversified into rice milling, and finally achieved dominance in Burma, handling half the crop on the eve of the Second World War. This was done by an aggressive system of what was called 'jungle buying'. During the 1930s the firm set up branches all over the Irrawaddy delta, manned by buyers equipped with speed boats, who offered ready cash for the crop and moved it quickly in large motor barges. Under the old system, small growers or village collectives had sold to local dealers and had had to wait for funds while their crops were sent forward to a broker in Rangoon who, in turn, sold to the miller.[66]

In Peru, where cotton producers were generally small, merchants were once again able to dominate. Duncan Fox, Graham Rowe, W. & J. Lockett, and other indigenous firms, were able to tie growers securely by advances against the crop and by the provision of central gins in the principal towns.[67] In India, too, up-country ginning and pressing provided the key to control of the Bombay cotton trade after 1850, because it created a more compact and standardised product which conformed to Liverpool classifications and could therefore be shipped to order, once telegraphic communication was established, at a firm price.[68]

Two further cases show the close interaction of credit and quality control. George Birnie, a tobacco exporter in Java, originally content simply to buy from small local growers, was drawn by the desire to secure uniform quality into the leasing of land to growers and even the supervision of planting, until, by 1900, he employed 60 Europeans and 500 Indians to oversee the work of 35,000 native growers bound by contract to supply his firm.[69] On a much smaller scale, Edward Lumb of Buenos Aires undertook to finance the development of sheep farming on land belonging to Bernardo de Irigoyen, but only on condition that Thomas Armstrong, whose experience of sheep farming far exceeded Irigoyen's, should participate in management and profits. Lumb also took the initiative in acquiring superior breeding stock.[70]

Yet the best of all examples of the use of credit and integrated commercial services to secure a niche for merchant firms is to be found in the Australian wool trade. It is a powerful example for two reasons: firstly, because some squatters appeared big enough to go past merchants if they wished, and, secondly, because the initial stages of processing and grading were neither mysterious nor capital-intensive, and could easily be handled by buyers acting on behalf of the major manufacturers. Indeed, both of these species of bypassing have already been remarked upon in the Argentine wool trade, where some of the largest *estancieros* consigned their clips direct to Europe, while a single manufacturer, Lorthois Frères of Tourcoing, bought 14 per cent of all Argentine wool exports in 1886 through its local agent, Gustave Hernan.[71] Here, the extent of the final victory of the manufacturers was extraordinary. 'The import-export merchant steadily lost his business to the manufacturing agents and to the consignment brokers,' noted Reber. 'By 1903, 75 per cent of the Argentine wool parcels were shipped directly to European manufacturers.'[72] Against this background, then, the achievement of Australian pastoral houses such as Goldsborough Mort & Co., Gibbs Ronald, and Dalgety, in holding on to the trade is impressive. Their strength ultimately lay in access to capital markets.

Though many of his most forward-looking schemes came to nothing and the firm he started foundered in the crisis of the early 1890s, the career of Thomas Sutcliffe Mort provides an obvious starting point because of his keen diagnostic skill. Mort realised, as early as the 1850s, that the only way to survive and prosper in the highly competitive wool trade of the future would be by a combination of vertical integration and pastoral finance. Mort's first entry to the trade was as an auctioneer. Like other auctioneers of the 1840s, he realised that small growers were being persuaded to sell their wool by private treaty at very low prices to dealers because they were needy and ignorant of current market conditions. The answer was to hold public auctions where small lots of variable quality could be sold for a modest commission to the major export houses or, increasingly, to buyers from overseas. But Mort's particular contribution was to hold the first regular auctions to be devoted solely to wool. During the 1850s Mort developed a consignment business, offering to sell wool on commission in London, where his brother, William, acted as his agent. In addition, he offered cash advances against consignments, and secured the funds for this by drawing on London and discounting the bills with the local joint stock banks. The general auction business was continued, but a second specialisation developed, namely the auctioning of sheep stations. By providing finance for the purchase of stations sold through his firm Mort was able to secure their town agencies, which brought commissions on the supply of provisions and the hiring of staff, and the consignment of their wool as well.[73] From the early 1860s, the creditors of encumbered stations even had the legal right to nominate the firm to which the clip should be consigned.[74]

The only weakness in this strategy was its reliance on short-term credit from the banks. When money was tight bankers would only renew bills, if at all, at punitively high rates of interest. Worse, the banks themselves began to move into the consignment business, in direct competition with their clients. Finally, it was reasonable to use short-term bank credit to provide advances against the same year's clip, but not to finance the purchase of a station over a number of years or support a floating debt that went on from year to year.[75] To overcome this, Mort tried, but failed, to form a joint-stock company in the 1860s. Thwarted, he fell back on a second line of defence, which was to compete with the intruders on quality of service, offering meticulous sorting and grading to suit the requirements of individual manufacturers, and using a company brand as guarantee of quality. Inadequate management and staffing robbed Mort of success, but he was thinking clearly, and others were to develop his ideas with more conspicuous success.

Gibbs Ronald & Co. of Melbourne and London was one such. This firm, established in the 1850s, consisted of linked partnerships managed by Robert Bruce Ronald in Victoria and Richard Gibbs in London. Like Mort & Co., Gibbs Ronald & Co. were consignment agents, receiving about 12,000 bales from 70 clients in 1865, of which a quarter was sold locally, while the remainder, amounting to about 5 per cent of Victorian wool exports, was sent to London for sale. To secure these consignments, Ronald, like Mort, had made advances to squatters amounting to £178,000, secured by liens on stock or, more rarely, mortgages. Since the partners' equity amounted to no more than £50,000, the firm had become dependent on its ability to discount squatters' wool bills at the banks.

The partners realised that independent access to a major capital market was necessary, and hit upon the brilliant scheme of hijacking a most respectable but somewhat muddleheaded public corporation which had been launched shortly before with a paid-up capital of £60,000 and a further uncalled liability of £440,000. The grandly named Australian Mercantile Land and Finance Company Ltd had been registered in London by a group of former politicians and merchants, many of whom had experience of Australia, with the intention of raising funds in England by the issue of debentures secured against the uncalled liability of the shares for employment at higher rates of interest in advances against urban land in Queensland. But soon after the company was set up, the Queensland land boom collapsed. A company with an impressive list of directors, a modest, widely dispersed equity, and no solid business was just what Gibbs, Ronald needed. Accordingly, they secured a merger, by the terms of which the partners of Gibbs Ronald & Co. were to continue to conduct their existing pastoral business on behalf of the Australian Mercantile Company for a fee of £1000 a year, receiving a new issue of 15,000 £25 shares, with £3 paid, to be divided among the partners, and a seat on the board for Richard Gibbs. Of the new shares, 4773 were held by Gibbs and an equal number by Robert Ronald, the remainder being divided equally between the two junior Australian partners. But since the average shareholding in the company before the merger had been only 44, with the two largest investors holding no more than 500 shares each, the board of directors soon found itself powerless to resist Gibbs, who controlled an effective majority of votes.

Disputes soon arose over policy questions, including control of the colonial management's access to short-term funds.

The original directors of the Australian Mercantile Land and Finance Company saw themselves as managing the Company and expected to notify the colonial officers when they could draw on London. Richard Gibbs, on the other hand, was the head of a firm which derived its main impetus from the colonies.

Gibbs organised a campaign to oust the secretary of the company, who, as was customary in Anglo–overseas companies of this time, was in effect the chief executive. At the 1866 annual general meeting he forced the issue and secured the appointment of his own candidate. The *coup* was soon followed by the resignation of the chairman, Sir Charles

Nicholson, and several of the original board, leaving Gibbs in virtual control.[76]

Like Mort, Gibbs and Ronald, Frederick Gonnerman Dalgety realised during the 1840s the value of a colonial house of a London branch from which it might draw funds each October in order to be in a position to make advances against the clip, thereby securing consignments. He was rather slower to accept the logic of incorporation as a means of access to long-term capital, and was only driven to this solution by circumstances and the pleas of his partners. This reluctance stemmed in part from Dalgety's wealth and success. By 1861, the total equity of the Dalgety partnerships in London, Australia and New Zealand amounted to £348,000 of which £200,000 stood to Frederick Dalgety's account. Eighteen years later this capital had increased to £934,000, partly by the admission of new partners, and partly by the consolidation of undistributed profits. Dalgety himself retained an investment of £300,000. This relatively large capital, coupled with the strength of their business and the credit balances of some of their squatter clients, made the Dalgety companies very acceptable to bankers and less likely to be squeezed by them than were second-rank firms.

Yet the Dalgety firms were reliant on the banks all the same, especially the Union, and were constrained in some measure by that bank's persistent efforts to reduce its Melbourne overdraft, which still stood at £500,000 in 1880, following the failure of the City of Glasgow Bank two years before. This reliance, coupled with the prospect of an eventual withdrawal of Frederick Dalgety's capital, was disheartening to his colleagues. E. T. Doxat, brought in to manage the London branch in 1879, soon declared himself in favour of incorporation, in spite of his chief's opposition. It was becoming increasingly difficult to compete in the financing of squatters with public companies which raised money by issuing debentures and with Anglo-Australia banks having access to fixed interest London deposits. 'I have always said these damned companies would play the very devil with us and have warmly advocated turning our firms into a limited company,' he declared. In the end, Doxat forced incorporation on his reluctant and elderly partner by the threat of resignation. In

1884 Dalgety & Co. Ltd was registered in London with a nominal capital of £4 million in £20 shares. Simultaneously, the company issued £500,000 in debenture stock. While Dalgety & Co. Ltd retained some of the features of a general import-export house, importing tea and tobacco and acting as agents for shipping and insurance companies, it now became more and more a specialised pastoral house, already handling 70,000 bales of wool a year by 1880. And when it diversified again, from the 1880s, it was into other export commodities, notably meat and grain, where the same combination of financial resources and integrated commercial services which it had developed in the wool trade could once again be brought to bear.[77]

PHYSICAL INFRASTRUCTURE

The provision of physical and commercial infrastructure must be examined next. Shipowning, warehousing, marine insurance and certain aspects of banking had been among the traditional interests of the general merchant. As the range of ancillary services relevant to international trade widened during the nineteenth century to include railway transport, urban utilities, dockyard services and fire insurance, each of these also became either more capital-intensive or more competitive, sometimes both. Merchants faced a difficult set of choices. Should surplus capital be spread across the whole range of infrastructural activities by investment in public corporations on the assumption that infrastructure was, to a degree, a collective good from the benefits of which it would be hard to exclude one's competitors? Or should some attempts be made to extract private advantage from the public need by retaining managerial control, perhaps even denying some essential service to competitors, or charging them the earth for it?

Shipping and Port Facilities
The pattern varied greatly from one sector to another. In shipping, British-based companies quickly took control of major routes in the 1860s, following the development of the

compound marine steam engine. These companies, managed from Liverpool, Glasgow or London, required agents at ports of call to obtain cargoes and handle provisioning and repairs. Very often, however, established houses seem to have been passed over in the search for assiduous agents in this sector, and new firms, linked by kin or credit with the home managers or owners, specially established.[78] These, in turn, became in rare instances independent centres for the deployment of locally accumulated—perhaps also locally managed—capital in diverse enterprises; more commonly they remained under the wing of their original mentors. The only cards which established local houses could play were their ability to operate feeder fleets of coastal or river craft, and their possession of developed branch houses. Some firms, including Andrew Yule in Bengal, or Russell & Co. and Jardine Matheson, both of Hong Kong, attempted to keep a foot in the door. Russells set up the Shanghai Steam Navigation Company in 1862 with local capital deriving in almost equal proportion from the partners, other European houses in Shanghai, and Chinese compradors. In 1873 Jardines floated the China Coast Steam Navigation Company, providing almost 60 per cent of the capital themselves and drawing on the local business community, including the ubiquitous compradors, for the remainder. But Russells soon sold out and Jardines were forced to share the trade with others, including John Swire's London-registered China Navigation Company and the China Merchants' Steam Navigation Company, which had been set up in 1873 by a former comprador of Jardines with financial support from the Chinese Imperial government.[79]

Port facilities were more promising. They neatly combined substantial capital requirements and natural monopoly with an appearance of philanthropy, even patriotism. Thomas Mort recalled, shortly after completion of the Waterview Dry Dock, that when the idea of such a scheme first came to him:

It was prompted by the great want of such a work. That was also the first, the moving cause with me. I also saw myself gradually becoming possessed of capital with which I did not know exactly what to do. It occurred to me that if I could only carry out a work which could be useful to this colony, and at the same time obtain a return for my capital equivalent to that which persons who leave the colony with a fortune are making in England, I should be killing two birds with one stone.[80]

Mort provided about £100,000, almost the whole cost of building the dock in the mid-1850s, and after failing to lease it he later invested further funds and assumed direct operational control, first through a new partnership, Macarthur & Co., quite separate from his pastoral interests, and later, in 1869, through a joint-stock company. The engineering workshops were to find many kinds of employment during the 1860s and 1870s, but very little of it was ship repair. Prolonged wrangles over mail contracts and the attendant subsidies delayed the establishment of regular steam services to Sydney, and Mort was left, appropriately, high and dry.

If the Waterview scheme demonstrates the dangers of lack of coordination between the provision of shipping services and shipping proper, the case of Carr Tagore & Co. shows how problematic a more integrated pattern could prove, and suggests one possible reason why the new British liner operators may have preferred their own protégés as agents. When the India General Steam Navigation Company was set up in Calcutta in 1844, Dwarkanath Tagore handled the flotation and took a substantial number of shares, but the other investors decided to appoint a managing director to run the undertaking, rather than a merchant or agency house. The vice-chairman left no room for doubt:

It generally happens in these Calcutta Companies that there are plenty of directors but no managers and no management, beyond that of a house of agency, at whose mercy the shareholders are placed. The directors of the new company have determined to avoid this.[81]

But Tagore managed to get his candidate appointed to the post, and over the next three years the India General was milked. It bought services and materials from the Calcutta Steam Tug Association, the Calcutta Docking Company, and the Bengal Coal Company, all of which were managed on a profit-sharing basis by Carr Tagore & Co. It was later claimed that transfer prices had been manipulated to the advantage of those enterprises in the group in which Tagore and his intimates were most directly interested, whether as shareholders, profit-sharing managers, or both.[82]

Railways and Urban Utilities

As for railways and urban utilities, local merchants certainly invested in them and helped, as directors, to manage them. Before long, many enterprises of this class were sold to British companies, and local men made substantial profits as vendors. Yet even the wealthiest were seldom able to gain and manipulate control of such companies for very long. They were so evidently monopolistic that public opinion and the local state were generally vigilant. In addition, few merchants had sufficient capital to undertake this kind of investment alone. Tramways, telephones, railways and the supply of gas, electricity and water, all required large initial expenditures, and profits could be very slow in coming. But to float a company locally would usually result in oligarchic management, while to seek funds in Europe, as we shall see, could have even more drastic implications for effective control. Exceptional political and financial skills were needed, therefore, to prevent utilities from becoming genuinely public. Robert Shewan, however, appears to have possessed just such skills. In 1891 he had managed to reconstruct the undertakings of the old-established Canton and Hong Kong firm of Russell & Co., which he had joined ten years before. The new firm, Shewan Tomes & Co., registered a Hong Kong company, the China Light and Power Company Limited, in 1901, to operate power stations and electricity distribution in Canton and Kowloon. Shewan kept a very tight grip on the company. Up to 1927 it was managed by a consulting committee in which he, a senior partner in the managing agency, was dominant. As managing agents, Shewan Tomes received $5000 a year general office expenses and 5 per cent of gross receipts from 1901 to 1919, and, over the next eight years, 5 per cent of the credit balance of the working account before allowance for depreciation, plus the fixed annual expenses allowance. The position of Shewan Tomes & Co., and hence of Shewan himself, was especially strong because the firm had been granted the managing agency in perpetuity. In addition, Shewan had used other companies in his group, notably the China Provident Loan and Mortgage Company, to take up debentures of the perpetually capital-hungry Power Company; and he appears to have used one such debenture issue, in 1907, which was tied to an issue of special shares, as a means of appropriating a disproportionate share of profits and enhancing his control. This seems to have been used to the advantage of the partnership. Indeed a rather precise measure of the value to Shewan Tomes of China Light and Power is available, for when the board of directors finally decided to break the perpetual managing agency arrangements and manage directly in the early 1930s, the Chief Justice of Hong Kong awarded $2 million to the agents in compensation for loss of future earnings.[83]

Yet the point is perhaps that to exert this kind of control Shewan did not, as Mort did with his dock, use his own capital and the partnership form of organisation. Even though availability of capital was the key factor in determining the capital-intensive style of response to competition adopted by these men, they suffered from a superfluity only in relation to those smaller companies which were nibbling away at the old import trades. They still needed to economise as far as possible on capital if they were to compete against London-based corporations, either directly or by the broad spread of their integrated activities; and this constantly pushed them, too, towards incorporation, and towards the unfamiliar business skills of organising groups of financially interrelated companies and placating shareholders.

COMMERCIAL BANKING

The difficulties presented by the need to diversify while retaining control are best illustrated in the banking sector. Almost all peripheral merchants who attempted bold adaptive strategies in the second half of the nineteenth century tried their hand at banking sooner or later. Certain banking functions—a trade in commercial bills and bullion, the collection of credit information, short-term lending to government, and the receipt of deposits—had been commonplace aspects of mercantile business until the rise of joint-stock banking. It made sense to try to build on accumulated skills and connexions in this field. Furthermore, a bank could be used to fuel favoured ventures—one's own, and those of selected clients and friends in government. Three cases, from Brazil,

Argentina and New Zealand, show the possibilities of such tactics.

Irineo Evangelista de Souza, Baron Mauá, orphaned at the age of nine, had served his commercial apprenticeship in the shop of a Portuguese storekeeper in Rio de Janeiro before securing the position of confidential clerk to an English merchant in the city, Richard Carruthers, in 1829. Towards the end of the 1830s, Carruthers returned to England, and left management of the business, in which he retained an interest, to the young Brazilian. Still only 27 years of age, Mauá made his first visit to England in 1840, and set up a new partnership, Carruthers De Castro & Co., in Manchester. Further Carruthers partnerships also fell under Mauá's control: Carruthers Souza & Co. in Buenos Aires and Carruthers Dixon & Co. of New York. The ostensible purpose of opening the Manchester house, managed by his close friend Joseph Reynell de Castro, may have been to buy Lancashire textiles direct from the manufacturers or the Manchester dealers. This would indeed have been a plausible, if suspiciously far-sighted, defensive tactic for a general import-export firm in Rio at this time. But the use which was actually made of Carruthers de Castro suggests that finance, not trade, was its *raison d'être*. Just like Frederick Dalgety, Mauá was starting to feel constrained by lack of access to capital markets. He now used the Manchester house to remedy this deficiency in his organisation, drawing on it and discounting the bills with local merchants or bankers in order to raise funds for his many projects. The first step into banking proper came in 1851, when the Baron opened the Banco Mauá e Companhia in Rio. In order to establish the new bank in the teeth of the existing Banco do Comercio, Mauá appears to have offered easy terms to borrowers. The Banco do Comercio responded, and a financial crisis in 1853 found both institutions dangerously overextended. With government assistance a new company, the Banco do Brasil, was formed, in which the proprietors of the old Mauá bank held 45 per cent of shares and those of the Banco do Comercio 27 per cent. But in spite of this the shareholders voted in a board of directors which placed Mauá and his allies in a minority. In effect, Mauá had lost control, and he resigned immediately to set up a new bank, Mauá

MacGregor e Companhia, specialising in foreign business. For this he used the French-style *sociedade em comandita*, in which sleeping partners were allowed limited liability while the managing partners assumed unlimited liability for the firm's debts.

This was not ideal. A decree of 1854 made clear that the shares of the 182 sleeping partners who had provided five-sixths of the capital were not transferable, so that the *sociedade em comandita*, fell well short of the backdoor incorporation for which Mauá had hoped. Full incorporation was in the gift of the state, which was not anxious to see Mauá competing with the Banco do Brasil. To make matters worse, the deed of partnership forming the *sociedade em comandita* placed supervisory powers in the hands of a council of sleeping partners who, to take one example, forbade expansion to Rio Grande do Sul in 1858, obliging Mauá to set up an independent partnership there to conduct business as agent of Mauá MacGregor. The way out appeared to lie, as it had in 1840, in England. Among the great wave of Anglo–overseas banks founded in the early years of general limited liability was the London and Brazilian Bank. Registered in London, this company had received Imperial permission to operate in Brazil through branches without incorporating under local law. If Mauá were to gain control of it through a merger, he might yet retrieve the position lost in 1853. Mauá plainly saw himself in the role taken by Gibbs Ronald about this time within the Australian Mercantile Land and Finance Company.

It is clear from his surviving correspondence—writes one recent historian—that Mauá expected to run the bank's affairs in South America, subject to oversight from the directorate in London. But the directors in London were veteran English financiers who did not take kindly to playing second fiddle to any foreigner. For them orders and control would naturally flow from London.[84]

During the merger negotiations, for example, Mauá failed to persuade the London directors to dismiss their inspector in Brazil, 'whose conduct he found hostile'.[85] Then, when the strength of the London and Brazilian was called in question by the Overend Gurney crisis of 1866, the merger went off the boil. Mauá held on to his shares until the downturn of 1873, but his banking operations passed from Mauá MacGregor, on the expiry of its evidently unsatisfactory deed of partnership, to a traditional partnership, Mauá e Companhia, which staggered on, perpetually overstretched, until the entire Mauá empire foundered in 1878.[86]

The same financial crisis of the mid-1870s brought down a second Latin American attempt to harness corporate organisation and British capital to a banking business that had originated in general international trade. It will be recalled from an earlier chapter that Edward Lumb was one of the most prosperous Anglo-Argentine merchants of the mid-nineteenth century. By 1844 he was trading chiefly through Nicholson Green & Co. of which he was the managing partner. Francis Falconnet, reporting to Baring Brothers, declared him 'a clever and active man of business, but ... said to be very unprincipled'.[87] The firm was clearly wealthy but rather speculative. A report by Falconnet for 1843 noted that a good deal of the business was conducted for account of the firm rather than on commission. It had become a firm of true merchants, rather than commission agents, and had in addition ships of its own running between Liverpool and the River Plate.[88] It is not quite clear how Lumb's relations with his firm developed. Barings' reports for the 1840s make no mention of a separate Lumb house, but in 1857 Edward Lumb & Co. is listed quite separately and described as 'importers, good business, well-managed, rich'.[89] What appears to have happened is that, some time between 1857 and 1865, possibly at the time of the marriage of Lumb's daughter to Frederic Wanklyn in 1859, the firm of Lumb Wanklyn & Co. was set up to provide an outlet for the energies of Lumb's new son-in-law, who had formerly been a junior partner in Zimmerman Fair & Co. The original partnership included at least one of Lumb's sons, Charles Poynton Lumb, who had returned to Argentina in 1846 after education in Britain. Later, Edward himself became an active partner.[90] In 1870, a local manager of one of the Anglo-Argentine banks noted that Ambrosio P. Lezica, son of a noted *porteño* merchant family of the previous generation, was also a partner.[91]

The partners in Lumb Wanklyn & Co., like other Buenos Aires merchants, found the credit provided by the London and

River Plate Bank, a London-based limited company, to be quite insufficient for their purposes. At the beginning of the 1870s, following the retirement of Edward Lumb to England, they determined to set up a rival, registered in London and drawing upon European capital, in order to build on the foreign exchange and public finance business they had developed over the past decade. Only the year before the firm had received a concession to issue $6 million in government bonds by offering an advance of $1 million *fuertes*, or about £200,000.[92] The London partner, John Bradshaw Wanklyn, Frederic's brother, had been busy for some time establishing contacts there, and at the end of 1872 it was unveiled: a grand coalition, more reminiscent of the Credit Mobilier than of any orthodox British joint-stock bank, the Mercantile Bank of the River Plate was registered in London with a nominal capital of £1.5 million. Initially, only £150,850 was called up, of which £30,000 was paid in exchange for the goodwill and business of Lumb Wanklyn & Co.

The founders of the Mercantile Bank may be divided into four groups, each centring upon one location.[93] First, and most impressive, was the Paris connexion which the Wanklyns had worked up in the course of their public finance business. Here were the Banque de Paris et des Pays-Bas, Henri Bamberger, Jacques de Stern, Alphonse Mallet and Samuel de Haber. With six other less illustrious names they held 7250 of the 49,950 ordinary shares issued by the bank up to 6 November 1872. A further 6250 were subscribed for by Liverpool and Manchester men. The Wanklyns came from a family of Manchester merchants active in trade with Latin America since independence. A Manchester house still existed in the 1880s— Hibbert Wanklyn & Bradshaw—in which James Wanklyn, Member of Parliament for Central Bradford, was a partner. So, now, shares in the new bank were taken by Edward Ashworth, director of the Lancashire and Yorkshire Bank, and a merchant with houses in Manchester, Rio de Janeiro, and Buenos Aires. In Liverpool, Josiah Stokes held 500 shares and Bates Stokes & Co., a firm comprising Henry and Edward Stokes and their partner, Alexander Mackinlay, held 3500. Bates Stokes & Co. were said to be 'interested in the house of Lumb Wanklyn, and implicated in precisely the same connexions'.[94] Among Argentine residents holding shares were Andrew Ure Mackinlay, local partner in Bates Stokes & Co., and another Anglo-River Plate merchant banking firm Isaac & Samuel, of Great Winchester Street, in the City. Frederick Simeon Isaac took 1250 shares. Alexander Isaac, of the Montevideo house, Twentyman & Isaac, took 200. Frederick's elder brother, Leon Joseph, at this time resident in Buenos Aires, took 750.[95] In Buenos Aires, aside from Isaac and Mackinlay, the shareholders were a familiar crew: S. B. Hale with 1250, Lezica with 2000, C. P. Lumb with 1250, and Frederic Wanklyn with 7500. Finally there was London, where nine names accounted for 9750 shares: F. S. Isaac, J. B. Wanklyn, John Blacker, Julius Beer, the London Banking Association, Henry Oppenheim, H. L. Posno, H. L. Raphael and Baron Herman de Stern. There was, as became an enterprise with such a strong Parisian participation, a markedly continental flavour even about its London shareholders.[96]

Table 1: Geographical Distribution of Major Shareholders in the Mercantile Bank of the River Plate, 6 November 1872

	Number of holders	Number of shares held
London	19	16,930
Paris	11	7,250
Buenos Aires	6	13,000
Liverpool	2	4,000
Manchester	2	2,500
Vienna	1	1,500
Other (Montevideo, Cork, Antwerp, Brighton and Birmingham)	5	2,045
Total	46	47,225

These 46 names held 94.5 per cent of the ordinary shares of the bank

Source: Public Record Office, BT31 1736/6406. The analysis is of all holdings of 100 or more shares. The number of shares issued was 49,950, each £3 paid. The 1000 £1 founders' shares are ignored here.

Management of the new bank was to remain firmly in the hands of its former proprietors. Frederic Wanklyn became managing director in Buenos Aires, advised by a local board comprising Norberto de la Riestra, Ambrosio P. Lezica, Andrew Mackinlay and Samuel B. Hale. In London, John Bradshaw Wanklyn was chairman of a board which included Julius Beer and Frederick Isaac. John H. H. Duncan, an accountant in the firm of Duncan Bryce & Co., was secretary, and Charles Raphael was appointed manager of the London head office.

The London and River Plate Bank were suspicious of the new rival from the outset, regarding the London board as 'far from strong'.[97] They had never had much respect for the Wanklyns and well knew the straitened circumstances of Lanus and Lezica and their Banco Argentino.[98] With Lezica on the board of the new bank it seemed all too likely that a large part of its funds would find their way into the Banco Argentino and related schemes. But the end of the year saw the Mercantile Bank seemingly healthy, having paid a dividend of 15 per cent to its shareholders on the first twelve months' operations and put £49,037 to reserve.[99] The only cloud, it would seem, was the death of J. B. Wanklyn, whose seat on the board was taken by his partner, A. J. Lambert.

Two years later it was a very different story. Lanus and Lezica had long enjoyed the support of top people in the Mitreist faction of Argentine politics. It was said to have been through their influence that Newman & Medici, a local firm, had been able to win the contract for water supply and drainage in Buenos Aires against a lower tender from the far more experienced British firm of Brassey Ogilvie & Withers.[100] A connexion such as this could work two ways, though, and when ex-President Mitre staged a rebellion towards the end of 1874, Anacarsis Lanus, along with other Mitreists, went into hiding. When the revolt collapsed, so too did Lanus y Lezica, to be followed soon afterwards by Norberto de la Riestra and the Banco Argentino.[101] De la Riestra and Lezica were obliged to resign from the Buenos Aires board of the Mercantile Bank, and it began to appear most unlikely that the very large advances made to Lanus, Lezica and Enrique Fynn, their Montevideo partner, for the construction of a waterworks there, could be reclaimed.

March was the crisis month. Events in Buenos Aires, exacerbated by the ill-health and subsequent death of Frederic Wanklyn, were met with what looked like panic measures.[102] Charles Raphael took ship for Buenos Aires and £50,000 in gold was sent out, part of the proceeds of a £4 call on the outstanding liability of the shareholders.[103] At this point a number of the large shareholders appear to have rebelled against the way in which the business was being managed. Early in 1876, A. J. Lambert and C. P. Lumb were forced to resign from the board, Samuel Hale left the local board, and Raphael was replaced, so breaking the last links between the bank and the discredited Wanklyn clique. In February it was vaunted that the bank might still be saved by a debenture issue.[104] A further call on the shareholders was out of the question, as several were already in arrears on earlier calls. In private, approaches were being made by the principal shareholders to the London and River Plate Bank to find out whether that institution would be willing to undertake a private liquidation of its crippled rival.[105] Anxious though they were to avoid a public failure which would cast doubt on the condition of River Plate companies generally, the management of the London Bank drew back from the burdensome responsibility of unravelling the Wanklyns' affairs, and it was left instead to the remaining directors and shareholders to sort out the mess as best they could, which, in the event, turned out to be very well indeed.

The premature deaths of the Wanklyn brothers within the space of two years, at a time of acute financial crisis, make it hard to judge whether this attempt to harness European capital to peripheral management could possibly have succeeded. More successful in attempting a similar manoeuvre was Thomas Russell. Russell, born in Ireland the son of a carpenter, had come to New Zealand by way of Australia as a child. Educated as a lawyer, he grew rich in partnership with a leading Auckland lawyer and politician, Frederick Whitaker. Unlike the other peripheral capitalists considered in this chapter, the basis of his early accumulation seems to have been local lending and land speculation rather than external trade. Russell played a leading part in founding the Bank of New

Zealand in 1861. The circumstances were as follows. During the 1850s, Russell had banked with the Oriental Bank Corporation, the first London joint-stock bank to gain entry to the preserves of the East India Company. When the Oriental withdrew from New Zealand, its business there was taken over by the Bank of New South Wales. But it appears that this company was reluctant to take on Russell's rather immobile account, and that Russell responded by organising a local competitor which might serve to finance his pet schemes. The Bank of New Zealand was locally owned, registered and managed, but had from the outset a manager and a local board in London, where it kept substantial deposits with the Bank of London. In New Zealand, as in Australia and South America, there was great demand for pastoral finance. But the Bank of New Zealand was forbidden from lending on mortgage by its Articles of Association. In 1865, therefore, the directors promoted a sister company, the New Zealand Loan and Mercantile Agency, with a nominal capital of £500,000. Unlike the Bank, this was registered in London, and included a number of prominent public figures on its board there. This was necessary if debentures were to be successfully issued on the London market against the uncalled share liability. But effective management was to be in the hands of the local board, which was virtually identical with the main board of the Bank of New Zealand. Then, in 1874, Russell moved to London, where he dominated the affairs of the Bank and the Loan Company, and established further British companies, closely linked to the Bank by overlapping directorships and common ownership. These included the Waikato Land Association and the Auckland Agricultural Company, formed to acquire the pastoral properties of the 'limited circle' of Auckland capitalists headed by Russell.

In these companies there were essentially three classes of investor. There were insiders: Aucklanders like Russell and Whitaker, who were frequently vendors of generously valued properties to the new companies and who also benefited indirectly in all sorts of ways from the influx of British capital through their various New Zealand interests. There were the British shareholders, who had paid cash. And there were debenture holders who, by their willingness to accept 4 to 4½ per cent, provided the gearing that would, in theory, allow high dividends on the ordinary shares, and very high effective rates to the vendors. Russell's task, in which he succeeded for many years, was to reconcile the interests of these groups. But from the end of the 1870s suspicions began to develop among the British members of the Loan Company board that management in the colonies was not all that it should be, and that they were not being kept fully informed. Doubts grew when the New Zealand economy deteriorated after 1886 and the Bank of New Zealand proved unable to pay a dividend the following year. In 1888, A. J. Mundella, as chairman of the board, sent Falconer Larkworthy out to Australia and New Zealand to investigate the affairs of the company and to effect a separation of its local management from that of the Bank of New Zealand. Larkworthy found considerable irregularities, but discovered, on his return, that Russell had kept his reports from the other directors. A prolonged conflict built up between Larkworthy and Mundella, favouring disclosure of the true state of affairs to the shareholders, and a majority of the board, who opposed this. Larkworthy was defeated in the short run, and resigned from the board of the Loan Company in 1890, but three years later the company had to go into liquidation, weighed down by advances to its sister company, the Waikato Land Association. Mundella, as President of the Board of Trade, and therefore the immediate superior of the Registrar of Companies and the Official Receiver, was widely felt to be in an anomalous position, and was driven to resign from the government in 1893. As for Russell, he survived the crisis by the narrowest of margins, greatly assisted by New Zealand government support for the crippled Bank of New Zealand, to die worth an estimated £160,000, some £100,000 less than his paper wealth on the eve of the crash.[106]

INVESTMENT BANKING, MANAGING AGENCIES AND DIRECT PRODUCTION

The last two paths of adaptation open to merchants may conveniently be taken together. The sale of management skills to corporations on an agency basis commonly went hand in hand with a substantial equity investment and the provision of loans. In the East, mercantile partnerships frequently came to dominate the conduct of plantations, mines, textile mills and other industrial enterprises in this way. Where local capital markets were less adequate, the managing agency system was less usual, and merchants were generally faced with a choice between more direct participation through their central partnership, or the creation of a British or European joint-stock company.

In India, Carr Tagore may be taken as typical of the many managing agencies which developed from the 1830s. The interests of Dwarkanath Tagore, the managing partner, went beyond import-export trade, shipping, port services and coalmining, to include land, money-lending, sugar refining, banking, insurance tea plantations, salt and the manufacture of indigo and silk. In many of these fields he employed the device of floating a company, usually with capital drawn from the expatriate and Indian communities, which was then managed by his firm. One historian, crediting Tagore with the invention of this system of management, has declared that:

Carr Tagore's chief innovation was to harness the commercial experience of the agency house to the greater financial resources of the joint stock company. Thus they led in the transition from international trade to the development of domestic industry in India.[107]

Others followed. Binny & Co. of Madras, established in 1799 by John Binny of Forfar, carried on a mixed business, engaging in the country trade with Java and the Malay Peninsula, and providing banking services to the local expatriate community. From the 1840s the firm began to diversify. It took on agencies of the new shipping companies operating to the East from British and European ports; it went in for plantation agriculture; and from the 1870s, it developed textile mills producing for the domestic market. Towards the end of the century further ventures were made into coalmining, ice manufacture, mica mining, sugar refining and distilling. In most cases the firm took shares in a corporation but were also appointed managing agents on a commission based on output or profits.[108] The system also operated in the China ports, where Shewan Tomes, managers of China Light and Power, handled the Green Island Cement Company, Hong Kong Rope Manufacturing Company, China Underwriters Ltd, the China Provident Loan and Mortgage Company, and the Sandakan Light and Power Company as well.[109]

Elsewhere the agency system did not take root to quite the same extent, but local entrepreneurs were able to go some way towards insulating their multifarious ventures from one another by the use of corporations which they controlled, if not by agency agreements, then as directors and significant shareholders. By such devices Mauá established a business empire spanning Brazil, Uruguay and Argentina. As well as trade, banking, shippping and utilities, this included directly productive ventures: ranching in the River Plate republics and a foundry near Rio de Janeiro.[110] Thomas Mort, in addition to pastoral finance and port services, went in for mining, railways, farming, milling and engineering. In some instances these enterprises were operated by Mort on his own responsibility or through partnerships; in others he set up local companies, though often drawing on a very limited circle of investors. From time to time there were hints of an incipient managing agency system, as when the sales agency of the Peak Downs Copper Mining Company was given to William Mort, in London. But ignorance of the extent to which Mort and his partner, Smart, were able to unload shares in the company obscures the degree to which they may have benefited disproportionately from the sales arrangements or drawn speculative profit from the sale of their vendors' shares. However, the general impression of Mort's career provided by Alan Barnard suggests a far less developed and inventive use of incorporation and the agency system here than was commonly to be found in the East.

Ernesto Tornquist, whose family had been active in Argentine international trade since the 1820s, moved rapidly from trade into banking and direct production in the closing years of the nineteenth century. A commercial apprenticeship in Krefeld and a spell with the Buenos Aires mercantile house of Altgelt Ferber, had equipped him for import-export business, which he entered for his own account in 1873, setting up the firm of Ernesto Tornquist y cía. Soon he was diversifying into sugar production, land development and investment banking. Early in the 1880s he played a leading part in setting up the Italo Land Company, a locally registered corporation in which he was joined by men of political stature, including Aristóbulo del Valle, a leading opposition figure, and Antonio Cambaceres.[111] But though he drew on local resources, Tornquist also attracted capital from Europe, especially Antwerp. In 1884, when a new five-year deed of partnership was signed, the capital of the firm was raised from 1.25 million francs to 8 million francs (£1 sterling: 25 Belgian francs), of which half was supplied by the partners in Buenos Aires and Montevideo, and half in ten equal shares by sleeping partners including the Nottebohms, the Osterrieths, Corneille David & Co., and Felix Grisar. All but one of the sleeping partners were residents of Antwerp.[112] Several were already deeply concerned in other River Plate enterprises, notably Liebig's Extract of Meat Company.[113]

At this stage the firm still handled a considerable general trade with Northern Europe through their Antwerp agents, Victor Lynen & Co., exporting foodstuffs and importing Belgian and German machinery.[114] But in 1894, when the partnership agreement was once again revised, the *de facto* conversion to a merchant banking business was finally recognised and the mercantile interests passed over to a distinct, though related, firm.[115] By the end of the century the business was acknowledged to be 'practically that of bankers' even by the bankers themselves.[116] But though Tornquists were later to move into retail banking, their operations at this point were largely in industrial banking. On the base of their European partnership capital they borrowed funds in Germany and from local retail bankers in Argentina at rates a shade above the prevailing discount rates, which they then pushed into pastoral finance, meat packing and, above all, into the sugar industry, in which the partners were directly and largely interested.[117]

In the northern province of Tucuman, the arrival of the railway in 1876 had opened up the major coastal cities to the traditional sugar industry. But a modern refinery was needed to produce a product of sufficient quality to replace imported refined sugar. Tornquist obtained from the federal government a concession to establish just such a refinery and established a corporation in 1887, La Refineria Argentina, which he controlled by a 48 per cent equity stake and an agency contract which gave his firm effective control over managerial appointments as well as commissions on the purchase of machinery.[118] In addition, Tornquist y cía, rather than the refinery company, financed the growers and took the commissions and profits on this large business. This was done through the creation of a further company, the Tucuman Sugar Company, to handle purchases for the refinery, which it was enabled to do by loans from the local joint-stock banks. The Refinery Company then processed the sugar at a fixed rate per kilo for the Sugar Company, which handled the eventual sale of the finished product.[119] Details of the relative equity stake of Tornquists' partners in the central partnership, the Sugar Company, and the Refinery are not clear from published materials; nor, perhaps not surprisingly, are details of transfer pricing arrangements within the group, though it is worth noting that Tornquists had increased the gearing of their substantial equity stake in La Refineria Argentina by a London debenture issue in 1889.[120] Yet this clearly was an arrangement not unlike the Indian managing agency system, and one which offered similar possibilities of wide and complementary diversification coupled with attractive opportunities for the appropriation by the central partnership of a share in profits disproportionate to the capital put up by the partners.

This chapter has examined international commerce and finance in the middle years of the nineteenth century by taking one activity after another—first trade, then physical and commercial infrastructure, and finally investment banking and management services. The contrast with the two preceding chapters, which were organised geographically, is no mere whim. While many international firms remained in a number of mutually reinforcing activities in the mid-nineteenth century, the rise of capital-intensity, by its effects on their own operations, on transport and communications, and above all on the raw material grading and final product marketing demands of the manufacturers they depended upon, made it more and more difficult for merchants to pursue the mercurial course of earlier years, when they had been used to shift from one commodity to another, move from port to port, and vary the scale of their operations just as it suited them. Now, if they wanted to survive, they had to choose their ground, occupy it and defend it. The siege mentality of oligopolistic competition was gradually destroying the hussar outlook of the merchants. For most firms this meant a degree of specialisation or a spurious diversification which consisted of the creation of groupings of interdependent firms rather than the successive and unrelated stabs in the dark of the previous generation.

Yet if this was the dominant strategy, why was it that so few of the firms examined in this chapter succeeded? For every Dalgety there appears to be a host of Mauás. In the chapter that follows it will be argued that location was decisive in the competitive battles of the late nineteenth-century commercial world. To be in London, at the centre of international finance and commerce, was to start ahead of the pack.

5 Concentration at the Centre

BRITISH-BASED MERCANTILE CAPITAL

Care was been taken throughout the later sections of Chapter 4 to limit illustration of mercantile diversification largely to firms which, while engaged in international trade, were firmly based in commercial centres outside the core industralised areas of Europe and North America. Thomas Mort, though born in Lancashire, spent his adult life in Australia and died there. Frederick Dalgety, son of a lieutenant in the Royal Irish Fusiliers, had been born in Canada, and arrived in Australia when he was only sixteen. Lumb had been no more than fourteen when he first visited Buenos Aires; Russell, nine, when he arrived in New Zealand from Ireland. All had made their fortunes in the countries of their adoption. Like the others, Robert Shewan was a young man of twenty-one years of age when he joined what was still at that time a New England house. Ernesto Tornquist, Charles Lumb and the Wanklyn brothers were second-generation immigrants. Tagore and Mauá could not claim European descent but were honorary Europeans through their partnerships with Carr, Prinsep, Carruthers and MacGregor. Binney and Co., though it recruited partners from Scotland, was under firm expatriate control. Madras was head office and 'partners in London were reluctant to interfere directly with decisions taken in Madras'.[1]

In other words, we have so far established only the first element in a model of mid-nineteenth century mercantile adaptation. Upon the manoeuvres of these peripheral capitalists must be superimposed the strategems developed in

141

response to very much the same stimuli—improved transport and communications, changes in commercial law, new processing technologies—by metropolitan merchants, pure financiers, and, in so far as they affected *international* business at this time, by industrialists.

In Britain, it was Liverpool, Glasgow, Manchester and, above all, London that housed the principal concentrations of international merchants by the middle of the nineteenth century. Firms managed from these four cities traded with almost every part of the world, and their partners were no less aware than their overseas competitors of new opportunities for adaptation. They had, however, the additional advantages of ready access to new technology and proximity to capital markets.

Liverpool

In Liverpool, the development of shipping services provided the principal route out of general trade. The Holts, perhaps most successful of the great shipowning families, first rose to prominence through the success of George Holt in the cotton trade during the first four decades of the century. He invested his surplus funds in urban property and insurance. But the third of his sons, Alfred, after an apprenticeship with the engineer of the Liverpool and Manchester Railway Company, gained valuable experience of the problems of designing and operating steamships through a brief appointment with Lamport & Holt in 1851. Holt worked on the technical problem of building a screw-driven iron steamer that could operate economically on long runs. He experienced some success during the 1850s. Relying on capital drawn from his family and its connexion, he ran steamers to the West Indies during the 1850s and early 1860s. But severe competition reduced profits so much that Holt sold out in 1864 and decided to operate along a much longer route, where the technical advantages of his newly developed tandem-type compound engine would provide an effective barrier against other firms. For this purpose, the Ocean Steam Ship Company was set up in 1865 with a paid-up capital of £156,000.

This was not a limited company, nor did it become one until 1902. Alfred and his brother Philip, who together managed the company, put up almost a third of the capital. Their family provided another fifth, and a further 14 per cent came from close friends and associates. Fresh injections of capital continued to be drawn from this select group. There were only 26 original shareholders, a number which had risen to 58 by 1875; and the new Articles of Association of that year provided that whenever a stockholder died or became insolvent or bankrupt or, if a woman, married, her stock had to be offered for sale to the company or its members unless a majority consented to the continued membership of the heir, creditor or husband. This rule kept the number of stockholders below one hundred.[2]

The same pool of capital was available to others born into the Liverpool mercantile elite. Alfred Booth, six years younger than Alfred Holt, also received his introduction to shipping through service with Lamport & Holt before working for two years in Rathbones' New York house. In 1860 he entered into partnership with his younger brother Charles and an American named Walden to export English light leathers to the United States. His Liverpool connexions secured him in addition the New York agency for Alfred and Philip Holt's steamers, still, at that time, operating in the North Atlantic. The capital for this new firm came largely from the Booth family, which had already made its mark in Liverpool. But the brothers also received substantial credits from the Holts, the Rathbones and other leading families, and continued for many years to rely on funds of this sort. In 1880, for example, the working capital of the firm amounted to £116,000, of which £44,000 consisted of deposits from family and friends. In 1896 such deposits amounted to just under a quarter of the firm's resources.

Because of their close connexion with the Holts, the Booths were quick to realise the implications of the new compound marine steam engines. Relatively short of capital themselves, but anxious to retain management and control of the new enterprise, they looked for a route long enough to yield the benefit of the new technology but short enough to be served and dominated by two ships. North Brazil seemed ideal, and in 1865, the same year that Holts started Ocean, Booths went into the steamship management for their own account. As with the Ocean Company, so with Booths' ships, ownership was not at all widely dispersed. When a limited company was formed in 1881 to take over the four ships then operated by the Booths, the shares were held largely by the partners in Alfred Booth & Co. and members of the Holt family. Up to 1873 Holts' engineers had serviced Booths' vessels.

As shipowners, the Booth family were subordinate to Holts. However, the firm were not simply specialist shipping managers, as Holts were. Rather, they continued the tradition of diversified mercantile enterprise. In addition to the 10 per cent of net earnings which it derived from the shipping company, the firm earned profits and commissions from a broad general trade with the United States, selling tinplate, soda ash, hops and paper in New York on commission, dealing in United States bonds for Liverpool friends, and continuing to handle the New York agencies of other Liverpool shipowners. But the principal counterweight to the Brazilian shipping line was the trade in leather, where Booths sold in the States both for their own account and, on commission, for British tanners. Gradually Booths were drawn into other stages of the business. In 1877 a major client, Kent & Stevens of Gloversville, New York, failed, owing Booths $70,000. One of the proprietors, John Kent, had been especially active in developing new methods of tanning and leather dressing, so Booth decided to pay off the other creditors and operate the factory jointly with Kent. Further integration into manufacturing took place in England, where Booths set up the Nuneaton Leather Company in 1882 to develop heavy grains that would be better suited to the New York market, and so avoid the build-up of unsaleable stocks there. The same concern for quality was starting to draw Booths into closer contact with the sources of supply of untreated skins at a time when these were beginning to be drawn into Europe and North America from a wider and wider circle of countries. By 1890, the firm had its own buying agent in Sydney selecting kangaroo skins which, along with Brazilian goatskins, had become a profitable raw material for the Gloversville factory.

If the ability to draw on a pool of sympathetic mercantile capital and expertise had been the foundation of Booths' prosperity, their position was very substantially improved after 1890 by exploitation of two new technological developments.

Chrome tanning, a new process which reduced the cost of producing kid, led to a massive increase in United States consumption of goatskins during the 1890s. Booths quickly established a brand name, 'Surpass', for their chrome-tanned kid, and used their mercantile skills and connexions to set up a reliable supply network, buying chiefly through Hen & Hirsch of Pernambuco, Rossback & Delmiro, of Ceará, Pará and Bahia, the Zurich-based firm of Cohn Brothers & Fuchs in Calcutta, and Liddell Brothers in China. At the same time, an extensive sales organisation was being created in the United States, where travelling salesmen, equipped with automobiles by the early 1900s, operated from branches in New York, Boston, St. Louis, Cincinnati and Rochester.

Quite fortuitously, Booths' position in Brazilian shipping put them in a position to profit by a second, concurrent, technological development—the invention of the pneumatic tyre in 1888, which brought massive demand for wild rubber from the Amazon basin. The firm moved quickly downmarket from their early specialisation in the carriage of high-value goods, operating much bigger ships that could handle the new traffic in immigrants, construction materials and rubber itself, thus deterring new entrants to the trade as far as possible. Investment in local feeder lines, investment in the construction and operation of port facilities and engineering workshops at the main rubber port of Manáos, and an amalgamation with their old Liverpool rivals, Singlehursts, in 1901, all but completed a defensive strategy designed to secure a monopoly of the Amazon trade. A brief rate war with the Hamburg-Amerika line in 1902 led to the creation of an effective oligopoly governed by a pooling agreement.[3]

A third Liverpool house within the Holt cousinhood was John Swire & Sons. John Swire Senior, the founder of the firm, had come to Liverpool, like George Holt, in the early years of the century and established a general import-export house. His sons, John and William, inherited a business embracing a broad trade in foodstuffs, hardware and earthenware, with ports in North America and on the Atlantic coast of Europe.[4] An abortive attempt to develop a trade with Australia in the 1850s was followed by a much more successful expansion in the Far East. Founding shareholders in Holts' Ocean Steam Ship

Company in 1865, the Swire brothers were appointed agents for the company and, in 1866, established a new firm, Butterfield & Swire, with a branch in Shanghai to handle this business and to develop and redirect their existing export trade in textiles. In 1868 the textile manufacturer, R. S. Butterfield, withdrew from this new firm, which became, in effect, the Shanghai branch of John Swire & Sons. Soon, further branches were established in several Chinese ports and at Yokohama.[5] The next twenty years saw John Swire's mercantile undertakings expand to include the sales agency of John Fowler of Leeds, manufacturer of railway locomotives and equipment, the export of tea to Britain, the United States and Australia, and the bottling and export of stout to Australia. The shipping side of the business grew apace, as Butterfield & Swire added the White Star agency to that of the Ocean Steam Ship Company. In addition, the firm broke into coastal and river shipping in the face of opposition from entrenched locally-managed houses such as Jardine, Matheson or Russells. Here, Swire had the advantage of support from Holts and other Liverpool capitalists and the ability to draw on the London capital market. For the river trade he used the device of a London registered company with limited liability for which the partnership could act as managing agents. In this way the China Navigation Company came into being in 1872 with a paid up capital of £300,000. Though its shares were publicly issued, the principal holders were the Swires, Holts, Rathbones and other Liverpool families, and the Greenock shipbuilder, John Scott.[6] On The China Coast a more old-fashioned financial structure was adopted up to 1883 because Scott and H. J. Butterfield (brother of the Swires' former partner), the original co-owners of the two vessels with which Swire had begun this venture in 1874, were opposed to limited liability. Then the two undertakings, the China Navigation Company and the Coast Boats Ownery, were amalgamated, the former absorbing the latter.[7] A final strand in Swire's Far Eastern business was the creation of the Taikoo sugar refinery at Hong Kong. Again, the device was adopted of a limited company, registered in London, and drawing on a relatively narrow community of friends and business associates, including the Holts, H. J. Butterfield, Ismay & Imrie of

Liverpool, and a sugar manufacturer, James Barrow. Once again, Butterfield & Swire in Hong Kong and John Swire in London were to act as agents, taking commissions on purchases and sales, recruiting staff and overseeing management.

This survey of strategies adopted by Liverpool merchants may best be concluded by an account of two firms operating on the West Coast of America. W. & J. Lockett & Co. had been established by two brothers in the late 1830s. The firm traded, often in its own vessels, to the maritime provinces of British North America, to Barbados and Trinidad, to Australia, and to Calcutta, Macao and Bombay, dealing in coal, wines, cotton textiles, raw materials and foodstuffs. It was a classic, general import-export trade, not dissimilar from that of John Swire & Sons before the revolutionary developments of the 1860s. But like the Swires, Locketts specialised increasingly towards the end of the century, restricting their interest to the ports of Peru and Chile, and concentrating on the export of cotton, sugar and nitrates. Locketts acted as joint promoters with John Thomas North, of four Chilean nitrate companies, including the immensely profitable Liverpool Nitrate Company of 1833, which averaged a 50 per cent yearly return on capital throughout the period 1885–1930.[8] They were also concerned in the creation of infrastructure companies such as the Nitrate Railways Company Ltd, in 1887, and the Bank of London and Tarapacá the following year. Members of the Lockett family held seats on the boards of these companies, and the firm received lucrative agencies from the new companies.[9] To the North, in Peru, the firm participated in the finance and sale of the cotton crop.[10] It also became drawn directly into sugar production, founding the British Sugar Company Ltd in 1900, with a capital of £260,035, to acquire its estates there.[11]

Balfour Williamson & Co. had similiar origins to general trade and shipowning. Like W. & J. Lockett, the firm was drawn into the promotion, finance and management of Chilean nitrate companies towards the end of the century.[12] They also became interested in milling in Peru, Chile and Argentina, and their Peruvian wheat milling interests were consolidated in 1913 and sold to a London company, the Santa Rosa Milling Company Ltd, for which the partnership acted as agents.[13] Perhaps more lucrative than either of these activities was the firm's interest in petroleum. In 1901, Alexander Milne, a Callao merchant and flour miller, formed a syndicate to explore for oil in the Lobitos region of Peru. By 1903 the signs were good but more capital was required. This was provided by Balfour Williamson and the Peruvian Corporation. Soon, however, the Corporation withdrew, and it was Balfour Williamson who handled the London flotation of Lobitos Oilfields Ltd in 1908, raising a paid-up capital of £360,000. The new company appointed Williamson Balfour, the Valparaiso branch of Balfour Williamson, as its agents in Chile, and Milne & Co., soon to be absorbed by Balfour Williamson, as its Peruvian agents. Archibald Williamson, senior partner in Balfour Williamson, was elected chairman. By the terms of the Peruvian agency, Milne & Co., which continued to be operated as a separate undertaking, received 4 per cent on sales, 2.5 per cent on the purchase of equipment, and further management fees, the total earnings over the period 1918–27 amounting to £310,000.[14]

Nor was this the limit of Balfour Williamson's concerns. The firm had opened a San Francisco branch in 1869. There, as in South America, it handled the agencies of British fire insurance companies and engaged in a general trade; but from 1880 it moved increasingly into investment banking, channelling funds from Britain into mortgage loans in California, Oregon and Washington through the Pacific Loan and Investment Company and the Pacific Trust Ltd, financing and distributing to English and Welsh smelters the output of the Anaconda copper mines in Montana, developing a new port through the medium of the Howard Company at Oakland Creek, and establishing a successful British company, California Oilfields Ltd, to exploit the Coalinga oilfield in the Coast Range, and so provide a hedge against a declining import trade in British coal.[15]

Manchester

Manchester was far less eminent than Liverpool as a centre for international firms of this sort. Until the completion of the ship canal at the end of the century it relied on Liverpool and Hull as its ports. As we have seen, however, a good deal of bypassing went on as Manchester merchants or manufacturers went overseas and Continental or American buyers set up in Manchester. In these firms were sometimes the makings of vertically integrated international firms. On a small scale, Edward Ashworth & Co., a Manchester firm with a branch in Rio de Janeiro from the 1840s, diversified into local textile manufacture, making canvas in São Paulo, woollens in Petrópolis, and operating a cotton mill with about 600 workers in Taubaté on the eve of the Great War.[16] Rather more impressive in the scale of its operations was the Knoop family. Ludwig Knoop came from Bremen to work for De Jersey & Co., a Manchester house exporting cotton yarns to Russia. Knoop appears to have taken over the business after 1847 along with the Russian sales agency of Platt brothers, manufacturers of textile machinery. By the 1890s, Knoop is thought to have helped set up more than a hundred cotton mills in Russia, often taking shares and sometimes retaining control. At the turn of the century, the Manchester house took a further step towards total vertical integration when it set up a cotton purchasing syndicate at Memphis, Tennessee, to supply the Knoop group.[17]

Glasgow

Textile interests had been merged with more general mercantile interests in the early years of the Glasgow house of James Finlay & Co. (see Chapter 2) This business was allowed to coast during the later years of its once energetic senior partner, Kirkman Finlay. Then after his death in 1842 it underwent a great revival engineered by James Clark and John Muir. Muir

... decided that the normal trading of the Company gave insufficient employment to the capital available and a too restricted prospect of securing profits. He considered that tea was a good investment for the surplus, and it became his policy to make advances to estates in order to secure agency appointments.[18]

Investments by the firm in the Sylhet tea companies secured their secretaryships for the Glasgow house and their managing agencies for the Calcutta branch, Finlay, Muir & Co. A Bombay branch, Finlay Clark & Co., was set up in 1862 during the cotton famine caused by the American Civil War to supply raw cotton to the firm's Glasgow mills, and rapidly became the biggest exporter of Indian cotton to Europe. These branches and others throughout South Asia took on shipping and insurance agencies, exported jute sacks to South America and tea to Britain, America and Australia, imported Canadian and Finnish newsprint to India, dealt in indigo, jute and sugar, sold piece goods from Finlays' own mills, and became concerned in local cotton manufacture, both for their own account and as managing agents.

London

The same style of diversified undertaking was evident in the capital. Shaw Wallace & Co., a London firm with a branch in Calcutta, commenced business in 1886. It had from the start some tea plantation agencies, also dealing in silk and exporting Manchester goods supplied mainly by Robert Barbour & Bro. Over the next twenty years the firm took on a wide variety of businesses. Local companies were floated in Calcutta to operate gold and mica mines. An import-export business was developed with Hamburg. A big managing agency business embraced cotton mills, coal mines and flour mills, in most of which the firm took some equity stake. Like Finlays, Shaw Wallace dealt in jute sacks or gunnies and took on local agencies of British insurance companies. Finally, there were sales agencies: some hardly worth the trouble, as with Jeyes fluid; some extremely lucrative, as with Burmah Oil. At different times the goods sold for American and European manufacturers included Hungarian locomotives, American sound insulation boards for cinemas, pesticides, paints, paper, tools and building materials. Later, after the Great War the range of activities broadened still further. Shaw Wallace took on shipping agencies, and the agencies of the Marconi Company and Imperial Airways. The need to supply the tea plantations in their care adequately led the firm into production of fertilisers and sulphuric acid and the manufacture, under licence from a British company, of crop-spraying equipment. The Burmah Oil agency led to the managing agency of another manufacturing concern, the Tinplate Company of India Ltd, a Burmah Oil–Tata joint venture originally set up to make kerosene cans. It also involved the firm in the early development of the Anglo-Persian Oil Company, which was initially staffed and serviced by the Bombay branch and by a new joint venture, Lloyd Scott & Co., at Mohammerah (now Khorramshahr).[19]

For Knowles & Foster, another London house with established mercantile interests in Brazil, diversification into flour milling was a natural move in the 1880s, because it kept the capital of the firm fully and continually employed in financing wheat purchases. In addition to providing about £100,000 at a time for this purpose up to 1904, and nearer £250,000 thereafter, Knowles & Foster organised the flotation of a company, Rio Flour Mills Ltd, in London in 1886, and provided senior local staff and the usual agency services.[20]

A third London house, Samuel Samuel & Co. had grown from small beginnings in the 1830s. Jewish merchants were already becoming dominant in the jewellery and fancy goods trades, and Marcus Samuel, founder of the family business, developed a special line, the trade in exotic shells, coral, ivory and mother of pearl, and the manufacture of boxes encrusted with these materials for sale in the tourist centres of England and France. In the 1860s a second generation of the family began to broaden the business. They moved into new commodities, and for the first time a member of the firm was sent overseas to buy goods direct from the producers, passing over the commission agents who had fulfilled their orders up to that time. Samuel began to trade in tea and to export British manufactured goods through British commission agents in the East. Marcus Samuel, Jr., later Viscount Bearsted, played an active role in the family business from the 1870s, developing a strong trade with Japan, and opening a branch house at Yokohama on the basis of an earlier agency in 1878. Here British machinery, hardware and textiles were imported, and silks, porcelain and lacquer wares consigned to London to meet the insatiable middle-class demand for cheap oriental goods. Here, also, a country trade was developed to other parts of the Far East in tea, jute, sugar, grains, ores and Japanese coal. The firm took on, in addition, the kinds of shipping, insurance and sales agencies which were part and parcel of the business of a major overseas house, acting for Asa Lees & Co., manufacturers of cotton spinning machinery, the Ashbury

Railway Carriage and Iron Company Limited, and the China and Manilla Steamship Company, among others. Further trading opportunities came with the start of the Sino-Jananese War in 1894. Samuel Samuel & Co. helped feed, clothe and arm the Japanese forces and, as a reward, received the management of the Formosan camphor and opium monopolies from a victorious government in 1895 and, by 1897, was acting as banker to the Japanese government in London, floating their first sterling loan.

By this time, Japan was no longer the whole of the Samuels' overseas operations. For years, the firm had been accustomed to commodity trading operations carried out on joint account with corresponding houses such as Syme & Co. of Singapore. In 1893, however, they hit upon a scheme which required a slightly more permanent organisation, since it depended upon substantial investments in specialised storage facilities and careful coordination of stocks and supplies. Kerosene, used widely for lighting, was being sold in the Far East by Rockefeller's powerful Standard Oil Company. But the Standard Oil product, sold under the 'Devoes' brand, was case oil, sold in metal cans in which it had been packed at refineries which were generally thousands of miles from the market, and transported, at great cost, in these cans. Samuel believed that by developing superior bulk transport and storage facilities and coupling these to the financial strength and local knowledge and marketing skills of a chain of major Anglo-Oriental houses, Standard Oil could be undercut and the market for kerosene seized. The oriental market had continued to be dominated by case oil after the West had gone over to bulk transport and storage because the early tankers of the 1880s had been considered too dangerous to be allowed through the Suez Canal. This was the problem which Marcus Samuel's colleague, Fortescue Flannery, solved in 1891, enabling the Samuels to build a fleet of oil tankers, the Shell fleet, with permission to use the Suez route to move Russian oil from Black Sea ports to the Far East. Until 1897 the fleet was owned and managed by the Samuels. The bulk storage and distribution operation was a cooperative venture conducted on a profit-sharing basis by a syndicate of Far East houses, the 'tank' syndicate, including Samuel Samuel & Co. in Japan,

Arnhold Karberg & Co., with branches along the China coast, Best & Co. of Madras, W. & A. Graham of Bombay, Graham & Co. of Calcutta, Boustead & Co. of Penang, Syme & Co. of Singapore, and A. Runge & Co.[121] In the meantime, the Samuels strove desperately to develop an independent source of crude oil in the East, which would free them from dependence on Russian supplies. Only in 1897 was the traditional partnership system abandoned and a limited liability company, 'Shell' Transport and Trading Co. Ltd, set up to acquire the production, shipping and storage facilities of the Samuels and their partners in the 'tank' syndicate.[22] Though it was to grow into something very different, this undertaking of the Samuels remained, thus far, characteristcally mercantile in its rapid response to market opportunity, light administration and employment of networks of friendly but independent houses. But it already pointed the way ahead in two regards. Firstly, it was an operation of such complexity—with its mixing of production, shipping, storage and trading, and its large number of participants—as could only be arranged in a city which combined financial and commercial resources on a gigantic scale: London and New York, perhaps Paris. Provincial centres were slipping into a second division. Secondly, it demanded investment in capital-intensive equipment to an extent that must considerably reduce the future flexibility of participants. There would be no skipping in and out of the oil trade; it required commitment.

CONVERGENCE ON LONDON

Attention has so far been restricted almost exclusively to the adaptive strategies of firms which were already engaged in the cosmopolitan world of international trade and finance by the middle years of the century. To simplify matters further, I have drawn an artificially sharp contrast between firms clearly based in overseas ports and those based in Britain, making use, for purposes of exposition, of distinctions which, as I was at pains to point out in the introduction, cannot be applied to the nineteenth-century business world without serious risk of anachronism. Many of the overseas firms referred to—Lumb,

Wanklyn, for example, or Binnys—were managed by Britons, but none was managed *from* Britain. Conversely, Knoop and the Samuels had Continental origins, but lacked significant Continental allegiances. But during this period a great many firms were on the move. Partners from the countries of European empire or settlement were despatched to develop closer links with major capital markets; limited liability companies were formed in London by overseas entrepreneurs to draw on these markets; and, in response to these changes, the locus of managerial control, which has been taken as the ultimate determinant of the nationality of an undertaking, also moved. A further simplification has been the setting aside of those bodies of capital accumulated *within* the major industrialised economies in domestic banking, in insurance and in manufacturing, which were being drawn into the international arena from the middle of the century, partly in reaction to the same stimuli to which the international houses were reacting, and partly by less obviously related factors. Once again, the locus of control in international business enterprise was greatly influenced by the growth of these firms. On the whole, they weakened the relative position of mercantile elites. Yet this outcome was not brought about simply by competition in the marketplace. It was also the result of changed contractual arrangements, as merchants were drawn into collaboration with metropolitan finance capital, often only to be thrown out again, in a much weakened condition, a few years later. Much more indirectly, the spread of finance capital, and the growth of explicitly foreign investment in politically sensitive sectors of the developing economies of the periphery, roused strong feelings of popular resentment which spilled over into animosity towards collaborating or comprador groups. Their political power suffered accordingly, and they began to find themselves supplicants and outsiders at the very time they most needed the protection of local states against metropolital capital.

The migration of merchants towards the major capital markets and commercial centres has already been touched upon in passing, Frederick Dalgety, Edward Lumb and Thomas Russell each followed this path, from Australia, Argentina and New Zealand. Wernher Beit & Co., established in London in 1890, provides a more complicated example of the same tendency. The firm was a reconstruction of Jules Porges & Co., a Parisian firm set up by a Bohemian diamond merchant, which had become an active buyer in the Kimberley diamond field in the 1870s and had diversified into gold mining after the discoveries in the South African Republic in 1886. The active partners were Julius Wernher, a protégé of Porges, who came from a Prussian military family, and Alfred Beit, whose German-Jewish father, a convert to Lutheranism, operated a diversified mercantile business in Hamburg with interests in gold refining, silk, wool, dyeing and banking.[23] By the mid-1890s, Wernher Beit was the largest of the Rand mining houses. Like the Anglo-Indian managing agencies or the nitrate firms of the West Coast of South America, these houses controlled operating companies by a system of minority shareholdings, sales and supply agencies, control over staffing, and board representation. They provided 'a pool of expertise, a purchasing depot, and secretarial and accounting services, as well as financing arrangements, for the individual mines the parent company controlled'.[24]

The Mosenthals followed a similar route. Born in Hesse-Cassel, Joseph Mosenthal went to Cape Town in 1839, perhaps as buying agent for a north German wool firm. By 1851 he had been joined by his brothers, Adolph and Julius, in a firm, Mosenthal Brothers, based at Graaff Reinet, with branches at Port Elizabeth, Murraysburg and London. The main trade was in wool and mohair, a business in which Julius, at least, had already some experience. The brothers introduced merino sheep and angora goats to South Africa in an attempt to improve indigenous stock and, in the 1860s, were pioneer ostrich farmers.[25] Following the discovery of diamonds in the Kimberley area in 1867, Mosenthals entered this trade, buying directly from the small diggers who were initially the predominant producers, and subsequently becoming involved directly in production as the industry moved towards a more capital-intensive and monopolistic structure.[26]

During the 1870s the Mosenthals took part in the promotion of Anglo-South African companies through their London branch, where Adolph and his son Henry drew in funds from London and Parisian diamond merchants and merchant bankers. The London and South African Exploration Company, a prospecting and mining company registered in London in 1870, brought together Julius Beer, Anton Dünkelsbuhler (formerly a buyer for Mosenthals), the Ochs brothers, Louis Floersheim, the Posnos and the Mosenthals themselves, with much smaller contributions from Knowles & Foster, concerned in the diamond trade through their Brazilian house, and from the Sterns, Baron Emile d'Erlanger, and the Frankfurt and Paris Rothschilds in what was, in essence, a financial syndicate of interrelated family firms rather than a public company.[27] Joseph Mosenthal & Co. of London and Adolph Mosenthal & Co. in Port Elizabeth acted as managers of the company's fund of £32,000, and Adolph Mosenthal took his place on the London board. Another, later, enterprise in which the Mosenthals were once again active was the Orion Diamond Mining Co. Ltd of 1881. Formed in London to acquire claims at Du Toits' Pan belonging to Martin Van Beek, Adolph Mosenthals & Co., Anton Dünkelsbuhler & Co. of London, and Thaine Allen and Jones & Co., both of Kimberley, the Orion had a paid-up capital of £250,000, of which £124,850, or almost precisely half, was listed in the names of the vendors in a return of November 1881, and may be assumed to have been given to them in exchange for their claims. Of the remaining shares, about 5000, of a nominal value of £50,000, were held by City merchants, stockbrokers and bankers, probably members of an underwriting syndicate who would gradually unload their holdings, while the rest were held, often in lots of considerably less than £1000 nominal value, by smaller shareholders clustered around the Bavarian towns of Regensburg, Fürth and Nürnburg. Adolph and Harry Mosenthal sat with Anton Dünkelsbuhler and Samuel Paddon on the London board, but in this case local management appears to have been in the hands of a local board of directors instead of an agency house, and the Mosenthal family was not represented.[28] Finally, after the emergence of a single dominant production company, De Beers Consolidated Mines Ltd, in 1888, Mosenthals joined other dealers who had been most active in the concentration process, including Wernher Beit and the Barnatos, to form a monopsonistic buying syndicate of which the object, like that of the later

Central Selling Organisation, was to stabilise the market and maximise long-term rents from the mines by contracting for the entire output of De Beers.[29]

Because of the convenience of London for operations of this sort, Harry Mosenthal, who took charge of the firm after the founding generation had retired, made it his headquarters, and the business, like that of Wernher Beit & Co., came more and more to resemble that of an investment bank. In the first case, authority had passed from Germany to South Africa and on to London. In the second, the transition from the Continent to London was more direct, as neither Porges & Co. nor Wernher Beit appears to have been managed by a South African resident at any stage.

Though far better known and far wealthier, the partners in Wernher Beit were responding to the same incentives that had drawn the Günthers to replace their Belgian company of 1863 with a London company, Liebig's Extract of Meat Co. Ltd, two years later, and to move from Antwerp to London themselves. In London, the Günthers operated a branch of the Antwerp hide merchants, Königs Günther & Co., provided general management for Liebig's, and participated as minor investment bankers in a wide variety of River Plate ventures. Charles, Charles Eugene, Charles John and Robert Louis Günther between them held a nominal paid-up value of £243,355 in the mid-1890s in 21 London-registered River Plate companies. Some of their ventures were mere extensions of the merchant firm. In the Western Buenos Aires Land Co. Ltd, for example, which was organised in 1883 to buy and operate *estancias* in Buenos Aires and Santa Fé provinces belonging to Königs Günther's Antwerp house, the firm and its partners continued to hold the great majority of shares.[30] In other cases they appear to have acted as underwriters in company with more prominent merchant bankers, helping to guide other Continental businessmen towards the resources of the City of London, and to feed out securities to the public through their Continental connexions. Charles E. Günther was founding chairman of the Forestal Land, Timber and Railways Co. Ltd, registered in London in 1906 to take over the assets of an Argentine company, Compañía Forestal del Chaco, controlled by Albert Harteneck, Frederick Portalis—formerly a partner in the Paris and Buenos Aires firm of Portalis Frères—and Hermann Renner, who manufactured dyestuffs in Hamburg using tannin extracted from Argentine quebracho wood by the company.[31]

Initially, the creation of a British company to acquire the Forestal appeared to be merely a financial device. The company was effectively controlled by the vendors, Harteneck, Portalis and Renner, who had received all of the 500,000 £1 preference shares, and £633,328 cash. Renner also controlled the company's Hamburg sales agent, Otto Bolms, who bought largely for account of the Gerb- und Farbstoffwerke H. Renner & Co. of Hamburg. The attraction of London had been the ability of Baron Emile d'Erlanger and Günther to unload the remaining 450,000 preference shares and £550,000 in 5 per cent debentures, so raising funds for a programme of expansion by acquisition of competitors and local transport enterprises, which was successfully carried out betweeen 1908 and 1910. Quite soon, however, the brass plate in the City developed a will of its own. Cut off from Bolms in Hamburg by the First World War, the company had to establish its own sales network. For this purpose it moved out of Erlangers and started its own office in 1916. Vertical integration into the manufacture of extract in Britain, the United States, South Africa and Kenya, and into research conducted in Britain, produced a further dilution of the control of the original vendors. So too did horizontal integration, as the Forestal acquired competitors with proprietors based in many different countries, who now became shareholders and sometimes directors of the company. Alberto Fontana of Barcelona, whose Argentine quebracho company was taken over by the Forestal in 1920, joined the main board and played a leading part in the development of the company's research laboratories. The acquisition of the Santa Fé Land Company in 1913 brought an influx of French capital.[32] In 1894, a very English board of directors had concealed the fact that the major shareholder in the Santa Fé Company, the de Camondos, the Banque de Paris et des Pays Bas, Maurice de Hirsch, and Michel Heine, who between them owned 48,036 of the 87,500 shares, were all based in Paris.[33] Dispersed operation and dispersed ownership concentrated authority increasingly in the hands of the executives of the company in London.

The Suárez family, from Bolivia, provide a final, extreme, example of the centripetal drift of peripheral merchants. Like Booths of Liverpool, Suárez did well out of rubber, establishing himself at Cachuela Esperanza, the only portage point on the Beni River, in 1881. There he bought rubber, provided supplies and labour, and developed ranching and river transport. The firm also sold Bolivian rubber through a branch in London, F. Suárez & Co. When the Suárez partnerships were reorganised in 1909 as a single London-registered company, Suárez Hermanos & Co. Ltd, their value was estimated at roughly £750,000. By 1925, the Suárez group was thought to be worth as much as £10 million. But Nicolas Suárez spent more and more time in London; his children, educated in England, were reluctant to return to Bolivia to manage their assets; diversification out of rubber at the end of the boom was grossly inadequate, and finally, when Suárez & Co. Ltd was dissolved in 1961, the dynamo of this anglicised rentier family was found to have assets worth just £1500.[34]

I am running ahead. Merchants like Suárez who moved to Britain and organised their overseas assets in family-owned joint-stock companies might just as easily have left control in the hands of competent local agents. Equally, they might take on a directorship or two in the City, yet still not be regarded as predatory figures out to gain competitive edge by transferring their authority from periphery to centre. Not all returning merchants resembled Suárez, Dalgety or Russell. Nor has it yet been established that Wernher Beit effectively controlled the Corner House group of mining companies any more than, say, their Johannesburg agents, Eckstein & Co. Not every peripheral enterprise which tapped the London capital market surrendered effective control to London through migration of its principals, as in the case of Liebig's, or in the course of the evolution of the company's proprietorship and operations, as in that of the Forestal.

Three questions need to be addressed rather more formally. The first concerns the extent to which merchants moving the base of their operations from the periphery of the world economy to London retained an allegiance to the country where they first accumulated capital. The second concerns the extent to which they retained economic autonomy in their new field of operations. The third has to do with the locus of control in corporations set up in London to do business on the periphery. Though they converge empirically, the three issues are analytically distinguishable.

We have already seen that London had long acted as a magnet for merchants and bankers. Industrialisation and the French wars brought an acceleration in this trend, and political upheaval on the Continent coupled with the sustained financial vigour of the City continued to attract new arrivals from Hamburg, Frankfurt and Antwerp well into the second half of the century. There were also returning partners from Anglo-Indian houses. For while settlement and integration were the usual pattern for British-born merchants in the temperate countries of European settlement, the tropics were generally felt to be too hostile in climate and too populous to admit of the creation of European civilisations. The Companies Act of 1862 and the development of liner services and submarine telegraphs shifted the balance of advantage even further in favour of London residence. The Act provided a convenient and cheap legal form through which to tap the London capital market. Liners and telegraphs made effective management from London of estates and undertakings in Cape Town or Melbourne more feasible. Besides, such enterprises could themselves be organised as London companies. And the new possibilities of corporate organisation and management at a distance, coupled with the availability among the growing group of returned merchants in London of men with local experience which they were willing to trade for a directorship, made it possible for the first time for pure financiers—City men who had long since ceased to handle merchandise and confined themselves to money—to create corporations which could compete directly in overseas markets, threatening to marginalise any peripheral merchants who chose to rest on their laurels and rely on local resources.

It was in this context that Frederick G. Dalgety gradually moved his headquarters to London during the 1850s and, eventually, reorganised his London and colonial partnerships as a single British company, which now ranks among the leading British industrial enterprises, with diversified interests in milling, animal feed, frozen foods, shipping, insurance and merchanting, spanning a wide geographical area. Dalgety soon came to see himself as an English gentleman. He chose an estate in Hampshire, centring upon Lockerley Hall, and threw himself into country life.[35] By 1890 many others had followed, and few appear to have gone out of their way to retain strong social or cultural affiliations with their original provincial or overseas bases.[36] Edward Johnston, Son & Co. originated in Rio de Janeiro in 1842. The founder, son of a lowland Scot, had travelled to Brazil in 1821 to serve as clerk in F. le Breton & Co., where he soon rose to the position of joint manager. In Brazil, he married the daughter of a German-born coffee planter. These origins might very easily have led on to fuller local integration, but the connexions of one of his partners, William Havers, appear to have drawn Johnston to Liverpool in 1845. Then, in the early 1860s, the growing specialisation of the firm in coffee made London a more convenient base. A branch was opened there in 1862, and shortly afterwards this became the firm's headquarters when the Liverpool branch was closed.[37] The scant sources available indicate little continuing social commitment to the lowlands, to Brazil, or to Liverpool. Instead, in the fullness of time, the family brought forth that quintessence of Englishness, a test match commentator.

Following the example of Johnston, Brown Shipley opened a London branch in 1863 and moved its head office there in 1888, abandoning Liverpool.[38] John Swire & Sons, in Liverpool since the 1830s, opened in London in 1868 and made it their headquarters from 1870.[39] Balfour Williamson finally left Liverpool for London somewhat later, in 1928.[40] Booths did not follow until 1946, when they finally sold off their shipping interests.[41] From further afield, the active partners and managers of Shaw Jamieson, which had begun operations in Calcutta in 1868, reconstituted themselves in a new group of partnerships, including Shaw Wallace & Co., centred firmly upon London, in 1886, while the Sassoons moved their headquarters from Bombay to London in 1872.[42]

This last case is instructive, because its social consequences are so much better documented than those of the others. In effect, the firm split in the 1860s. When the original house of

David Sassoon & Co. came under the control of Abdullah or Albert Sassoon, his brother Elias, unwilling to play second string to Albert in Bombay, set up on his own as E. D. Sassoon & Co., also of Bombay. It was control of David Sassoon & Co. which passed to London, when Reuben Sassoon was joined there by Arthur from Hong Kong, and Albert (the eldest son of David Sassoon) from Bombay. On the whole, the London house was the less vigorous, remaining largely committed to international commodity trading; E. D. Sassoon & Co., by contrast, diversified into textile manufacturing and developed into one of the leading managing agencies in the East, with interests in China as well as South Asia. It is said that David Sassoon was worth £4 million when he died; there was room for a little high living and neglect of business. The English Sassoons appear to have devoted themselves almost exclusively to Society and the Court, taking little interest in the business. Victor Sassoon, on the other hand, who took over the management of E. D. Sassoon from his father, Edward, in 1924, was a more than competent administrator, but no politician. He sold out in the face of advancing Indian nationalism, netting something in excess of £4 million, but managed to pull out only £1.4 million, perhaps a fifth of the post-war value of his Chinese assets, before 1949.[43]

But if there is a contrast to be drawn between the economic histories of the two branches of the family, their social histories are convergent. All but a handful turned their back on their oriental and Jewish backgrounds. Philip Sassoon epitomised this. A younger son of Albert, he devoted himself to politics, sitting as a Conservative for Hythe, holding a succession of minor ministerial posts, entertaining lavishly, and continuing the family tradition of abject devotion to royalty. He could not accept his Jewishness, repeatedly trying to pass himself off as a Parsee. 'Though Jewish, he hated Jews,' a friend remarked.[44] Victor, less strident, may nevertheless have been in earnest when he declared the Derby a greater race than the Jews.[45]

The same divorce from their social origins is evident in the lives of many leaders of South African business. 'Despite long experience in South Africa,' writes Kubicek, 'many of the controllers, either resident in the Transvaal or Britain, cultivated life-styles and business practices far removed from or indifferent to the local scene.'[46] Joseph E. Robinson, born in Cape Colony, had graduated from wool through diamonds to gold, much as the Mosenthals had, but 'after 1894 remained mostly abroad and chose to live in grotesque opulence in London's Mayfair'.[47] The influx of Randlords and nabobs undoubtedly contributed to the almost paradoxical condition remarked upon by Davidoff in which, while 'by the 1880s the basis of London society membership was beginning to widen', there was also an 'excessive concern with propriety and social placing' by comparison with the period before 1870.[48]

For many of the second rank, the settlement into English society and the divorce from active business were more gradual and unspectacular. German in origin, but trading between London and Uruguay by the 1860s, the im Thurns may be typical of a good number of the merchant firms of foreign or provincial origin that we have considered. They were well enough established by the 1860s to send a son, Everard, through Marlborough and Oxford, from where he graduated to the Colonial Office and a knighthood. By 1938, their portfolio holdings in one River Plate company in which Frederick Charles im Thurn had taken an active interest a century before demonstrated their absorption into the solid ranks of the English middle class: Dr Robert im Thurn of North Finchley, Mrs Gladys im Thurn of St John's Wood, John im Thurn at Milford-on-Sea, Miss Mildred im Thurn at Eastbourne, Miss Margaret in South Kensington, and only one, Robert, with an address in the City.[49]

Those merchants who settled in London may, therefore, almost without exception, be considered to have become, or to have aspired to be, English. We may therefore group them now with merchants who first accumulated capital while resident in England, and examine the fate of what may be termed British-domiciled mercantile capital as a whole in the face of challenges from financial and industrial capital. Mercantile capital elsewhere faced the same threats, naturally, and would find its own ways of meeting them. The uniqueness of British mercantile capital is that it met the opposition on common territory, with access to similar institutions and resources. It stood some realistic chance of gaining control of or successfully imitating the creations of finance and industrial capital, and, if it failed, it had nowhere to retreat to and was wide open to predation.

The score in this contest so far is very clear. Those British-based merchants whom we have examined up to now appear to have been uniformly successful in keeping control of their various enterprises, usually retaining a family controlling partnership at the centre of things with a group of satellite companies in which control was assured by management contracts or sales and purchasing agencies. The contrast has been between them and the peripheral entrepreneurs, like Maúa, Mort or Tagore, many of whom failed to master or utilise fully the new legal devices of incorporation, or else suffered from inadequate local legislation.

But by no means all London-based merchants did succeed in retaining control of their enterprises, and of those who did, many found themselves obliged to resort to corporate structures which mimicked those of City commerce and manufacturing industry in their struggle to avoid absorption by a new kind of multinational corporation, based no longer on initial accumulation in the sphere of international exchange, but spilling over, instead, from massive success in the domestic market. Still others found themselves losing ground to the new multinationals as these rapidly growing organisations took direct control of agencies formerly handled by merchant houses or absorbed whole firms to serve as adjuncts to their central operations. The questions of the ability of merchants to retain control of their diversified overseas business operations and the locus of control in the new generation of City-based overseas banking and insurance corporations or international manufacturing concerns therefore resolve themselves into one. Our attention is drawn to the struggle between mercantile capital and finance and industrial capital: in the market to be sure, but, most of all, *within* corporations established in Britain by alliances formed between representatives of these three quite distinct bourgeois traditions during the half-century before the outbreak of the First World War.

STRUGGLES FOR CONTROL

The great problem for City bankers or northern industrialists who contemplated operations overseas was that they did not know the territory, they did not know the market, and they did not know the people. For those in extractive industries there was the additional problem of communications. Oil might turn up in the middle of a desert or a jungle, far from the telegraph and far from a port.[50] It frequently proved impossible to run manufacturing operations from nearby commercial centres, as Shaw Wallace found when they acquired the Bengal Hagpur Cotton Mills at Rajnandgon, almost 500 miles from Calcutta.

Mr Frederick, brought out in 1897 to learn his work with a view to controlling the mill for the firm from Calcutta, has almost uninterruptedly lived thereat ever since, and has long superintended it.

So wrote a colleague, almost 30 years after Frederick's arrival.[51] The options for outsiders were three. A management team could be sent out to build up the business from scratch. Local assistance could be bought on a contractual basis: a managing agent as substitute for or supervisor of a salaried executive from home, or else a local board of directors recruited from local politicians, lawyers and business. Last, a going concern could be bought, and its business and staff used as the foundation for expansion.[52]

Viewed from the perspective of the merchant, the problem was of access to cheap sources of long-term funds, and the answer appeared to lie in the use of London-based corporations. The most intractable clashes between mercantile and finance capital came, therefore, when British financiers with an active determination to retain control of their capital merged their interests with mercantile entrepreneurs who expected to retain control of their undertakings and saw London as no more than a source funds. Mauá and the London and Brazilian Bank were set on this course, but never completed their deal. Gibbs Ronald successfully captured the Australian Mercantile Land and Finance Company, but were only able to do so because that company lacked a directorate with sufficient acumen to spot glaring weaknesses in the merger terms. Other cases were to lead to more prolonged disputes.

The East
Such wrangles were to be expected above all in India and

China, where British mercantile capital, both home-based and expatriate, was most developed. As early as 1786 there were hints of this sort of conflict in the opposition of the agency houses to the General Bank of India, set up by servants of the East India Company to compete for their banking business.[53] Tension between London and British India outlasted the Company, and was complicated by the fact that while a considerable pool of expatriate British capital existed in India, so that many joint-stock companies could be set up as Indian companies with shares denominated in rupees, expatriate investors had a way of drifting back to Britain, taking their shares with them. Such shareholders could play a useful role, especially in industrial companies, where they might liaise on behalf of the management in India with British suppliers of machinery and equipment. But, constituted as London committees, or shadow boards of directors, they could sometimes sought to gain control of the whole enterprise.[54] A challenge of this sort was successfully fought off by the Hong Kong board of the Hong Kong and Shanghai Bank in the 1870s, and this continued to be an institution quite independent of the City of London.[55]

The Hong Kong and Shanghai Bank had had, from the start, a majority of its shareholders in the East. The position of the Assam Company was very different. Here conflict originated in a merger between a London group and the Bengal Tea Association controlled in Calcutta by Carr Tagore & Co. Both groups had had as their objective the purchase and operation of the experimental government tea plantations in Assam which, it was hoped, might come in time to rival China. From the terms of the merger it was clear that the London committee would be sovereign. London, after all, was providing four times as much capital as Calcutta. Operations in India were to be funded from London and the Calcutta committee were forbidden to raise local capital independently for new projects. Even so, London found it difficult to manage through the Calcutta committee, which was disinclined to account for expenditure or hold regular meetings of local shareholders.[56] A London committee appointed to look after alternative forms of management in 1846 urged the Board to abolish the Calcutta committee and manage through a disinterested firm of agents.

But the Calcutta committee held fast to their rights. It was, after all, an Indian company, and they were required to meet, and to take ultimate responsibilty for its affairs, under Indian law. Disagreements continued, first Calcutta then London wanting to force the pace of development when the others did not, while Calcutta criticised the London board for their lack of commitment to the company's affairs and their refusal to accept on to the board men with recent practical experience of the plantations. The position was only resolved in the 1860s, and then not without difficulty. A sterling company was set up to acquire the undertaking. This removed the legal necessity for a Calcutta board of directors, and this body was indeed replaced by an agent and general manager in 1864. But this, too, proved unsatisfactory, and three years later the original 1846 recommendation was adopted when Schoene Kilburn & Co. were appointed managing agents.[57]

Southern Africa
The same clash between local and London boards developed, and was resolved, very much more quickly within the Standard Bank of South Africa. Before the founding of the London and South African Bank in 1860 and the Standard Bank two years later, banking in South Africa had been conducted by local merchants often operating through narrowly-owned joint stock companies as 'mere discounting establishments of a few leading merchants'.[58] At first the Standard Bank was simply this writ large. The *Argus* might puff itself up and claim that the initiative for the creation of the London-based banks had come from 'some old and respected heads of commercial houses connected with this Colony, now resident in London', but one of these, John Paterson, the founding chairman of the Standard, had already, in three short years, brought the bank close to disaster by allowing it to operate as a loose federation of formerly independent local houses, each feathering its own nest and refusing cooperation either with London or the other colonial branches. In 1865, made suspicious by a lack of adequate information from the Cape, the directors in London had sent out Robert Stewart, trained at the Bank of Scotland and the National Provincial Bank of England, as general manager. He rapidly broke up the local boards or reduced

them to purely deliberative status, introduced a system of inspection of the branches, and exposed irregularities in the lending policies of the Port Elizabeth board which led swiftly to the resignation from the London board of the chairman, implicated through his connexion with Paterson, Kemp & Co., and James Black, whose family also had a house in Port Elizabeth and had been represented on the local board of the Bank there. The Standard was only saved by the decision of London to choose a disinterested bank official of orthodox training, and his willingness, in turn, to refuse further accommodation to his chairman's firm and so precipitate its failure.[59]

A generation later, Cecil Rhodes, like Paterson before him, felt the strength of the City. Rhodes was fortunate in his partner, Charles Rudd, when the time came to organise his Witwatersrand gold mining interests into a British company. His brother, Thomas Rudd, was a director of the London Joint Stock Bank, and was also able to get support for the new company, Consolidated Gold Fields Ltd, from Arbuthnot Latham and its large Anglo-Indian connexion. At the outset the positions of Rhodes and Rudd as managing directors appeared impregnable, and the London board, too, was packed with two ex-colonial friends of Charles Rudd. Charles Rudd and Rhodes proceeded more or less to ignore the mundane affairs of the company while they pursued fresh schemes. Local management was delegated to two of Rhodes' brothers, and was loose and unsatisfactory. But soon London were able to seize upon Rhodes' disgrace over the failure of the Jameson Raid of 1895 to get a grip on the affairs of the company and begin pulling its resources out of South Africa into mining ventures in Australia, West Africa, Canada, Siberia and Colombo, oil in Mexico and Trinidad, and power generation in the United States.[60]

Control was also disputed within the Corner House group. In the early 1890s Julius Wernher begged the partners of his Johannesburg agents, Eckstein & Co., to avert conflict in South Africa by fostering an accommodation with President Kruger in the Transvaal, and meanwhile plotted the gradual diversification of the group's interests away from South African mining. But the local partners ignored him, identifying the group with anti-republican activities. Once again the victory lay with London in the long run. Lionel Phillips was implicated in the Jameson raid, and later another partner in Eckstein's, the fiercely imperialist Percy FitzPatrick, left the firm.[61]

Some of the magnates acted as if they were local entrepreneurs, able to control capital from the metropolitan area, Kubicek concludes ' . . . but if Rhodes's financial activities were motivated by strong regional or local objectives, it is difficult to discover other controllers with such priorities. Certainly after his downfall local entrepreneurial aggression was sharply reduced. Thereafter, entrepreneurs resident in South Africa had to endure local government or cooperate with the imperial factor, and accept business strategies enunciated in London, or Paris, or Berlin.'[62]

The River Plate

In Argentina, the early experience of London-based banks bore striking resemblances to that of the Standard Bank in South Africa. Formed, like the Standard, in 1862, the London and River Plate Bank was controlled by a London board which included four British bankers: John Bruce, formerly of the Colonial Bank, John Elin, a director of the Alliance Bank and the London and Brazilian Bank, James Hackblock, who represented the new bank's own bankers, the City Bank, and was also a director of the London Financial Association, and Thomas Richardson of the Midland. The remaining directors were merchants, but only one, John Fair, had direct experience of the River Plate.[63] Fair had come to London in 1857 to set up a new branch of Zimmermann Fair & Co., of Buenos Aires and Montevideo. Between them, the directors took up almost 10 per cent of the shares, and there was no question of their intention to exert strong control over the branches and pursue orthodox policies.[64] But distance made it necessary to rely on branch managers and local directors to begin with, and it was felt advisable to draw in local merchants for the clientele and local connexions they would bring. So in Buenos Aires, John H. Green, formerly of Darbyshire & Green, was made manager, under the supervision of two local directors, Norberto de la Riestra, a past partner in Nicholson Green & Co., and Thomas Fair, Jr.[65] In Montevideo, after two false starts, James Lowry, a private banker in the city, was offered

£2000 a year, free accommodation, and 5 per cent of any surplus profits from the River Plate branches over and above those needed to pay a dividend of 7 per cent to the shareholders. In return for this generous remuneration he was to bring 'as many of his present customers as possible'.[66] Once again supervision was felt to be necessary. Lowry was teamed as joint manager with Thomas Hyne Jones and the two of them placed under the supervision of Vicente Fidel López, an Argentine lawyer and academic, as local director.

All these expedients failed. Green, De la Riestra, and López all regarded the Bank as a source of funds for their friends and associates and made injudicious advances. Green was discharged in 1870. De la Riestra resigned in 1865. López was dismissed after recommending a great deal of discount business which Jones and Lowry could not accept.[67] In their place professional bank officials, Georg Wilhelm Maschwitz and Louis Behn, were appointed to take over in Buenos Aires and Rosario.

Perhaps it was to counteract the loss of local expertise at the branches that George Wilkinson Drabble, a merchant newly returned from Buenos Aires, was elected chairman of the bank in London. Born in Sheffield in 1823, Drabble had travelled to Argentina in 1849 with his brother Alfred to establish an agency there for the family firm, Drabble Brothers, exporters with houses in London, Manchester and Sheffield.[68] There, he had been a director of the Banco y Casa de Moneda, and had served as President of the Buenos Aires Stock Exchange in 1862–63, and as the elected *municipal* for the parish of Socorro in 1867. He had also bought land in Argentina and Uruguay. Then, in 1867, he returned to join the family's Manchester house and was immediately offered a seat on the board of the London Bank. Within two years he had moved to London and the chairmanship, an office he was to retain for over 30 years. Drabble brought no change in policy at the bank. He presided over increasing professionalism and impeccable orthodoxy. In essence, he abandoned his identity as an Anglo-Argentine on the path to full integration into Buenos Aires society and became, instead, a City man. By 1880s he was on the boards of the Buenos Aires Great Southern Railway and the City of Buenos Aires Tramway and had been elected chairman of the

Central Uruguay Railway Company of Montevideo. Ten years later he had added to these the directorships of four more Anglo-River Plate companies and was, in addition, chairman of the River Plate Fresh Meat Company and trustee of the Western Railway of Buenos Aires and the Buenos Aires Harbour Works.[69] In his later years he was a wealthy man who, like his fictitious near contemporary, Nicolas Forsyte, 'had made a large fortune, quite legitimately, out of the companies of which he was a director'.[70]

Besides his fees as a director, Drabble had the dividends on a healthy River Plate portfolio with a paid-up value in excess of £180,000. But Drabble created no enduring business enterprise. Where he ruled, he ruled by consent and not by gaining effective voting control. The only exception to this was the River Plate Fresh Meat Co. Ltd.[71] His influence in the City was strictly personal, a reflection, in some degree, of the strength of the bank he had helped create, and passed, on his death, to the long-serving chief executive of the London and River Plate Bank, H. G. Andersen. It is even hard to say whether Drabble gained personally from returning to England when he did and forsaking trade and land for the City. For the attractions of the metropolis, substantial yet anonymous wealth, and a large, ugly house in Pembridge Square must be set against the fortune and high public position which he might easily have attained had he remained in Argentina as his brother did. In 1928 the Argentine branch of the family owned more than 75,000 hectares in Buenos Aires province, said to have been worth more than m$n 17 million (£1 = $5.2 moneda nacional).[72] Then there were Uruguayan interests, for which no figure is available, but which were of the same order as the Argentine estates.

Neither in London, nor in the River Plate, did mercantile capital override the bankers and the mass of investors in the London and River Plate Bank. Those who tried failed. Drabble, for his part, never appears to have tried to bend the policy of the bank towards his pet schemes or gain unreasonable accommodation for the enterprises of his family. The objectives of the Wanklyn brothers in creating the Mercantile Bank of the River Plate in 1872 were quite different, as we have seen. What remains to be studied is the way in which the failure of that bank led on to a transfer of authority over several River Plate enterprises from local merchants to City men.

As the Mercantile Bank rapidly sank during the 1870s, a number of the original shareholders sold out or reduced their holdings, while others, including the Isaacs and Edward Ashworth, stood firm. Only one man came into the market to buy shares in any quantity, and this was Charles Morrison, son of James, who now managed the family's investments from a small office in Coleman Street. By 1880 he was the second largest holder with an investment worth £32,000 at par, equalled by Ashworth and exceeded only by Elizabeth Wanklyn, Frederic's widow.[73] A purge of management left only John H. H. Duncan, the London secretary, untouched. As others were dismissed, he was elevated to the board of directors, and a new secretary, James Anderson, appointed. Two new companies were set up in London. The object of the Montevideo Waterworks Company was to acquire the new works from the Montevideo firm of Lezica Lanus y Fynn. The Mercantile Bank had financed the construction of this new utility to the extent of more than £300,000 by 1876.[74] Now 10,000 fully paid £20 shares were allotted to the bank in settlement, while 7500 went to Lezica Lanus y Fynn. Next, in 1881, a second company was registered to acquire the remaining assets of the Bank. To attract public subscription a prestigious board was contrived, including the Tory Member of Parliament, John Gorst, the Hon. S. Herbert and Lord Norreys. The financial weight came from a syndicate including Charles Morrison, Edward Ashworth, Falconer Larkworthy, Emile d'Erlanger and Charles Schiff, John Bruce of Edinburgh, and two London stock jobbers, Alexander Henderson and William Cuthbert Quilter. These, along with many smaller investors, provided new funds, while the capital of the old bank, much written down, was represented in the new company by 50,000 £5 B shares, issued fully paid.[75]

The initial object of the River Plate Trust was to liquidate the remaining assets of the Mercantile Bank. Its longer-term objectives were two. It was to provide a channel for the investment of British capital in mortgages on pastoral properties, on established Australian and United States lines.

And it was to serve as a managing agency house, coordinating the affairs of a group of related companies, of which the Montevideo Waterworks was only the first. Soon the founding directors retired, and a more businesslike board emerged. John Morris, as chairman, had experience of mortgage lending to the United States, but owed his position chiefly to his being senior partner in Ashurst Morris Crisp & Co., solicitors to the Morrison family. John Duncan remained, valued for his skills as an accountant. Charles J. Günther of Liebig's, William Wilson and Reginald Neild provided knowledge of Argentine *estancias* and *estancieros*. A. J. FitzHugh, a south coast solicitor, was able to market securities to a wealthy clientele, while the function of Thomas Farrell is less clear, though he may have been an engineer, and certainly was the director chosen in 1891 to travel to the River Plate on business connected with the Montevideo Waterworks. Between them, these seven held a total of 52 directorships in 28 Anglo-River Plate companies by 1895. Together with their partners in various private firms, the Trust Company itself and its sister company, The River Plate and General Investment Trust, they held almost £1 million (paid-up nominal value) in Anglo-River Plate companies in the mid-1890s, while Charles Morrison held a further £500,000. To back up this investment, Ashurst, Morris, Crisp acted as solicitors for 18 Anglo-Argentine companies in London, while the Trust Company were managing agents for several in Buenos Aires.[76] Ironically, what had begun as a revolt by local merchants against the conservatism of the City-based London and River Plate Bank ended up as heart of the strongest single London-based financial group in nineteenth-century Argentina.

North America
It is hard to resist the conclusion that in Argentina and South Africa the City made considerable gains at the expense of mercantile capital. In the East and in Australia the two were more evenly matched. Given this record, it is hard to see why merchants went on hoping to manipulate the City for so long. The answer may lie in the experience of the United States of America. Here there was a well-established tradition of passive British portfolio investment in locally-managed railroads.[77]

Also, developed local capital markets gave local management greater freedom of action. It would have been easy, therefore, for merchants from other parts of the world to confuse long-term investment groups with managerial capabilities with mere underwriting syndicates, and to believe that company directors were part-timers and dilettantes, and shareholders a rabble, so that in the event of any challenge to their management, they, the Americans, would triumph because of their superior expertise.

It is perfectly true that there were specialist firms, from the 1860s, whose business was to direct rentier capital into new ventures. Chadwick Adamson & Collier of London directed the investment of about 5000 clients into companies which it promoted. At least half a dozen similar firms existed, some of them drawing on provincial sources.[78] In many parts of the country solicitors performed a similar intermediary role.[79] These firms appear to have taken no continuing interest in the companies they promoted and played no part in their management. However, extensive losses in the United States during the 1870s showed the weakness of this system of portfolio investment and inclined British capital in the following decade, even in its dealings with the United States, to a more active stance. This produced collisions between investors intent on controlling the mid-western ranches, mines, breweries and mills into which they poured their funds, and vendors who had thought that they, like their predecessors, were simply raising capital, not conceding control, and that the move from local to London registration was merely a fashion, of no practical consequence. In scarcely any of the cases that have been chronicled in any detail do the British appear to have come out on top. Very frequently one of the vendors provided local management, and conflicts such as those we have seen in South African and Argentine banking developed.

In the case of the Pillsbury-Washburn Flour Mills Co. Ltd, registered in London 1889 to buy one of the largest mid-western milling groups for little short of £2 million, the British investors failed to get a grip on the vendor, who bought back control soon after the turn of the century.[80] Pillsbury, it turned out, had been 'less efficient as a manager than as an entrepreneur'.[81] As for the Spur ranch, in West Texas, this was one of a number of enterprises put together, fenced and stocked on a speculative basis for sale to the British in the early years of enclosed ranching. No sooner was the land acquired than one of the promoters, Colonel A. M. Britton of Denver, took ship for Europe to find a buyer. A syndicate was formed by Alexander McNab of Clackmannanshire, and a company, the Espuela Land and Cattle Co. Ltd, formed to acquire the new range in 1884 for just over £100,000. The details of what followed are not clear. Spottswood W. Lomax, a well-travelled and cultivated Virginian who had been Britton's partner in the venture, was retained as manager by the British company on a salary of $7000 (£1400) a year. He appears to have been a responsible and meticulous manager, but something in his conduct alienated the board, it would seem, and they voted in 1889 that his salary be reduced to $3750, prompting his resignation. Management then passed to a young Scot who had been set out as local representative of the board while Lomax was in charge, and subsequently to another Scot, closely related to Alexander McNab. But these were hard years. The company had bought at the start of a period of declining cattle prices. Conditions changed frequently, and the directors too often reacted, belatedly, by pursuing policies which demonstrated their ignorance of local conditions. There was little profit, and in 1907 the ranch was sold to a United States group.[82]

The reasons for failure of so many of the British ventures of the 1880s in the United States are not entirely clear. It would appear, though, that a major difficulty must have been the maturity and independence of the United States economy, which meant that there was not, as in India, China or the new lands of European settlement, a system of mercantile houses with a foot in both camps. Pillsbury and Lomax plainly needed the kind of firm control that the local management of the River Plate Trust Company was able to exert when vendors such as the Cassels brothers tried to milk the London companies to which they had sold out or initiate policies out of line with the wishes of their London boards.[83] But those Anglo-American houses of the first half of the century which might have provided these services, such as Barings or the Morrisons, had now moved on to areas where the prevailing rates of return were higher.[84] American investment bankers presumably developed the pick of the bunch with domestic resources. British investors in United States enterprises in the closing years of the century in a weak position, with no coordinated and centralised network of specialist intermediaries. This hypothesis is made all the more plausible by the experience of British direct investment in Canada before 1914, which resembled that in the United States in many respects, including its poor profit record, but succeeded best in the salmon fisheries of British Colombia, where long-resident Scots provided the required intermediating managerial group, combining local knowledge, technical skill and the lack of any alternative capital base.[85]

Direct Foreign Investment?

A strange consequence of concentration on North America in some recent literature has been that historians ignorant of the position in other parts of the world have concluded from the very specific United States experience that the syndicate system, by which they mean the use of an apparently independent company with relatively dispersed share-ownership for each overseas undertaking, was irretrievably weak: so incapable of producing effective management, in fact, that it should not be counted as direct foreign investment at all, but as portfolio investment. This error, which originated in a dissertation by T. C. Coram in the 1960s and has since achieved a wider audience through the work of Peter Buckley and Brian Roberts, rests on four major misconceptions. First among these is the assumption that dispersed ownership necessarily meant a lack of centralised managerial control. Syndicates, according to Buckley and Roberts, though they might own a majority of the shares in an Anglo–overseas corporation, failed to manage effectively because they could not reach decisions.[86] This might have been true for North American syndicate investment, but not for Latin American. Executive authority in the River Plate Trust Company and its immediate affiliates rested firmly with John Morris and company secretary, James Anderson. The commanding role of Morris within the group is clear from his correspondence, and it is noteworthy that Coram, in reaching his view, employed no business archives, for these might have enabled him to see through the veil of legal forms to the realities of power. Second, Coram failed to realise how enduring and stable an investment syndicate could be. He assumed that syndicates set up to acquire going concerns in the United States were *ad hoc* arrangements, got up for the purpose. This led him to contrast the syndicate form of investment with the case where a branch or subsidiary was set up in the United States by 'an established British company'. But Morrison, Morris and their City colleagues, coming together at the beginning of the 1880s, soon constituted 'an established British company': a permanent administrative, though not strictly a juridical individual.[87] So too did the Samuels and their colleagues in the tank syndicate in the period before incorporation of Shell.

These errors, based on a narrow range of cases and generalised to embrace the syndicate system as a whole, have led to a third, consequential, blunder. This was to suggest that in view of the apparent lack of specific expertise of syndicate members in ranching, milling, brewing, or anything else for that matter, their investment should be regarded as 'akin to a portfolio flow, since capital organised for the purpose flowed to the area where the host (not the source) country had the advantage'. This is a nonsense. It is like saying that when I run badly I am *really* walking. After the civil war a high proportion of British capital invested in the United States went into enterprises 'which demanded and received continuous supervision on the part of the investors'.[88] If they made a hash of it it was not because they were poor ranchers, or millers or brewers. If John Morris or Marcus Samuel, Alfred Beit or Frederick Dalgety succeeded, it was not because they were good engineers, oilmen, miners or sheep breeders. This sort of expertise was available on a contractual basis. No, all of them—Alexander MacNab as much as Alfred Beit—were administrators and investment bankers first and foremost. It was in this capacity that they succeeded or failed. And management and investment banking were fields in which the source (not the host) country had the advantage. The exception, the United States, may simply prove the rule.

In short, the style of syndicated foreign investment typically employed by British mercantile and finance capitalists in the late nineteenth century was just as much direct investment as the later system of wholly-owned subsidiaries pioneered by industrial capitalists at the end of the century and soon almost universally adopted. It can happily be accommodated to the explanatory models of contemporary economists. In the style of Raymond Vernon, for example, the City may be portrayed as building up special forms of expertise in response to a peculiarly British demand for managerial services and financial expertise. When economies overseas began to develop similar characteristics and exert the same demand, the British were ready and able to provide what was required, first by exporting and later, in response to the challenge of local competition, by 'local production'. There is a little sorting out to be done. In this model, for example, an Anglo–overseas bank was still a British-based exporter and its overseas branches simply sales outlets to the extent that it relied upon capital supplied from the United Kingdom. Only when it developed a firm basis of local deposits could it begin to be regarded as true direct foreign investment, because only then would it have reached the stage analogous to local production of goods by a manufacturing firm. Anglo-Australian banks before 1893, with their heavy reliance on London deposits, must be cast as exporters.[89] Anglo-Latin American banks, forced to insulate operations in each country where they did business by the perpetual threat of rapid exchange fluctuations, may be seen as local producers. The River Plate Trust Company was exporter in its mortgage operations, which drew in British capital to some extent, but a local producer in its provision of management services.

Internalisation poses no problems either. Financiers like Morrison or Beit may be seen to have acquired control, albeit often in a most economical way, by the acquisition of quite modest equity stakes, in companies to which they might have preferred to sell financial and administrative skills. They did so because there was really no adequate market mechanism available at the time for unpacking and pricing these intangible assets.

These are the merest sketches. But they may be enough to show that there is no difference of substance between British-style and American-style or, as we may now call them, finance-capitalist and industrial-capitalist styles of direct foreign investment, and that the classification of investment hinges quite simply upon two things: firstly, the attempt to exert control—whether successful or not—of an undertaking in one country by investors in another country; and secondly, the nationality of the controllers. So, in the struggles examined in this chapter, what has been at issue is whether control of British investment in British-registered companies would fall to British or foreign entrepreneurs, and, therefore, whether it would qualify as direct or portfolio investment. And the conclusion is that control showed a broad tendency to settle in London, in unambiguously British hands, and under the control of finance capitalists rather than merchants, either because British finance capitalists defeated their rivals in the marketplace or were the victors in intrafirm struggles for control, or else because merchants translated themselves into financiers, or foreigners became British, in their efforts to preserve control and defend their enterprises against established metropolitan finance capital.

THE VIEW FROM THE PERIPHERY

On the periphery of the world economy this long process of increasing concentration of ownership and control was frequently experienced as a progressive marginalisation of local entrepreneurs and a loss of social contact with high-level decision-makers. There were several facets to this. Central authorities, because of their preference for routine operations, often alienated enterprising employees, partners or clients. The desire of central decision-makers to spread risks could easily be interpreted by managers and politicians in the country where a company had first risen to prominence as a hostile drain of capital. The greater resources of British-based organisations could often drive out of business local competitors providing extra-economic services, producing copy-cat conservatism in surviving local firms. Local firms acting as selling agents of British companies faced the risk that they might be bypassed as their principals integrated forward into full local production. Finally, subordinate partners or salaried managers in major agency houses or Anglo–overseas companies were frequently distanced from general management by the gradual formalising and bureaucratisation of corporate and group structures or by the acquisition of their original employers by progressively larger and more remote corporations in successive waves of mergers.

The unwanted enterprise of loyal employees or directors could take a variety of forms. One, the attempt to manipulate metropolitan capital, has already been dealt with. Another was fraud. It was following a defalcation by one of their English bookkeepers that Shaw Wallace first took on a professionally trained accountant, J. B. Lloyd, in the mid-1890s. Other managers were apt to continue to do private business on the side. The speciality of one manager of the Oriental Banking Corporation, in charge of a small rural branch at Kilmore, Victoria, in the 1850s,

. . . was to supplement his salary by speculative ventures in farm produce, for which his position as manager gave him special facilities, such as buying up for forward delivery growing crops and cereals already garnered—what the Yankees call 'cornering'.[90]

In much the same way Francis Neild and John Ripley of Buenos Aires used funds entrusted to them by the Australian Mortgage Land and Finance Company and the Trust and Agency Company of Australasia for investment in pastoral mortgage loans to pay off the bank loans of their own *estancias* and to finance industrial ventures in paint and Portland cement.[91] Such schemes sometimes damaged and occasionally even ruined their victims, but more commonly it was the perpetrators who were shrugged off, their reputations gone, to make their way in the financial underworld.

The tendency of London managements to wish to limit risks was a source of frustration to local managers, clients, and governments alike. Many overseas governments disliked the preference of the major British fire insurance offices for home investment. Insurance companies built up their funds from local premiums. Why, then, should these funds not be invested in the countries that had generated them?[92] Local propaganda against London-based banks made much of their lack of financial commitment to the countries in which they intended to operate. 'We have repeatedly shown that the Anglo-Australian banks perform their operation with the deposits of their customers', grumbled the *Sydney Morning Herald*, 'leaving the larger portion of their paid-up capital in England, much of it resting on what Sydney Smith called "the sweet simplicity of the three per cents".'[93] As early as 1869, Thomas Armstrong's *Estrella* insurance company in Buenos Aires was being advertised as 'an Argentine Company, whose only investments are in the country'.[94] The investment policies of the South African Randlords have already been remarked upon. All of them appear to have drawn on funds generated in South Africa for investment elsewhere. Harry Mosenthal turns up in 1890, for example, taking a large share in the first abortive syndicate organised by Ashurst Morris Crisp to build a central London underground railway. He acted, somewhat anomalously, through the Exploration Company.[95] Channelling capital away from the country where it was generated was offensive; channelling from the periphery towards the very centre of the world economy doubly so.

The third facet of peripheral marginalisation is more problematic. Of course local firms failed. Most firms anywhere, any time, fail; success and longevity are the exception. British firms failed too. Yet it is hard to avoid the impression that firms with strong British links fared better than those without. Moreover, the competitive process was not an entirely anonymous one. It was often clear—as when one bank refused to hold the notes of another, or when the acquisition of a local firm was effected through foreclosure by its foreign creditor— just who was precipitating a failure. It was foreclosure that first drew James Finlay & Co. into direct ownership of tea plantations, and Dalgety, the Australian Mortgage Loan and Finance Company, and Liebig's into direct participation in ranching.[96] Though the ultimate causes might run far back and the final act be, in truth, a matter of reluctant prudence, it could easily be perceived as vindictive, and it sometimes was.[97]

Certainly, local entrepreneurs feared the intrusion of British companies and appealed to their clients and to local states to protect them on nationalistic grounds. Thomas Russell, in Auckland, complained of the new, London-based and presumptuously named National Bank of New Zealand in

1872, describing it as 'a foreign institution got up and managed from London'.[98] Forty years before, arguments about the likely drain of profits from the colony had been deployed by local bankers against the proposed Bank of Australasia.[99] Sometimes an edge was given to this hostility by the tactless or bullying way in which a London institution broke into the local market. The Standard Bank was felt by local people to have got the better of the bargain when it bought the Fauresmith Bank in the Orange Free State because it had access to inside information transmitted by the cashier, Barret, who became manager under the new dispensation.[100] In Argentina, especially in the Provinces, incoming British bankers who took over local establishments entirely failed to realise that these had performed an important political function in the past, pursuing politically determined lending policies, providing funds for the virtual purchase of votes, and acting as centres of patronage. Plainly, the British could not have continued to operate in this way, but if their eyes had been open they might have avoided actions of their own which were interpreted, though not intended, as provocatively political in character.[101] Local businessmen were not simply that. They were also politicians, community leaders, public men. To defeat them in the marketplace was to damage the social fabric to which they belonged and alter the balance of local politics in favour of other groups: petty industrialists and leaders of recent immigrants in Argentina, western-educated bureaucrats and lawyers in India.

Did more local men fail than British? It is hard to see how a properly quantified answer to this question could be devised, partly because changing nationality was a possible, indeed not infrequently resorted to, move in the game. The British grew to dominate some sectors of business in some economies. From others, such as the import of consumer goods, they were largely excluded. In the end, the cosmopolitan petty bourgeoisie of brokers and fixers, those denizens of Conrad novels, drifting from partnership to partnership and port to port, were squeezed between the giant multinationals and the protected enterprises of indigenous entrepreneurs; so, too, were distinctive client groups of the British: Indians in East Africa or the Chinese in Malaysia. Yet it often appeared, and it was sometimes true, that firms of British origin, and above all firms with direct representation or headquarters in Britain, were quicker than their competitors to seize on new methods of organisation, new technologies, and new sources of capital, and were consequently more successful in riding out the periodic commercial crises of the nineteeth century, and more successful, too, at consolidating their positions by the acquisition of weaker rivals in the aftermaths of these crisis.[102] This example, in its turn, often fostered more conservative policies among local lending institutions and defensive organisation or consolidation by local processors and middlemen, which were felt by those small producers of export commodities and other provincial folk who were the natural constituency of populist politicians.[103]

A particular threat to the most successful mercantile houses was the prospect of losing agencies to principals as British-based corporations gradually expanded their bureaucracies or as the local operations reached the point where direct representation was justified. British insurance companies, which had operated through agencies for many years in provincial Britain as well as overseas, were sensitive to the fact that even the most influential of local agents, commanding very extensive business among the various manufacturing and utility companies for which they acted as managing agencies, might none the less lack real incentive to drum up new business. Shaw Wallace, for example, had a big insurance department by 1912, acting for several British offices. But they allocated business in a way that can hardly have satisfied the Royal Exchange. 'The "Royal" received the lion's share of Shaw Wallace & Co.'s fire insurance business and the best outside business we could introduce,' wrote a former employee.

Then followed the 'London, Liverpool, and Globe' ... 'L'Union', 'British Dominions' and 'Excess'. The 'Royal Exchange' agency came to us at the instance of a Director of one of the Oil companies (Burmah or the Anglo-Persian Oil Company) who was on the 'Royal Exchange' Board. Although we could not give them much business, they were very useful to us in handling excesses.[104]

Similarly, the Sun found that their Buenos Aires agent, in spite of his impressively wide business acquaintance, was disinclined to extend their business.[105] This problem of motivation, coupled with legislative changes to which we shall return, led the British companies to replace agencies by branches, and, finally, by local subsidiaries, in one market after another from the closing years of the nineteenth century.[106]

For the merchant houses this entailed the loss of a business which they had perhaps had for half a century, and with it, as often as not, the loss of trained staff who went to set up the new branch, and a loss of influence and patronage for the firm.[107] Sales agencies for manufactured goods went too, of course, but this might be less damaging, since they were often shortlived and, individually, formed only a small part of any firm's business.[108] Most damaging of all was the loss, during the 1920s, of the great oil distribution agencies. Standard Oil, Asiatic (a Shell offshoot), Anglo-Persian and Burmah Oil all sold through agents in Asia until the 1920s.[109] The same system operated in parts of Latin America, and perhaps elsewhere.[110] At this point, however, the desire for a more centralised system of administration, clearer information flows and rational accounting came to outweigh the value of local expertise. In 1925 Burmah Oil gave three years' notice to Shaw Wallace of the termination of its agency. In the view of R. I. Watson, Burmah's chairman from 1918 to 1946, and a determined centraliser, the 'building-up of an efficient whole-time company organisation' had made the managing agency system no longer appropriate.[111] But this one agency had accounted for half Shaw Wallace's profits and had tied down its staff and resources at a time when other houses had been moving into new trades and local manufacture. And with the agency went the staff. Anglo-Persian had already claimed J. B. Lloyd, a former senior Indian partner in the firm, as its managing director in 1919.[112] Now, at the termination of the agency in 1927, Burmah-Shell took over 42 Shaw Wallace executives, perhaps a third of the senior staff.[113] On the West coast of South America, Balfour Williamson and its subsidiary, Milne & Co., held on to the valuable sales agency of Jersey Standard's local affiliate, IPC, in spite of their 'unaggressive and costly' marketing, only because as controllers of the Lobitos field they could have obstructed attempts by Standard to set up its own marketing system, either directly, or by the sale of Lobitos to a rival company or the Peruvian state.[114] Those companies which dropped managing agents were often first to abandon compradors, for much the same reasons. Standard Oil, along with British American Tobacco, were among the first western firms to do so in the early twentieth century.[115]

A final facet of marginalisation had to do not with discarding over-enthusiastic staff, the defeat of rivals in the market place, risk-aversion, or the rupture of old contractual and organisational arrangements, but rather with social relations within surviving international mercantile firms and the new City-based international corporations. Changes in scale and business methods had a profound effect. As staff and clients began to be numbered first in dozens, then in hundreds, personal acquaintance with each became impossible for partners or directors, and they were obliged to fall back on routine procedures, hierarchical structures and explicit definition of managerial functions. Marcus Samuel, who thought two clerks in a single office in Houndsditch enough of a bureaucracy to manage the Shell fleet of eight tankers, not to mention other vessels on long-term charter, never really adjusted to the scale of his vast enterprise, which operated in an extraordinarily pragmatic, ramshackle fashion, until control ultimately passed to Henri Deterding of Royal Dutch, the consummate bureaucrat and centraliser, in an agreement of 1902 which epitomised the transformation from a nineteenth century to a twentieth-century style of management.[116]

In the rule-bound atmosphere of the newer, more bureaucratic companies, the prospects of clerks suffered a serious deterioration. They may have been made a little more comfortable and paid a little better, but they could not look forward to promotion with the same certainty as in the past. When Robert Thurburn first went out to the River Plate in 1870, he went as the nephew of a City bank director to work in an organisation which, though it had the form of a public company, was owned by a proprietorship many of whom knew each other well. It was possible for the family to make representation to directors on Thurburn's behalf when questions of promotion cropped up. He could not know quite how high he would rise nor how quickly, but he never had any doubt, nor any reason to doubt, that he was destined for senior management positions in the bank.[117] This was even more clearly the case for clerks recruited into merchant houses of the mid-nineteenth century from among the kind of the partners and their correspondents.[118] If they did not rise to partnerships in the firms to which they were apprenticed, they could look forward to financial support in an independent or loosely affiliated venture, such as John Swire or the Booths received from the Holts and other Liverpool families.[119] Towards the end of the nineteenth century many men who had set out with aspirations to set up their own firms were obliged to settle for salaried management posts. Many who would have been satisfied to have done that well remained clerks to the end, performing routine and repetitive work. Kinship and community were giving way to a meritocracy in which the skills of the clerk were less highly valued than those of the new professionals: accountants, lawyers, engineers and salesmen.[120]

One of the arguments of this book has been that twentieth-century economists, looking back at the nineteenth century, have confused dispersal of ownership with dispersal of control in the many Anglo-foreign joint-stock companies organised on what they called the 'syndicate' basis, and in the managing agencies which retained the partnership form. It was possible for these extremely flexible forms of business organisation to be used effectively to govern large undertakings and great concentrations of capital. Gradually, however, the syndicates moved to tighter structures of majority or wholly-owned subsidiaries under holding companies, while the partnerships incorporated and adopted similar group structures. The imperative was not managerial, but financial and fiscal.

As we have seen, incorporation offered easier access to cheap capital through the issue of debentures and avoided the problem of withdrawal of partners' capital on retirement.[121] But a new urgency was given to incorporation by the rise of personal taxation, which became an ever stronger influence on business structure during the twentieth century, and by the growing need to organise integrated groups of capital-intensive undertakings, which could be met by incorporation, which released substantial sums of partnership capital for new ventures while allowing retention of effective control over going concerns through minority holdings and board appointments. More tight-knit defensive grouping arrangements were simultaneously prompted by the growing threat of a new stock exchange phenomenon, the takeover bid, which loomed larger as the proprietorships of companies became more numerous and anonymous.[122]

At Shaw Wallace, incorporation was finally resorted to in 1946, and the (Indian) company went public in 1947, a judicious move, as India attained independence.[123] But as a limited company the firm still faced problems. How was it to retain control of its own equity? How was it to hold on to companies in which it had only a minority stake, but on whose agencies it depended for its profits? In the event, former partners and their families who received shares in Shaw Wallace & Co. Ltd as vendors gradually sold these to R. G. Shaw & Co. Ltd, the incorporated successor to the firm's London branch, which now became, more than ever, 'the pivot of the much enlarged Shaw group'.[124]

The experience of the Inchcape Group was similar. Born in 1852, the first Lord Inchcape, James Lyle Mackay, had risen through various salaried positions to a partnership in Mackinnon Mackenzie & Co. by the 1880s. Returning from the East he was elected to the Board of the British India Steam Navigation Company, another of William Mackinnon's creations. Later, as chairman, he engineered its amalgamation with P. & O. During a long life, Inchcape acquired substantial shares in a number of partnerships affiliated to Mackinnon Mackenzie. His successors, driven by the usual taxation and financial consideration, converted many of these into private limited companies in the 1940s and 1950s. Then, in 1958, Inchcape & Co. Ltd, was formed as a holding company, and a process of financial reorganisation began in which the Hon. Simon Mackay and other members of his family consolidated their control of Gray Daws & Co. Ltd, Duncan Macneill & Co., and St Mary Axe Securities and, through them, of an extensive network of operating companies through the East.[125] With financial consolidation came centralisation of authority. Mackay took over Binnys in 1906, and 'under the new set up there was never any doubt that, in the last resort, decisions would be taken in London'. The Madras partners of the encumbered firm became its managers, part of their salaries going each month to repay their creditors.[126]

Those who neglected to attend to the financial organisation and managerial efficiency of their groups fell prey to those who did not. Lloyds Bank acquired control of the major Anglo-Latin American banks, organised as the Bank of London and South America, an organisation which, by 1944, was operating in fifteen states, and had more than 1000 employees in Argentina alone. At various times in the mid-twentieth century the old-established Greek cotton and general merchants, Ralli Brothers, fell to Slater Walker; Balfour Williamson to Dalgety; and the tea growers and distributors, Brook Bond to Liebig's. Plainly, the close relations—even identities—formerly obtaining between staff, management and proprietorship could not survive these financial and organisational gymnastics unimpaired. The few surviving giants of mercantile origin slowly became indistinguishable in management style, in the increasing public and diversified character of their undertakings, and in their relations with states, employees and shareholders, from multinational corporations rooted in finance or manufacturing industry. It was no longer possible for those on the periphery of the world economy to have the same intimate and continuous relations with leading business decision-makers that had prevailed in the days of resident partners. The new executives did not stay as long, never intended to settle, and worked with one eye on head office, looking for notice, for approval, and for promotion back to the heart of things.

CONCLUSION

This chapter has chronicled the fortunes of mercantile firms as they adapted to new economic conditions in competition or partnership with metropolitan finance capital. On the whole this is seen as a process of spatial concentration of control over capital. Not only independent firms overseas and in the provincial ports, but managers of agencies, branches and subsidiaries within large European-based corporations found their autonomy increasingly restricted.

Technological and institutional changes examined in

Chapter 4 had contributed, by the closing years of the century, to low interest rates and overcapacity in many commercial activities, which emphasised the power of the centre by favouring oligopolistic competition strategies in which high-level negotiation was vital. These strategies often depended for their success on unaccustomed restraint on the part of the subordinates. Cartels, such as shipping conferences or the London Fire Offices Committee, were not only arranged on high, but obliged local management to curb their competitive impulses, something they generally did not like.

With this centralisation of authority came closer links with the state. This was part cause, part effect. Government contracts and concessions, always important, became increasingly so as the significance for modern government and warfare of secure supplies of oil, rapid communications, public health and full employment became fully apparent. At the same time the state began, often reluctantly, to take cognisance of the effects which private collusion between firms were having on public welfare. The keel of competition policy was being laid.

In this closer relationship with the state—a phenomenon as much of the periphery as of the centre of the world economy—were to be found the seeds of capitalist imperialism. It is taken for granted here that for all its anti-imperialist and nationalist rhetoric, the militarism, populism and state-capitalism of many Third World regimes is just as symptomatic of imperialism as the expansionist foreign and commercial policies of the USA and other major capitalist powers—that capitalist imperialism is, in short, a condition of the *whole* world economy, not merely of its most powerful states.

For this reason the precise ways in which remnants of the old cosmopolitan merchant class were prised away from their liberal ideology and intensely private style of business into a more imperialist (or nationalist) and bureaucratic frame of mind are of the first importance to a theoretical understanding of the onset of imperialism. It is to this theme that the final chapter is largely devoted.

6   Conclusion

THE NATIONALISATION OF THE BOURGEOISIE

By the first chapter of the twentieth century the profound social and political consequences of recent structural changes in business organisation were already apparent. They were evident in new ideals of the businessman—a new self-image and a new public image. They were evident also in business itself, which took on a more public character. They were evident most of all in a new and closer relationship between big business and the state, sometimes symbiotic sometimes antagonistic, but never neutral.

Images

The merchant or merchant banker of the mid-nineteenth century had been, on the whole, a very private figure, working with the grain of the market and accepting its judgement with resignation. Charles Morrison, writing in 1854, set the tone. The businessman should be:

> ... a man sparing of words—close in disposition—often intuitively seeing what is best to be done without being fluent in explaining to others his reasons for doing it—wary in his choice of men—cautious and balanced in his opinions—careful never to promise as much as he expects to perform—innovating only in a gradual, practical, and tentative manner—averse to tumult and verbal contention—willing to work in obscurity for a result only to be realised after years of patience—instinctively distrustful of everything showy and popular—and punctiliously correct in the minutest pecuniary detail.[1]

'There had never been a distinguished Forsyte,' Galsworthy

190

observed. 'But that very lack of distinction was the name's greatest asset. It was a private name, intensely individual, and his own property.'[2]

This was an old tradition. Commerce, though not the quickest way of attaining a fortune, was the least violent. To many seventeenth-century commentators it had appeared '*doux*' or '*innocent*'.[3] 'Divine Providence', wrote one,

. . . has not willed for everything that is needed for life to be found in the same pot. It has dispersed its gifts so that the mutual need which they have to help one another would establish ties of friendship among them. This continuous exchange of all the comforts of life constitutes commerce, and this commerce makes for the gentleness [*douceur*] of life.[4]

It is easy to see how this fitted into the Cobdenite vision of the nineteenth century, yet still a little uncanny to observe the similarity of Cobden's phrasing to that of Savary two centuries before.[5] Cobden stood on a well-prepared platform. Adam Smith had explained how the pursuit of individual self-interest could redound to the collective good. Immanuel Kant and Tom Paine, in their different ways, had emphasised the connexions between commerce, civil liberty and international peace. The middle years of the nineteenth century had seen an apparently causal conjunction of the removal of constraints on international commerce, its rapid growth, and the maintenance of a general peace. But now, towards the end of the century, as they started to adopt more bureaucratic and centralised institutional forms, those in commerce and finance adopted a new style, owing much to industrial models. Aggression, daring, publicity and a Napoleonic command of detail were the new virtues.

The shipowner, Sir Alfred Jones, scarcely a generation younger than Alfred Holt and John Swire, was a world away from them in culture. Every inch the tycoon, he rose early and spent his life amid a swarm of secretaries. Travelling down to London he would dictate to several of them, despatching one to the telegraph office at each station while the train stood waiting. To create a market for bananas in Liverpool he is said to have sent barrowloads out into the streets to be given away.[6] In this new world the avowed object was to master the market, catch out competitors and hoodwink customers:

Think of having all the quinine in the world, and some millionaire's
pampered wife gone ill with malaria, eh? That's a squeeze, George, eh? eh?
Millionaire on his motor car outside, offering you any price you liked.[7]

H. G. Wells, it will be said, was no friend to the businessman.
But this is to miss the point. For almost a century now,
muckrakers and entrepreneurs alike have emphasised the
power of the tycoon: the former because they dislike it, the
latter because they desire it. Only in relatively recent years, and
not yet in all large corporations, have the virtues of flexibility,
delegation and decentralisation been rediscovered, while
voices have been raised on the Left to proclaim the relative
immunity of the state from manipulation by businessmen and
admit that a great war could indeed be waged even if the house
of Rothschild and its connexions set their face against it.[8] The
comfortable thing to do for much of this century was to
emphasise the prevalence of order and control in the face of the
evident complexity, even chaos, of twentieth-century life by
exaggerating the power of big business. And if Left and Right
were agreed on the reality of rational bureaucratic control, they
were agreed too on the substance of its obverse. While the Left
vested rationality in the state and in planning, centring its
demonology on visions of international capitalist conspiracy,
the all-knowing computer, and the heartless and remorseless
production-line, the Right set up the firm as the paradigm of
rationality, lodging its opposite—black or demonic
rationality—in the supposedly tight-knit and disciplined
organisation of left-wing parties and terrorist groups and
organised crime.

Francis Chevallier Boutell, Buenos Aires manager of the
River Plate Trust Company, warned head office in 1903 that:

It is even now all the authorities can do to keep down the exceptionally well
organised army of socialists, which society is so constituted and disciplined
that it has only to send out the order and all the adherents, whose numbers
run into thousands, obey it to a man implicitly.[9]

Conan Doyle established the new myth of criminal conspiracy
in the character of Professor Moriarty, building ingeniously
upon fragmentary folk memories of an earlier mythology,
concerned with the power of freemasonry, which had been

thrown up in the disruptive aftermath of the French Revolution.[10]

'The man pervades London,' Holmes cried, 'and no one has ever heard of him. That's what puts him on a pinnacle in the records of crime. . . . For years now I have been conscious of some power behind the malefactor, some deep organising power which for ever stands in the way of the law. . . . For years I have endeavoured to break through the veil which shrouded it, and at last the time came when I seized my thread and followed it, until it led me, after a thousand cunning windings, to ex-Professor Moriarty of mathematical celebrity. He is the Napoleon of crime, Watson. He is the organiser of half that is evil and of nearly all that is undetected in this great city.'[11]

In a melodramatic novel of 1908, *The Man Who Was Thursday*, G. K. Chesterton perfectly married and attempted, rather too subtly perhaps, to expose the twin traditions. He described:

. . . first a band of the last champions of order fighting against what appeared to be a world of anarchy, and then the discovery that the mysterious master both of the anarchy and the order was the same sort of elemental elf.[12]

In the meantime, in a more prosaic world, hundreds of managing partners, each travelling with a microphone in his knapsack, emerged from the quiet parlours of family firms, took the chair to address shareholders and press, and attempted to convey to them at least the illusion of an organisation, and a world, under control. For indeed, 'civilisation is possible only through confidence, so that we can bank our money and go unarmed about the streets'.[13] And the less secure the world became, the more necessary it became for public men to puff themselves up and proclaim its security, in business as much as politics.

At the same time that they were adopting a more public role, the merchants were moving to the Right. Shaken as much by the failure of property-owning democracy to achieve tranquillity at home as by the rising tide of xenophobia and populism abroad, the commercial bourgeoisie crossed the floor of the House of Commons to join the Conservatives in 1886 and allowed themselves to drift into an accommodation with values quite alien to those of their parents. 'By the late nineteenth century the City was as firmly Tory as it had been Liberal a generation before,' writes Rubinstein.[14]

Cobden's dream had become a nightmare. The suspicion, voiced in 1838, that English manufacturers were developing into 'toadies of a clod-pole aristocracy' developed into a certainty.[15] 'Manufacturers and merchants as a rule seem only to desire riches that they may be enabled to prostrate themselves at the feet of feudalism,' he lamented.[16] Even republican Americans were not immune.[17]

The Public Face of Business
How had this disaster befallen the bourgeoisie? Most of all, how had the *mercantile* bourgeoisie been polluted: the element who, because of their direct participation in international commerce, might have been thought most resistant? The answer lay partly in the scale of business organisation, partly in the characteristics of those kinds of business which demanded increased scale, and partly in the style of competition to which large-scale organisation and naturally monopolistic activities gave rise. Of the first of these, Cobden had been well aware by the 1850s, though he observed it at work in manufacturing; trade was still untouched. The social and political state of Birmingham, he declared:

. . . is far more healthy than that of Manchester; and it arises from the fact that the industry of the hardware district is carried on by small manufacturers, employing a few men and boys each, sometimes only an apprentice or two; whilst the great capitalists in Manchester form an aristocracy, individual members of which wield an influence over sometimes two thousand persons.[18]

Next come the specific characteristics of those enterprises which demanded large-scale organisation. As we have seen, merchants, whether at the centre or on the periphery, moved into banking and land, insurance, railways and public utilities, manufacture, distribution and mining. They developed more vertically integrated systems for the finance, processing and shipment of internationally traded primary commodities. They exchanged the partnership for the corporation. Each of these steps brought them into contact and political confrontation with a new and numerous group. Each brought the merchant more clearly into public view.

Banking, which had originally been limited largely to the

mutual accommodation of merchants in the countries of settlement, had now grown into a vast business linking thousands of small depositors with equal numbers of small debtors. Moreover, in countries which still lacked central banks, the privately-owned joint-stock banks often had responsibility for the circulating currency, sometimes uneasily shared with government. A run on the bank was a very public event; a bank failure had public consequences; the calling in of loans at a time of crisis might save the bank, but at a visible cost in ruined farmers and mortgages foreclosed. Insurance, less obviously, created a pool of funds for investment. Where they were invested and how was a matter of public concern. Railways and urban utilities were used by the millions. Produce was moved to market, men and women to work, public safety was assured, and the business system sustained by railways and shipping lines, by trams and buses, by systems of water supply and drainage, and by telephones and telegraphs. Manufacturing, where it substituted for imports, was a matter of public concern because of its effect upon the balance of payments. In addition, it proclaimed national maturity and strategic capability, created employment and, through direct distribution, brought merchants for the first time into contact with the mass of consumers and with new techniques for manipulating their tastes.

In all these capacities, but most of all in mining, where the original isolation of discoveries heightened the difficulties, merchants were brought into contact also with large aggregations of labour: labour lacking the bonds of community and kinship which had underwritten the deferential relations of clerks to partners; labour capable of organisation and concerted action because of its concentration, because of the cheap transport system available to it, and even because of the structures imposed upon it by new work disciplines.

Finally, more integrated export procedures for primary products brought those who remained merchants face to face with growers, often as their creditors and as virtual monopolists. To take only one example, the Calcutta office of James Finlay & Co. found itself by 1939 with '139,260 employees under its jurisdiction', most of them on plantations and in mills, of whom just 354 were Europeans.[19] The firm still lives with the consequences of this most unmercantile relationship. 'The annual attack on conditions at Bangladeshi tea plantations owned by the Glasgow-based James Finlay and Company passed off quietly yesterday,' reported *The Guardian* of 2 August 1986, before providing a characteristically whimsical account of protests and justifications at the AGM concerning the conditions of the workforce. Fear of labour soon became tainted with racism. Kiernan found that in general the planters, those in the front line of organisations like Finlays, to be the most resolutely and viciously anti-Indian of all European groups in the sub-continent.[20] For Chevallier Boutell in Buenos Aires, seemingly unaware of the irony imparted to his remark by a Huguenot ancestry: 'Socialism should come under the heading of immigration.'[21] For Joseph Chamberlain, amply confirming Cobden's hypothesis about the interconnexion of increased scale and political degeneration, free trade and immigration were both weapons of a fanatical cosmopolitan liberalism directed against the national economy. 'You are suffering from the unrestricted imports of cheaper goods,' he told an audience in Limehouse, as the Aliens Act of 1905 went before Parliament. 'You are suffering also from the unrestricted immigration of the people who make these goods . . . I am now in favour of giving the Executive Government the strongest power of control over this alien immigration.'[22]

Reaching for the Apron Strings: Abroad . . .
Is it any wonder that merchants who had formerly been protected from all this by the opacity of complex market relations should react in fear and embark upon a frenzied search for legitimacy, the one great prize still held by the aristocracy, and for power, which remained the prerogative of the state.

The fear was certainly widespread. From Buenos Aires, Chevallier Boutell painted the picture of a situation barely under control:

The government is well aware of the steady growth and development of this socialistic mass of malcontents—he wrote—and is usually cognisant of the fact that for the safety of society and for the general peace of the country, it is necessary to keep its foot well down on the neck of this mob.[23]

On Mafeking night, Soames Forsyte, the fictional counterpart of John Morris, 'was bewildered, exasperated, offended' as the East Enders invaded the West End. 'A youth so knocked off his top-hat that he recovered it with difficulty.' Not long afterwards, at Hyde Park Corner, 'he ran into George Forsyte, very sunburnt from racing, holding a false nose in his hand.

'Hallo, Soames,' he said, 'have a nose!' Soames responded with a pale smile. 'Got this off one of these sportsmen', went on George, who had evidently been dining; 'had to lay him out—for trying to bash my hat. I say, one of these days we shall have to fight these chaps, they're getting so damned cheeky—all radicals and socialists. They want our goods.'[24]

Small wonder that the wealthy should search for 'a union of conservatism with liberality; of a love of steady quiet and strong government with concession to the spirit of the age and enlightened legislation'.[25] They yearned for a replication in class relations and in the political sphere of the benevolent despotism to which they still aspired in the world of business, where 'not only are the shareholders passive, but the Board of Directors is little more than a Committee of Control upon the management of one highly paid officer of the Company'.[26]

Similar pressures were at work on the periphery of the world economy. There, native and expatriate international merchants alike found their ambiguous nationality and comprador status more and more of a liability in countries where the political tide had turned against cosmopolitan liberalism in reaction to the damaging commercial crises of the 1870s and early 1890s and to the patterns of concentric marginalisation and increasing centralisation which had followed. Those who were committed to the economies of the periphery had been driven into the same range of activities as their metropolitan contemporaries, but were rather differently distributed across that range being, in general, rather stronger than them in local manufacture and distribution, rather weaker in insurance and shipping, with the balance in banking and public utilities varying considerably from one country to another under the influence of local government policies.[27] These men found themselves under threat at one and the same time from local populist pressures and the competitive force of metropolitan capital. Almost always they sought an escape not only through establishing barriers to entry, which could easily arouse popular resentment, but by seeking a close accommodation with local states which could grant and defend new privileges and monopolies, and by laying claim to national authenticity through social and cultural adaptations.

On the Gold Coast:

> . . . there had emerged by 1850 in the urban centres . . . a class of indigenous merchants who were in no way inferior in education and culture to their local European counterparts . . . by the 1850s these African merchants were more numerous, more influential, and wielded more power than their predecessors.[28]

Many of these men and women had one white or mulatto parent. It had been the almost universal custom in the first half of the century for Europeans on the Coast to take native wives, who were often active partners in their trading ventures.[29] It was from such liaisons that many of the African merchants of the middle years of the century came. Similar anglicised mercantile elites were to be found elsewhere in West Africa. A number of the freed Yoruba slaves who had been settled at Freetown by the British made their way to Lagos and settled there after 1851, adopting English dress and religion. But towards the end of the century they suffered reverses in trade, diversified into farming, and turned their backs on British culture, adopting Yoruba names and African dress, and setting up an independent church.[30] The same scurrying of denationalised bourgeoisies towards a spurious ethnic authenticity may be seen in many countries in the late nineteenth and early twentieth centuries. Faced with Sinhalese-Buddhist cultural revivalism in the 1920s, the westernised Sinhalese elite,

> . . . hastened to discover their forgotten past. They learnt the Sinhalese language, abandoned Christianity, re-embraced Buddhism, discarded Western attire and donned improvised local attire, calling it the 'Aryan-Sinhalese' dress.[31]

As the nineteenth century progressed there was less and less room for Eurasian populations and other comprador bourgeoisies to flourish between the rigid notions of respectability pursued by Europeans in the East and the drive for cultural authenticity among indigenous elites. To continue mixing cultures indiscriminately, as did the Maharajah of Cooch Behar, discovered by a British guest one evening shortly after the First World War 'roller-skating in the great central hall of [his] palace, to the strains of a really excellent string band', was to court ridicule and political impotence.[32] More and more the thing to do was to be an Australian in preference to a Pom, Boer instead of Briton, African not Creole, a Gaucho sooner than a *porteño*, a Quebecois not a Scot, and almost anything rather than a Yankee. For those with poor credentials, or with none, the best course was to cling to the coat tails of government and the governing class. So, Farran & Zimmermann, in Buenos Aires, the final local expression of one of the oldest North European commercial families in Argentina, acted largely as town agents for *estancieros*, as did the Buenos Aires subsidiary of the River Plate Trust, by this time independent, in the 1970s, after Peronist nationalisation had largely wiped out its London-based corporate clientele.[33] While in the South African Republic the *déraciné* Hungarian engineer, Alois Nellmapius, courted President Paul Kruger, winning monopolies of distilling and the manufacture of gunpowder.[34]

On the whole, local states were willing to help those businessmen who identified with and resided in the country, regardless of their origins. Barman has argued convincingly that Baron Mauá did not, as used to be claimed, fail because of the opposition or indifference of the Brazilian state.[35] Indeed, there was a good deal of political advantage to be gained from legislation which hit out at foreign capital while discriminating in favour of local entrepreneurs. It echoed authentic folk traditions—the early nineteenth-century gang fights between Brazilian students and Portuguese clerks, or the Mexican mid-century fashion for kidnapping wealthy foreigners and holding them for ransom.[36] It satisfied popular discontent arising from the ever-more direct contact of local people with foreign capitalists as creditors and suppliers of essential services.

Initially, until they realised the advantages to the state of lower local interest rates, governments in the British colonies and in India opposed the influx of London-based banks.[37] The government of India, even before independence, had been brought round to the nationalist view that the managing agencies were 'an irrational and part-time system of management' and had begun to hedge the agencies around with legislative constraints.[38] In the United States, populist xenophobia and local interest alike were served in the 1880s by a spate of anti-alien laws covering the national territories and many western states, which prohibited the acquisition of land by absentee aliens or by corporations in which more than a small percentage of stocks was owned by aliens while limiting the length of time that alien mortgagees could hold properties on which they had foreclosed. British investment, particularly in land, was regarded by the farmer:

... either as a step toward the formation of great monopolies, or, even worse, as part of an imperialistic design conceived by London bankers to enslave the American people.[39]

At the end of the decade 'the complete prohibition of land-ownership to this alien became an article of agrarian faith'.[40] But much of this was mere rhetoric, and the laws were only very selectively enforced, presumably in ways that catered to the interests of the legislators rather more than to the passions of the populists.[41] In Queensland, colonial socialism was first cousin to nationalism. State abattoirs received a monopoly of slaughter for the local market. Foreign-owned abattoirs could kill only for export. While on the other side of the Tasman Sea, New Zealand governments of the early twentieth century discriminated against the British firm, Borthwicks, by refusing to approve its purchase of two slaughterhouses and through discriminatory export quotas.[42] Aggressive competition with local institutions led to the exclusion of the Standard Bank from the Orange Free State in 1868 and to the confiscation of assets and temporary closure of the Rosario branch of the London and River Plate in Argentina.[43] In the Transvaal, the National Bank of South Africa was set up in 1890, the state providing two-fifths, and a consortium of European bankers the remainder of its £250,000 capital, in an effort to relieve the government from dependence upon the Standard Bank.[44] Many countries introduced protective tariffs. Many legislated to force foreign insurance companies to invest large sums in government bonds as a condition of doing business. Some, including Argentina, introduced discriminatory corporation taxes.[45]

... and at Home

All this partiality towards national business was not without its complement in Britain, although it was perhaps more strongly resisted there than elsewhere. A handful of Radicals resisted protectionism not simply, or even primarily, on economic grounds, but because it opened up vistas of public corruption reminiscent of the days of the old East India Company. John Brunner spoke of the ease with which he and other ' "wealthy business men" in the House might propose "import duty after import duty" to augment their private fortunes "at the cost of their fellow countrymen" '.[46] He preferred to meet foreign competition by direct state intervention to improve the competitiveness of British industry. As a first step he proposed railway nationalisation, James Morrison's hobby horse of the 1840s, which would have the additional merit of helping retain the support of organised labour for the Liberal Party.[47]

'I have encouraged Asquith to go in for Railway Nationalisation, [which] would in my opinion go like wild-fire', Brunner wrote to Lord Crewe. 'I know all the risks, but what I have seen and heard of the results in Germany . . . have convinced me. And the risks are as nothing compared to the risks of Protectionism.'[48]

The trouble was that, since 1886, these views had been held by an ever-diminishing number of the *haute bourgeoisie*: Brunner himself, Mond, Samuel Montagu, George Cadbury or Sydney Stern, but not many more. And on some issues the country was firmly behind the new, imperialist Right. Perhaps the deciding one was war: first the Boer War and then the Great War. While they continued to believe, in general, that war was inimical to capitalism and that commerce would ultimately bring about and sustain a general peace, many businessmen could also see the short-term material advantages to be gained from a little war here or there. Far more seductive, however, to the class as a whole, was the chance to demonstrate publicly their new status in relation to those traditional warmongers, the aristocracy. The Crimean War had seen a brief bourgeois foray into the fundamental business of organised coercion. During the disastrous early phase of the war it became evident that heroism was not enough.

There was more to the war than fighting. As this truism gripped the British public, war began increasingly to be seen in terms of matching supply with demand, in terms of organisation and administration and the manipulation of material resources, rather than of personal bravery and leadership. From this economic conception of war it was but a short step to the equation of military strength with practical efficiency, and this in the 1850s was inevitably associated with the middle class and modernity, not with the aristocracy and tradition.[49]

As revelations of gross military inefficiency piled up, the railway contractors, Brassey & Betts, came forward to offer a line at cost price to link the Balaklava supply depot to the allied forward positions. Joseph Paxton despatched navvies to build huts and roads.[50] 'Thus in 1855 the ultimate historic defence of aristocracy—its supreme value in time of war—received for the first time in England an outright denial.'[51]

The same vanity seduced a new generation of British businessmen at the end of the century. Trust the aristocracy to get the country bogged down in South Africa! Trust the businessman, with prefabricated huts and other novelties, to get it out.[52] In the bellicose atmosphere of the period, bourgeoisie and state drew closer. Marcus Samuel and Lord Fisher plotted the conversion of the British fleet in liquid fuel.[53] With the outbreak of war in 1914, oil became a vital strategic resource. But so too did imported foodstuffs and raw materials, and whole companies and groups of companies were abruptly incorporated wholesale into the machinery of state.[54]

After 1918, though the privacy of these enterprises was promptly and firmly restored, the atmosphere of insecurity remained. Imperial Chemical Industries—the name alone enough to have sent a shiver of disgust down the spines of John Brunner and Ludwig Mond—was formed by an amalgamation of their undertaking with others in 1926 in direct response to the German creation of I.G. Farbenindustrie in this strategically important area.[55] The initiative came from Reginald McKenna, wartime Chancellor of the Exchequer and now chairman of the Midland Bank. Strategy dictated not merely the organisation of the new concern, but its investment strategy. In the 1930s, millions were poured into the development of an uneconomic oil-from-coal process which might help secure Britain from dependence on overseas supplies.[56]

The very geography of London changed as major companies moved their headquarters westwards from the old heart of the City, at the junction of Lombard Street and Threadneedle Street, to Holborn, Millbank and the south bank of the Thames, often to within sight and smell of Parliament. Internal organisation also reflected the change. Immediately after its formation, ICI set up a registry on civil service lines. Wells parodied this bourgeois redemption of the traditional landed classes. 'We got to Buck-Up the country,' he had Edward Ponderevo muse. 'The English country is a going concern still; just as the Established Church is a going concern. Just as Oxford is—or Cambridge. Or any of those old, fine things. Only it wants fresh capital, fresh ideas, and fresh methods. Light railways, f'rinstance—scientific use of drainage. Wire fencing—machinery—all that.'[57]

If vanity was the downfall of the meritocratic, Manchester School elements in the bourgeoisie, their more romantic cousins were susceptible to a different ploy: the use of history as a means of social control.[58] Growing from antiquarian and literary roots in the late eighteenth century, this tradition offered a place for everyone. In the novels of Antony Trollope it re-emphasised the title of a Norman nobility and gentry to their role in country life. Lord De Guest, the unostentatious but productive countryman, whose 'peerage dated back to the time of King John', was contrasted with that upstart Whig grandee, the Duke of Omnium, than whom:

... perhaps, no man who had ever lived during the same period, or any portion of the period, had done less, or had devoted himself more entirely to the consumption of good things without the slightest idea of producing anything in return![59]

By contrast, some entrepreneurs, ludicrously, would squeeze

themselves into this mould. Julius Drewe, sitting in the solid granite castle built for him by Lutyens on an eminence in Devon amid sombre Spanish furniture bought cheap from the Murrietas after they had gone too deep into Argentine provincial bonds, could seriously regard himself as the descendant of William of Normandy's companion in arms, Drogo, or Dru. William Armstrong, first Lord Armstrong, sold battleships to Japanese and Brazilian admirals in a mock Tudor mansion in Northumberland.[60] Emulation and deference between them were gnawing away at the Radicalism of the middle classes. Cobden, while welcoming 'the breakdown of our aristocratic rulers, when their energies are put to the stress of a great emergency' as 'about the most consolatory incident of the [Crimean] war', doubted nevertheless whether 'it will so far raise the middle class in their own esteem as to induce them to venture on the task of self-government. They must be ruled by lords,' he concluded, ruefully.[61]

And there was room for Radicals, too, in this ludicrous fantasy, dressed up as honest Saxons defending local rights against the centralising Normans, or as latterday lairds in the Highlands and Islands, an illusion which was all the pernicious since it exposed potential opponents of militarism to all the chivalric nonsense of Hereward the Wake, Robin Hood and King Arthur, the authentic, truly national leader who would one day return, and provided literary models for later self-deceptive justifications by the Left of war to save the underdog, to save a little Belgium, Poland or the defenceless Falklanders.

However hardheaded in their business affairs, the romantics were distinguished by their inability to resist ceremony and titles. The trickle of peerages awarded in the middle decades of the nineteenth century to those who did not derive their wealth from land had gone almost entirely to bankers and merchant bankers, notably the Barings, who acquired several titles. There was little point in apeing the aristocracy on this account. Then, from the end of the century, the floodgates opened: an earldom for James Lyle Mackay, first Lord Inchcape; a viscountcy for Marcus Samuel, Lord Bearsted; and baronies galore, for Sydney Stern, Lord Wandsworth, or Alfred Mond, Lord Melchett.[62]

Honours came to Marcus Samuel before his enoblement. He processed in triumph through the streets of London as Lord Mayor in November 1902. On top of a London omnibus one passenger was heard to exclaim: 'Ours is not the climate for pageantry'; while another replied, 'we have outgrown all this.' To Henry Deterding, who would later swallow Fascist ceremonial, hook, line and sinker, it seemed 'very fine, according to the view here, but in Dutch eyes like the ceremonial parade of Oscar Carre's circus'.[63] In this innocent, pre-war atmosphere, public ceremonial seemed so very vulgar that it need not be taken seriously. Yet the durbah mentality was already gaining ground. As Samuel went from one engagement to another during his mayoralty, business tossed to one side, control of Shell passed to Deterding, the former bank clerk. Each man had one element of the new business style: Deterding, the Napoleonic rationality; Samuel, the exuberance and the feel for publicity.[64] Together they made Royal Dutch-Shell an emblem of twentieth-century business: merchant adventure transformed by diligent administration and harnessed to the war machine of the state.

By these two routes—the illusion of war as the supreme administrative problem and the illusion of war as chivalric crusade—all but the most clear-minded of the British bourgeoisie could be drawn into an accommodation with the state. Resistance had been fatally weakened by the shift in power from Liverpool and other provincial centres to London, and from truly mercantile to financial leadership. For London banking and commercial wealth was already closely integrated with the aristocracy.[65] The reassertion of metropolitan over provincial wealth is evident in W. D. Rubinstein's analysis of British wealth-holders. The City had been the dominant source of fortunes in the first half of the nineteenth century. Of those leaving estates in excess of £1 million between 1809 and 1879, almost half based their operations in the City. But of those who died as millionaires between 1880 and 1899, less than 20 per cent were City men. However, this trend was reversed after the turn of the century, and during the first two decades more than a third were from the City, including the richest of all, Charles Morrison, who died in 1909 worth an estimated £10.9 million.[66]

POINTS OF STRESS

Neither at the centre nor on the periphery of the world economy was the new accommodation between burgeoisie and state without its moments of unease. Politicians and businessmen could be quite ruthless in their exploitation of each other, as the generally dismal history of the new chartered companies at the end of the nineteenth century demonstrated.[67] William Mackinnon was taken up all of a sudden by the Foreign Office when they needed a stop-gap British presence in East Africa after years waiting in the ante room. Just as suddenly, after a brief bailing out during the crisis years following 1890, the state took over direct administration of British East Africa. But Mackinnon, philanthropist and imperialist though he might be, was in a position to manipulate transfer prices between the British East Africa Company and its managing agents, Smith Mackenzie & Co., which he controlled, and which long survived the company.[68] Cecil Rhodes was happy to obtain the blessing of the state for his British South Africa Company, and cared not a whit for the effect his aggressive behaviour towards the Portuguese or African nations might have upon imperial foreign relations.[69]

In Germany, Gerson von Bleichröder was drawn reluctantly into token investments in Samoa and Central Africa, underwriting the imperialist schemes of his clients, Bismarck and King Leopold of the Belgians. This was money tossed away to secure the larger prizes of prestige and patronage.[70] Chevallier Boutell, who held back from close contacts with the Argentine state, could observe with satisfaction 'that our friend Tornquist has too many influential friends who have a knack of expecting accommodation from time to time to make things quite as pleasant as they might be for the Belgian Company'.[71] Sir Alfred Jones, whose operations centred on West Africa and the Canary Islands, found it impossible to refuse Joseph Chamberlain's invitation to develop banana plantations in Jamaica.[72] In the closing years of the colonial era, many British overseas firms were diverted from their prime concerns by pleas from the Colonial Office. Steel Brothers were forever developing businesses they knew in places they didn't—timber in Guyana and Tanganyika, oil in the Punjab—in response to requests from officials.[73] And this is to say nothing of the gymnastic adjustments of investment planning performed in wartime. The question is not whether they profited. By and large they did. It is whether they ended up with strategic dispositions that made economic sense and could be defended against competitors. Often they did not.

Then there was regulation, which businessmen, in spite of the rapidly increasing bureaucratisation of their own undertakings, insisted on regarding as solely a characteristic of the state. The Phoenix Fire Insurance Company looked forward to a bleak post-war prospect, as they thought. 'By imposing minimum requirements as to capital, fixed deposits, investment of reserves, remittance of funds home, returns, and published accounts, the business becomes full of problems,' grumbled the Victory Committee. Even where state intervention created business, as through compulsory motor insurance, it was on the basis of maximum services at minimum cost.[74] The London general manager of Dalgety concurred. 'One would not mind', he concluded, after surveying the effect of the war in expanding bureaucratic influence, 'if one could believe that it would be for the benefit of the community as a whole, but all the evidence points the other way.'[75]

There was unease, too, in the industrialising countries of European settlement, where state subsidisation and support of the local bourgeoisie was often qualified by a specifically military or strategic view of industrialisation which, in Brazil, placed greater stress on the production of small arms and ammunition than on basic industrialisation; in Argentina, brought an overemphasis on self-sufficiency in oil and a premature move into the manufacture of aircraft;[76] or in India, made the state almost as hostile toward large privately-owned industrial conglomerates such as Tata as to foreign capital.

This was the new game. As much time would now be devoted by managers to relations with states, the manipulation of opinion, and collusion with competitors as to research, cost-minimisation and production. It was a world which was as utterly alien to that of Edward Lumb, Thomas Mort, Baron Mauá or Dwarkanath Tagore as theirs had been from the mercantilist era which preceded it. It is the condition of capitalism known to Marxists as imperialism.

CONCLUSION

This has, quite intentionally, been a social more than an economic history of international business. Accepting that competition in the marketplace is the most visible and well-documented aspect of business history, I have chosen to lay stress instead upon the development of firms by integration, upon changing patterns of authority within the firm, and upon the development of relations between firms and families, controllers and owners.

The social character of interpretation has been further emphasised by the central place given to what turned out in the end to be the chimera of a cosmopolitan bourgeoisie. The reason for this was that the progressive role of the bourgeoisie was a vital element both in liberal and in classical Marxist accounts of capitalism. Equally, Lenin's imperialism was, centrally, an attempt to explain why the bourgeoisie could *not* be expected, as Kautsky had believed they could, to overcome national divisions, and why, this being so, war was a necessary accompaniment of monopoly capitalism and must finally destroy it.

While this was a most acute analysis of capitalism as it existed during the first half of the present century, it seems far less plausible now. This is largely because, for all the continuing rhetoric of individualism and anti-communism on the one side and anti-imperialism and state capitalism on the other, major Third World industrial states and multinational extractive and manufacturing companies have, by and large, reached accommodations over the past quarter of a century which suit them both, while the major capitalist economies, too, have shown a sustained ability to prevent complete breakdown of relations, even in the most difficult economic conditions. These phenomena have more than a flavour of ultra-imperialism about them.

The history of international business provided in these pages speaks to those recent accommodations in two ways. Firstly, it addresses a question to the cosmopolitan technocrats who manage the multinationals and staff great government departments that deal with them. Have they, over the past generation, gone any way towards developing the webs of family connexions, the shared interpretations of history and future visions, and the sheer power which will enable them to survive the challenges which will undoubtedly come their way in the future? Have they acquired, in what I take to be Gramsci's sense of the word, hegemony? The earlier experience, and failure, of the liberal merchants who are the main protagonists in this book, offers a yardstick for this new managerial class.

Secondly, the book makes clearer than before that present-day multinationals have roots reaching down not only to the great manufacturing corporations of the turn of the century, but also to older mercantile and financial firms with very different traditions. This places the American challenge of the 1960s, as Servan-Schreiber termed it, in historical context. If my interpretation of nineteenth-century international business history is accepted, then the relative quantitative significance of post-war United States direct foreign investment will be seen to be reduced, and—more important—it will be seen that United States direct foreign investment of the post-war years, based as it was in industries that had done well out of the war and aimed at markets that were open because of the war—was the apotheosis of capitalist imperialism. I would go on to argue, though I shall not attempt it here, that part of the process of accommodation between multinational corporations and Third World states has been, in effect, the result of a reassertion of the commercial or private over the imperial or public in international business—sometimes by the substitution of European or Japanese for United States capital, and sometimes by changes of policy within United States firms. As just two illustrations of what I have in mind I would cite, firstly, the contrasting fortunes of the imperialist Chilean strategy of ITT and the more pragmatic—and successful—defensive policies of Kennecott in Chile and Asarco in Peru in the 1970s.[77] Secondly, I would contrast the way in which the doggedly centralist United States giants, IBM and Coca Cola, fell foul of Indian government policy in the 1970s while more pragmatic companies, many but by no means all of them European, found acceptable compromises.[78]

In each case the waters were soon muddied by changes of regime and policy, it is true, but they do provide an indication of the tendency of the past two decades.

Whatever view one takes, these issues—the strategic purpose of the present-day managerial technocracy and the changing relations between international firms and states—are second only in importance to the question of war and peace. I defy anyone to take a serious position on either of them which does not rest, at bottom, on an interpretation of the past. This is why business history matters and, indeed, is too important to be left to a small community of specialists tucked neatly away (for however much practitioners may protest, this is the public perception, such as there is): business history, within economic history, within history proper, within the Arts, within education, at the centre of a nest of Russian dolls labelled 'non-productive'.

Notes

CHAPTER 1

1. R. H. Coase, 'The Nature of the Firm', *Economica*, 4 (1937), pp. 386–405; J. H. Dunning, *International Production and Multinational Enterprise* (Allen and Unwin, London, 1981); Alan M. Rugman, *Inside the Multinationals: the Economics of Internal Markets* (Croom Helm, London, 1981).
2. Frederick C. Lane, *Venice and History: the Collected Papers of Frederick C. Lane* (Johns Hopkins Press, Baltimore, Md., 1960).
3. D. C. North, 'A Framework for Analysing the State in Economic History', *Explorations in Economic History*, 16 (1979), pp. 249–59.
4. D. C. North, *Structure and Change in Economic History* (W. W. Norton & Co., New York and London, 1981), Chapter 5.
5. V. I. Lenin, *Imperialism, the Highest Stage of Capitalism* (Foreign Languages Press, Peking, 1973; reprint of Vol. I, Part 2 of *Selected Works* Foreign Languages Publishing House, Moscow, 1952).
6. See Charles Jones, ' "Business Imperialism" and Argentina, 1875–1900: a Theoretical Note', *Journal of Latin American Studies*, 12, 2 (November 1980), pp. 437–44.
7. Norman Etherington, *Theories of Imperialism: War, Conquest and Capital* (Croom Helm, London and Canberra, 1984); Eric Stokes, 'Late Nineteenth-Century Colonial Expansion and the Attack on the Theory of Economic Imperialism: a Case of Mistaken Identity?', *Hist. J.*, 12, 2 (1969), pp. 285–301.
8. J. A. Hobson, *Imperialism: a Study* (James Nisbet & Co., London, 1902); J. A. Schumpeter, *Imperialism and Social Classes* (1919, 1927; Meridian Books, New York, 1955), 'The Sociology of Imperialism', Chapter 5.
9. The argument is analogous to that deployed by Brenner against Wallerstein. See Robert Brenner, 'The Origins of Capitalist Development: a Critique of Neo-Smithian Marxism', *New Left Review*, 104 (July–August 1977), especially p. 55.
10. Charles Dickens, *Dombey and Son* (Bradbury & Evans, London, 1848; first published in parts, 1846–48).

11. John Morley, *The Life of Richard Cobden* (T. Fisher Unwin, London, 1905), p. 80.

12. Ibid., p. 433.

13. See, for example, Lord Palmerston's attitude, in Jasper Ridley, *Lord Palmerston* (Panther Books, London, 1972), pp. 576–7.

14. Tom Paine, *The Rights of Man* (1791–92; Pelican Books, 1969), p. 185.

15. Ibid., p. 190.

16. Ibid., p. 99.

17. T. S. Willan, *Studies in Elizabethen Foreign Trade* (Manchester University Press, Manchester 1959), p. 34.

18. Immanuel Kant, 'Idea for a Universal History with a Cosmopolitan Purpose', in Hans Reiss (ed.), *Kant's Political Writings* (Cambridge University Press, Cambridge, 1970), p. 50.

19. Peter Cain, 'Capitalism, War and Internationalism in the Thought of Richard Cobden', *Brit. J. Inter. Stud.*, 5 (1979), p. 241.

20. J. Schumpeter, *Social Classes and Imperialism*, pp. 64 *et seq.*

21. For economic nationalism, see Henry Charles Carey, *Principles of Political Economy* (Carey, Lea & Blanchard, Philadelphia, 1837, 1838); Friedrich List, *The National System of Political Economy* (1841; trans. Sampson S. Lloyd; Longmans & Co., London, 1885); Gustav Schmoller, *The Mercantile System and its Historical Significance* (1884; Macmillan & Co., New York, 1902), esp. p. 80.

22. Morley, *Cobden,* pp. 141–42.

23. J. A. Hobson, *Richard Cobden, The International Man* (T. Fisher Unwin, London, 1918), p. 194, quoted in Cain, 'Thoughts of Richard Cobden', p. 241.

24. On the second of these routes see Linda J. Jones, 'Public Pursuit of Private Profit? Liberal Businessmen and Municipal Politics in Birmingham, 1865–1900', *Bus. Hist.*, 25, 3 (November 1983), pp. 240–59.

25. A. G. Hopkins, 'Imperial Business in Africa, Part 1: Sources', *J.A. Hist.*, 17, 1 (1976), p. 29.

26. Leslie Hannah, *The Rise of the Corporate Economy* (Methuen, London and New York, 1976; 2nd edn, 1983), p. 4.

27. See, for example, Herbert Simon, 'Theories of Decision-Making in Economics and Behavioural Sciences', *Amer. Econ. Rev.*, 69 (1959), pp. 253–83; David C. Colander (ed.), *Neoclassical Political Economy: the Analysis of Rent-Seeking and DUP Activities* (Ballinger, Cambridge, Mass., 1984); or Peter Earl, *The Corporate Imagination: How Big Companies Make Mistakes* (Wheatsheaf Books, Brighton, 1984).

28. For the old interpretation see, for example, John H. Dunning, *Studies in International Investment* (George Allen & Unwin, London, 1970), p. 2; Christopher Tugendhat, *The Multinationals* (Eyre & Spottiswoode, London, 1971), p. 10, n.; Robert Gilpin, *US Power and the Multinational Corporation: the Political Economy of Foreign Direct Investment* (Macmillan, London, 1976), Chapters 3 and 5; or Louis Turner, *Invisible Empires: Multinational Companies and the Modern World* (Hamilton, London, 1970), pp. 1–3.

29. See especially John M. Stopford, 'The Origins of British-Based Multinational Manufacturing Enterprises', *Bus. Hist. Rev.*, 48, 3 (1974), p. 307; Irving Stone, 'British Direct and Portfolio Investment in Latin America before 1914', *J. Econ. Hist.*, 37, 3 (September 1977), p. 691; and Peter Svedberg, 'The Portfolio-Direct Composition of Private Foreign Investment in 1914 Revisited', *Econ. J.*, 88, 4 (December 1978), p. 765.

30. Stopford, 'Origins', p. 305.

31. Svedberg, 'Portfolio-Direct', p. 768; Stone, 'Direct and Portfolio', p. 696, Table 3; John H. Dunning, 'Changes in the Level and Structure of International Production: the Last One Hundred Years', in Mark Casson (ed.), *The Growth of International Business* (George Allen & Unwin, London, 1983), p. 87.

32. T. A. B. Corley, 'Communications, Entrepreneurship and the Managing Agency System: The Burmah Oil Co. 1886–1928' (unpublished paper, ESRC Business History Conference, 1981?), p. 5.

33. P. J. Buckley and B. R. Roberts, *European Direct Investment in the U.S.A. before World War I* (Macmillan, London, 1982), p. 61.

34. A. W. Coats, 'The Historicist Reaction in English Political Economy, 1870–90', *Economica*, 21, 2 (May 1954), pp. 143–53.

35. Individual publications are referred to in the text. I have in mind Francis E. Hyde, John Harris, Sheila Marriner, A. H. John and T. C. Barker, all writing, at first, on Liverpool and Merseyside, and a comparable group, including Alan Barnard, on Australia.

36. For a thorough and persuasive critique see Martin Hollis and Edward J. Nell, *Rational Economic Man: a Philosophical Critique of Neo-Classical Economics* (Cambridge University Press, Cambridge, 1975).

37. There are, for example, very few studies of merchant communities which attempt even the most primitive quantification. An exception to the rule is E. W. Ridings, 'Business, Nationality, and Dependency in Late Nineteenth-Century Brazil'. *J. Lat. Amer. Stud.*, 14, 1 (May 1982), pp. 55–96.

38. One such area is the study of institutional influences on capital markets. See Charles Jones, 'Who Invested in Argentina and Uruguay?', *Bus. Arch.*, 48 (November 1982), pp. 1–23, and Lance E. Davis and Robert A. Huttenback, 'The Political Economy of British Imperialism: Measure of Benefits and Supports', *J. Econ. Hist.*, 42, 1 (March 1982), pp. 119–32. There is a long way to go. The first of these is entirely descriptive. The second has an argument of sorts, but it is launched against the non-existent Hobson–Lenin thesis once so beloved of cold warriors (see above, n. 7, for the antidote) and suffers from a serious error over the social significance of the term 'gentleman', which is wrongly taken to be a reliable indication of elite status.

39. Tony Hopkins is more sympathetic than most, though of this school. See A. G. Hopkins, 'Imperial Business in Africa, Part II: Interpretations', *J. Af. Hist.*, 17 (1976), pp. 267 *et seq.*

40. Cf., Yen-P'ing Hao, *The Comprador in Nineteenth Century China: Bridge between East and West* (Harvard University Press, Cambridge, Mass., 1970), p. 13.

41. The list is a long one. Among the most recent contributions are Charles Wilson, *First with the News: the History of W. H. Smith, 1792–1972* (Jonathan Cape, London, 1985); and Clive Trebilcock, *Phoenix Assurance and the Development of British Insurance, volume I— 1782–1870* (Cambridge University Press, Cambridge, 1985). The latter, in fairness, goes a long way towards escaping the bounds of corporate history.
42. This has deleterious effects when dilettantes nibble at the edges of the subject. Note for example the way in which Buckley and Roberts derive their descriptive categories (pp. 2–3), and many of their illustrations (Chapter 5) from the present, quite failing to grasp the variety of institutional forms available in the nineteenth century. Buckley and Roberts, *European Direct Investment*.
43. Cf. John Maynard Keynes, *The End of Laissez-Faire* (Hogarth Press, London, 1927), pp. 41–4.
44. ICI was no sooner founded than it set up a registry modelled on those of the Diplomatic Service. For other aspects of the close relationship of this company with the state see W. J. Reader, 'Imperial Chemical Industries and the State, 1926–1945', in Barry Supple (ed.), *Essays in British History* (Clarendon, Oxford, 1977).
45. David Bloor, *Knowledge and Social Imagery* (Routledge & Kegan Paul, London, 1976).
46. Karl Mannheim, *Ideology and Utopia: an Introduction to the Sociology of Knowledge* (Routledge & Kegan Paul, London, 1936), p. 5.
47. Loc. cit.

CHAPTER 2

1. *An Account of a Voyage up the River de la Plata and thence over land to Peru, with observations on the inhabitants*, by Mons Acarete du Biscay (for S. Buckley, London, 1698).
2. Miron Burgin, *The Economic Aspects of Argentine Federalism, 1820–1852* (Harvard University Press, Cambridge, Mass., 1946), pp. 10–11.
3. Samuel Wilcocke, *History of the Viceroyalty of Buenos Aires* (London, 1807), pp. 517, 524.
4. John Robert Fisher, unpub. paper, Conference of the Society for Latin American Studies, University of Warwick, 1985.
5. John Lynch, *The Spanish American Revolutions, 1808–1826* (Weidenfeld & Nicolson, London, 1973), p. 17.
6. The main published sources on the Anchorena is J. J. Sebreli, *Apogeo y ocaso de los Anchorena* (Buenos Aires, 1972); and Andres M. Corretero, *Los Anchorena: politica y negocios en el siglo XIX* (Buenos Aires, 1970).
7. T. Halperin Donghi, *Politics, Economics and Society in Argentina in the Revolutionary Period* (Cambridge University Press, Cambridge, 1975), pp. 83–8.
8. Juan Oddone, *La burgesia terrateniente argentina* (Buenos Aires, 1930),

pp. 185–6; Andres M. Carretero, *La propiedad de la tierra en la epoca de Rosas* (Buenos Aires, 1972).

9. Lynch, op. cit., p. 17.
10. Wilcocke, op. cit., p. 528.
11. Benjamin Keen, *David Curtis DeForest and the Revolution of Buenos Aires* (Yale University Press, New Haven, 1947).
12. Karl Wilhelm Körner, 'El consúl Zimmermann, su actuación en Buenos Aires, 1815–1847', *Boletín del Instituto de Historia Argentina 'Doctor Emilio Ravignani'*, 2nd series, VI–VII, 11–13 (Buenos Aires, 1966).
13. Albion notes the persistence of Baltimore in ship-building and South American trade in the face of nineteenth-century New York expansionism. Robert Greenhalgh Albion, *The Rise of New York Port 1815–1860* (2nd edition, Newton Abbott, 1970), p. 275. Until the French occupied Hamburg in 1806, a good share in the Silesian linen trade had fallen to a Galician firm with a branch in Hamburg: Brentano Vobara & Urbieta. Andrew J. Murray, *Home from the Hill: a biography of Frederick Huth, 'Napoleon of the City'* (Hamish Hamilton, London, 1970), pp. 26 *et seq*. But the sack of Hamburg and the subsequent capture of Corunna and declaration of the Continental System in the Berlin Decrees of 1807 made this route impossible.
14. Körner, 'Zimmermann' p. 11, n.
15. Ibid., pp. 11–12.
16. George H. Nelson, 'Contraband Trade under the Asiento, 1730–1739', *Amer. Hist. Rev.*, 51 (1954), p. 55.
17. Ibid., p. 61.
18. Wilcocke, *History of Buenos Aires*, pp. 513–14.
19. John Arthur Gibbs, *The History of Antony and Dorothea Gibbs and of the early years of Antony Gibbs & Sons*, (Saint Catherine Press, London, 1922), pp. 13–19.
20. A. D. Francis, *The Wine Trade* (A. & C. Black, London, 1972), p. 274.
21. H. E. S. Fisher, *The Portugal Trade: a Study of Anglo-Portuguese Commerce, 1700–1770*.
22. Memorial of the British Merchants Trading to Spain to Lord Grantham, Bedfordshire County Record Office, Lady Lucas's Collection, L29/598.
23. H. E. S. Fisher, op. cit., p. 48.
24. William Graham, *English Influence in the Argentine Republic* (J. Peuser, Buenos Aires, 1890), p. 7.
25. Vera Lee Brown, 'Contraband Trade: a Factor in the Decline of Spain's Empire in America', *Hispanic-American His. Rev.*, 8 (1928), pp. 178–89.
26. Elizabeth Boody Schumpeter, *English Overseas Trade Statistics, 1697–1909* (Clarendon Press, Oxford, 1960), Table V, quoted by D. C. M. Platt, *Latin America and British Trade, 1806–1914* (A. & C. Black, London, 1972?), p. 34.
27. Francis, *The Wine Trade*, p. 274.
28. Murray, *Frederick Huth*, pp. 26, *et seq*.
29. Hannibal Evans Lloyd, *Hamburg: or, a particular account of the*

transactions which took place in that city, during the first six months of the year 1813 (London, 1813).

30. John Quincy Adams, *Letters on Silesia written during a tour through that country in the years 1800, 1801* (J. Budd, London, 1804), p. 139. This was common practice in the eighteenth century in the international cloth trade. See Ralph Davis, *Aleppo and Devonshire Square: British Traders in the Levant in the Eighteenth-Century* (Macmillan, London, 1967), pp. 103–4. Later, British linens would bear German names. See W. O. Henderson, *The Rise of German Industrial Power, 1834–1914* (Temple Smith, London, 1975), p. 62.

31. John Thomas James, *Journal of a Tour in Germany, Sweden, Russia, Poland, during the years 1813 and 1814* (London, 1816), p. 25.

32. The Berlin Decrees were proclaimed in Buenos Aires in September 1807 but never enforced. Liniers allowed enemy merchants to remain in the city to dispose of their goods after the British forces were defeated in July 1807, and this tolerance continued in spite of orders from Europe. Keen, *DeForest*, p. 54, n. Anderson notes that though trade with Russia was badly hit during 1808, especially at Kronstadt where there was a watchful French mission, the normal level of trade was attained the following year because of the relaxation of local authorities, their willingness to accept false papers, and the general weakness of governmental authority at some of the outports, such as Riga, where British ships continued to call, flying United States or Hanse flags.

33. François Crouzet, *L'Economie Britannique et le blocus continental, 1806–1813* (Paris, 1958), especially vol. I, p. 184 *et seq*. 'Lord Grenville, d'abord mefiant, se laissa bientôt entrainer à croire que la Grande-Bretagne pourrait, en quelques mois, conquerir la plus grande partie des colonies espagnoles, et Windham affirmait qu'elle pourrait s'indemniser dans le Nouveau Monde des revers qu'elle avait subis dans l'Ancien.'

34. Murray, *Frederick Huth*, pp. 26 *et seq*. and p. 60; Körner, 'Zimmermann', p. 8.

35. Some further instances of continuity appear in R. A. Humphreys, 'British Merchants and South American Independence', in his *Tradition and Revolt in Latin America* (Weidenfeld and Nicolson, London, 1969), pp. 106–29. These include the Parish family, whose distinguished background is sketched in Paul H. Emden, *Money Powers of Europe in the Nineteenth and Twentieth Centuries* (Sampson Low, Marston & Co. Ltd, London, n.d.), pp. 20–6.

36. On the general characteristics of the trade see Platt, *Latin America and British Trade*, Chapter 2.

37. Public Record Office, FO.354/3, Enclosure with Parish to Canning, 30 July 1824, 'Report of the British Committee on the Trade of the River Plate'.

38. Wilcocke, *History of Buenos Aires*, pp. 517, 524; Sir Woodbine Parish, *Buenos Aires and the Provinces of the Rio de la Plata* (2nd edn, London, 1852), p. 353. The importance of judging decline in the Potosí trade from figures for Buenos Aires exports rather than those for overland

pack mule and ox cart arrivals in Buenos Aires is pointed out in Jonathan C. Brown, 'Dynamics and Autonomy of a Traditional Marketing System: Buenos Aires, 1810–1860', *Hispanic-American Hist. Rev.*, 56 (4 November 1976) pp. 605–29.

39. Platt, *Latin America and British Trade*, pp. 24–6.
40. R. G. Wilson, *Gentlemen Merchants: the Merchant Community in Leeds, 1700–1830* (Manchester University Press and Augustus M. Kelley, Manchester and New York, 1971), Chapter 6.
41. T. M. Devine, 'Glasgow Colonial Merchants and Land, 1770–1815', in J. T. Ward and R. G. Wilson (eds), *Land and Industry: the Landed Estate and the Industrial Revolution* (David & Charles, Newton Abbot, 1971), pp. 205–44.
42. Ibid., pp. 217, 229.
43. Ibid., pp. 229–30.
44. Stuart Weems Bruchey, *Robert Oliver, Merchant of Baltimore, 1783–1819* (Johns Hopkins Press, Baltimore, 1956), pp. 360–1.
45. *Gran Bretaña en la Evolución de la Economía Argentina* (Buenos Aires, 1945); Körner, 'Zimmermann', p. 19.
46. Carretero, *Los Anchorena*, p. 147. Pollard mentions Samuel Swann Brittain & Co., established by Samuel Swann Brittain in 1824, manufacturers and exporters of high-quality cast steel, files, edged tools and especially saws, and says that they concentrated on exports to South and Central America. Sidney Pollard, *Three Centuries of Sheffield Steel: the Story of a Family Business* (Sheffield, 1954), pp. 70–2. There is nothing firm to link this firm to Brittain Wilkinson & Brownell, or to James Brittain, who retired to Blackheath in the late 1820s and died there in 1832, nor, indeed, is there anything to link any of them to George Alfred Brittain, of Aylesbury, owner in the mid-1890s of just shares in British-registered River Plate companies to a nominal paid-up value of just over £50,000, except, of course, their shared interest in South America.
47. PRO, BT 3/3923 (i).
48. Some accounts suggest that the estate exceeded 100,000 acres. MacCann, however, thought it extended to about 90,000 acres when he visited in the 1840s. William MacCann, *Two Thousand Miles Ride Through the Argentine Provinces* (London, 1853), p. 73 *et seq*.
49. Wright Papers, c/o Hugh MacIntyre, Alticry, Port William, Wigtownshire DG8 9RT. Part of this account is based on the uncatalogued Wright papers, and part on family traditions for which I am indebted to Mr MacIntyre, who is a direct descendant of Duncan Wright.
50. Baring Papers, Guildhall Library, London. HC 16/1.
51. MacCann, loc. cit.
52. Baring Papers, HC 16/2.
53. K. N. Chaudhuri, 'Markets and Traders in India during the Seventeenth and Eighteenth Centuries', in K. N. Chaudhuri and Clive J. Dewey (eds), *Economy and Society: Essays in Indian Economic and Social History* (Oxford University Press, Delhi etc., 1979).

54. P. J. Marshall, *East India Fortunes: the British in Bengal in the Eighteenth Century* (Oxford University Press, London, 1976), p. 7; George H. Nelson, 'Contraband Trade under the Asiento, 1730–1739', *Amer. Hist. Rev.*, 51 (1954), p. 61.
55. Percival Spear, *Master of Bengal: Clive and his India* (Thames and Hudson, London, 1975), p. 46.
56. Marshall, *East India Fortunes*, Chapter 8.
57. Ibid., pp. 6–9.
58. Ibid., Chapter 7; Spear, *Master of Bengal*, p. 137.
59. Spear, *Master of Bengal*, pp. 112, 137.
60. Pamela Nightingale, *Trade and Empire in Western India, 1784–1806* (Cambridge University Press, Cambridge, 1970), p. 25; Holden Furber, *John Company at Work: a Study of European Expansion in India in the Late Eighteenth Century* (Harvard University Press, Cambridge, Mass., 1947; reprint edn, Octagon Books, New York, 1970), p. 194; Amales Tripathi, *Trade and Finance in the Bengal Presidency, 1793–1833* (Oxford University Press, Calcutta, 1956); 2nd edn, 1979), p. 11.
61. Tripathi, *Trade and Finance*, p. 29.
62. K. N. Chaudhuri, 'Foreign Trade and Balance of Payments (1757–1947)', in Dharma Kumar and Megnad Desai (eds), *The Cambridge Economic History of India*, II (Cambridge University Press, Cambridge, 1983), evidently uses the same source as Tripathi at p. 817, Table 10.1. Unlike Tripathi (p. 29) he gives figures for value, not tonnage, and it is from these that the proportions cited here are calculated.
63. W. E. Cheong, *Mandarins and Merchants: Jardine Matheson & Co., a China Agency of the Early Nineteenth Century* (Curzon Press, London and Malmö, 1979), p. 8.
64. Tripathi, *Trade and Finance*, pp. 111, 203.
65. Ibid., p. 157 *et seq.*
66. Ibid., p. 195.
67. N. Benjamin, 'Arab Merchants of Bombay and Surat (*c.* 1800–1840)', in *Indian Econ. and Soc. Hist. Rev.*, 13, 1 (Jan.–Mar. 1976), p. 88.
68. Radhe Shyam Rungta, *Rise of Business Corporations in India, 1851–1900* (Cambridge University Press, Cambridge, 1970), pp. 23–8, 57–61; Dosabhai Framji [Karaka], *History of the Parsis* (Macmillan & Co., London, 1884) II, Chapters 2 and 6, pp. 47–145, 242–95.
69. Benjamin, 'Arab Merchants', p. 94.
70. R. W. Beachey, 'The East African Ivory Trade in the Nineteenth Century', *J. Af. Hist.*, 8, 2 (1967), pp. 269–90; E. A. Alpers, 'The Coast and the Development of Caravan Trade' (University of East Africa, unpublished conference paper, n.d. [before 1970]).
71. Colin N. Crisswell, *The Taipans: Hong Kong's Merchant Princes* (Oxford University Press, Hong Kong, 1881), Chapter 8.
72. Tripathi, *Trade and Finance*, p. 20.
73. Ibid., pp. 191, 205, 213 and 217; Rungta, *Rise of Business Corporations*, pp. 19, n. 1, and 58.
74. Tripathi, *Trade and Finance*, p. 122.

75. Crisswel, *The Taipans*, p. 186 *et seq*. On Armenians in an earlier period see R. W. Ferrier, 'The Armenians and the East India Company in Persia in the Seventeenth and Eighteenth Centuries', *Econ. Hist. Rev.*, 2nd series, 26, 1 (1973), pp. 38–62.
76. Sir Percival Griffiths, *A History of the Inchcape Group* (Inchcape & Co. Ltd, London, 1977), p. 17.
77. Crisswell, *The Taipans*, p. 21.
78. James Morrison, who was not a Scot, chose Edinburgh University for his son, Charles. He went on to Trinity College, Cambridge, but not without some qualms in the family circle. James noted in his diary that James Mill 'doubts the propriety of Charles going to Cambridge—it might spoil him for commerce'. It did not, but the prejudice was widely held. Richard Gatty, *Portrait of a Merchant Prince: James Morrison, 1789–1857* (privately printed, Pepper Arden, Northallerton, Yorkshire, n.d., *circa* 1976), p. 171. Elizabeth Gaskell, as narrator comments that '. . . according to the prevalent, and apparently well-founded notions of Milton [a northern industrial town], to make a lad into a good tradesman he must be caught young, and acclimated to the life of the mill, or office, or warehouse. If he were sent even to the Scottish universities, he came back unsettled for commercial pursuits; how much more so if he went to Oxford or Cambridge, where he could not be entered till he was eighteen?' Elizabeth Gaskell, *North and South* ([1854–55] Penguin Books, 1970), p. 107.
79. C. N. Cooke, *The Rise, Progress and Present Condition of Banking in India* (Calcutta, 1863), cited in Rungta, *Rise of Business Corporations*, p. 6, n. 1.
80. Cheong, *Mandarins and Merchants*, p. 8.
81. Sidney G. Checkland, *The Gladstones: a Family Biography, 1764–1851* (London, Cambridge University Press, 1971), pp. 31–2.
82. Ibid., pp. 115–16.
83. Sheila Marriner, *The Economic and Social Development of Merseyside* (Croom Helm, London and Canberra, 1982), pp. 38–40.
84. Checkland, *The Gladstones*, pp. 120–3, 181, 317–18, 341, and, on Rathbones, who also went into the China trade in the 1840s, Sheila Marriner, *Rathbones of Liverpool, 1845–73* (Liverpool University Press, Liverpool, 1961), p. 5.
85. Nigel Cameron, *Power: the Story of China Light* (Oxford University Press, Hong Kong, 1982), p. 17; Tripathi, *Trade and Finance*, pp. 115–18.
86. Tripathi, *Trade and Finance*, pp. 9–10.
87. Alexander Allan Cormack, *Susan Carnegie, 1744–1821: her Life of Service* (Aberdeen University Press for the author, Aberdeen, 1966), p. 141.
88. Hoh-cheung Mui and Lorna H. Mui (eds), *William Melrose in China, 1845–1855: the Letters of a Scottish Tea Merchant* (printed for the Scottish Historical Society by T. & A. Constable Ltd, Edinburgh, 1973), pp. v–xxv.
89. Griffiths, *The Inchcape Group*, p. 153.

90. *James Finlay & Company Limited: Manufacturers and East India Merchants* (Jackson, Son & Co., Glasgow, 1951).
91. S. D. Chapman, 'The International Houses: the Continental Contribution to British Commerce, 1800–1860', *J. Euro. Econ. Hist.*, 6, 1 (Spring 1977), pp. 5–48.
92. S. G. Checkland, *The Gladstones*, p. 120: *James Finlay*.
93. In the rush to identify high fixed costs with the use of expensive machinery, and so restrict this hypothesis to the high-technology sectors of the industrial revolution, there is a danger of neglecting the considerable costs to merchant-manufacturers still operating a putting-out system of preventing the break-up and migration of a skilled workforce during a period of trade depression. See, for example, W. H. B. Court, *The Rise of the Midland Industries, 1600–1838* (Oxford University Press, London, 1938), p. 147, n., where Wolverhampton and Birmingham employers, giving evidence against the 1812 Orders in Council, said that they felt it vital to keep skilled labour teams together and would sacrifice much to this end.
94. R. G. Wilson, *Gentleman Merchants*, Chapter 6.
95. Hoh-cheung Mui and Lorna H. Mui (eds), *William Melrose*, Introduction, pp. xxv, *et seq.*
96. C. H. Lee, *A Cotton Enterprise, 1795–1840; a History of M'Connel & Kennedy, Fine Cotton Spinners* (Manchester University Press, Manchester, 1972), pp. 53–4.
97. Sydney J. Chapman, *The Lancashire Cotton Industry: a Study in Economic Development* (Manchester University Press, Manchester, 1904), p. 5.
98. S. D. Chapman and S. Chassagne, *European Textile Printers in the Eighteenth Century: a Study of Peel and Oberkampf* (Heinemann, London, 1981), pp. 86–9.
99. Lee, *Cotton Enterprise*, p. 49.
100. George Unwin, *Samuel Oldknow and the Arkwrights: the Industrial Revolution at Stockport and Marple* (Manchester University Press, Manchester, 1924; 2nd edn, 1968), pp. 55–7.
101. Ibid., p. 19.
102. Ibid., pp. 67–8.
103. Ibid., pp. 88–9, 96.
104. Ibid., p. 104.
105. R. S. Fitton and A. P. Wadsworth, *The Strutts and the Arkwrights, 1758–1830: a Study of the Early Factory System* (Manchester University Press, Manchester, 1958), pp. 309, 318.
106. Gordon Jackson, *Hull in the Eighteenth Century: a Study in Economic and Social History* (Oxford University Press, London, 1972), pp. 117 *et seq.*
107. A. H. John, *The Industrial Development of South Wales, 1750–1850* (University of Wales Press, Cardiff, 1950), pp. 122–9.
108. S. D. Chapman, *The Rise of Merchant Banking* (George Allen & Unwin, London, 1984), pp. 5–6.
109. Dorothy E. Adler, *British Investment in American Railroads, 1834–1898*

(University Press of Virginia, Charlottesville, 1970), pp. 36–8.

110. T. S. Ashton, *An Eighteenth-Century Industrialist: Peter Stubbs of Warrington, 1756–1806* (Manchester University Press, Manchester, 1939) pp. 51–60.

111. Elva Tooker, *Nathan Trotter: Philadelphia Merchant, 1787–1853* (Harvard University Press, Cambridge, Mass., 1955), p. 80.

112. Colin N. Crisswell, *The Taipans*, p. 85; Rhodes Boyson, *The Ashworth Cotton Enterprise* (Clarendon Press, Oxford, 1970), p. 60.

113. Norman Sydney Buck, *The Development of the Organisation of Anglo-American Trade, 1800–1850* (Yale University Press, New Haven, Conn., 1925; reprinted by David & Charles, Newton Abbot, 1969), pp. 153–4.

114. Harold Pollins, *Economic History of the Jews in England* (Associated University Presses, London, Toronto, and East Brunswick, N.J., 1982), pp. 107, 170; James Strachey, 'Sigmund Freud: a Sketch of his Life and Ideas', in Sigmund Freud, *Introductory Lectures on Psychoanalysis* (Penguin Books, 1973), p. 11.

115. Richard Gatty, *James Morrison*, pp. 11–24.

116. Ralph W. Hidy, *The House of Baring in American Trade and Finance: English Merchant Bankers at Work, 1763–1861* (Russell & Russell, New York, 1949), Chapter 5, pp. 124–63.

CHAPTER 3

1. William Blackwell, 'The Russian Entrepreneur in the Tsarist Period: An Overview', in Geoffrey Guroff and Fred V. Carstensen (eds), *Entrepreneurship in Imperial Russia and the Soviet Union* (Princeton University Press, Princeton, N.J., 1983); Gordon Jackson, *Hull in the Eighteenth Century: a Study in Economic and Social History* (Oxford University Press, London, 1972).

2. Alexander Allan Cormack, *Susan Carnegie, 1744–1821: her Life of Service* (Aberdeen University Press for the author, Aberdeen, 1966), pp. 147, 192.

3. Eugene W. Ridings, 'Business, Nationality and Dependency in Late Nineteenth Century Brazil', *J. Lat. Amer. Stud.*, 14, 1 (May, 1982), pp. 55–96.

4. J. Dorfman, 'A Note on the Interpretation of Anglo-American Finance, 1837–41', *J. Econ. Hist.*, 11 (1951), p. 147.

5. See, for example, works referred to in George Watson, *The English Ideology: Studies in the Language of Victorian Politics* (Allen Lane, London, 1973) Chapter 11.

6. The works of Guy Thorne were much reprinted. See his portrayal of the Jewish inventor and financier, Professor Pentique, in Guy Thorne and Leo Custance, *Sharks: a Fantastic Novel for Business Men and their Families* (Greening & Co., London, 1904).

7. Frank Richards, *Billy Bunter of Greyfriars School* (Charles Skilton, London, 1947), etc.

8. R. C. J. Stone, *Makers of Fortune: a Colonial Business Community and its Fall* (Auckland University Press, Auckland; Oxford University Press, London, 1973), p. 41.
9. David Avery, *Not on Queen Victoria's Birthday: the Story of the Rio Tinto Mines* (Collins, London, 1974), Chapter 12; H. E. W. Braund, *Calling to Mind: being some account of the first hundred years (1870–1970) of Steel Brothers and Company Limited* (Pergamon Press, Oxford, 1975), p. 20.
10. Avery, *Not on Queen Victoria's Birthday*, Chapter 12.
11. Andres M. Carretero, *Los Anchorena: política y negocios en el siglo XIX* (Ediciones 8ª Decada, Buenos Aires, 1970), p. 154.
12. Tulio Halperin Donghi, *Politics, Economics, and Society in Argentina in the Revolutionary Period* (Cambridge University Press, Cambridge, 1975), p. 68; Karl Wilhelm Körner, 'El consúl Zimmermann, su actuación en Buenos Aires, 1815–1847', *Boletín del Instituto de Historia Argentina 'Doctor Emilio Ravignani'*, 2nd series, VII–VIII, 11–13 (Buenos Aires, 1966), p. 54. On the failure of Lezica y hnos in 1835 see Vera Blinn Reber, *British Mercantile Houses in Buenos Aires, 1810–1880*, (Harvard University Press, Cambridge, Mass., and London, 1979), p. 107.
13. Körner, 'Zimmermann', pp. 103–5.
14. Carretero, *Los Anchorena*, p. 147.
15. Luis V. Sommi, *La Minería argentina y la independencia económica* (Buenos Aires, 1956), p. 15.
16. Carretero, *Los Anchorena*.
17. Guildhall Library, London. Baring Papers, HC16, Part 1.
18. Wilfrid Latham, *The States of the River Plate* (2nd edn, London, 1868) p. 319. For Rosas' response see Reber, *British Mercantile Houses*, p. 43.
19. Latham, *States of the River Plate*, p. 260.
20. Liverpool University Library, Rathbone Papers, XXIV/2/36(26): Brownells Grey & Co. to Rathbone, 31 August 1856.
21. Baring Papers, HC16, Part 1, 'Mercantile Houses in Buenos Aires, 1857'.
22. The same Lumb who played host to Charles Darwin when the *Beagle* called at Buenos Aires.
23. H. S. Ferns, *Britain and Argentina in the Nineteenth Century* (Clarendon, Oxford, 1960), pp. 316, 348; Nottingham University Library, Hadden Papers, Ha A 8, 1851–66, ledger of J. & H. Hadden & Co., hosiers, Nottingham, shows that Haddens conducted an extensive export trade to South America, much of it (in the region of £10,000 a year) through Joseph Green & Co., Liverpool, to the Buenos Aires, Manchester, and Valparaiso houses.
24. Baring Papers, HC16, Part 1, Falconnet's report of June 1844.
25. Reber, *British Mercantile Houses*, p. 46.
26. Loc. cit.
27. Thomas George Love, *A Five Years' Residence in Buenos Ayres during the Years 1820 to 1825 . . . by an Englishman* (London, 1825), pp. 45–6.
28. What follows is based on notes kindly made available by Charles Lumb,

of London, a genealogist distantly related to Edward Lumb.

29. Buenos Aires Herald, *Gran Bretaña en la evolución de la economía argentina* (Buenos Aires, 1945) shows William Wanklyn among the donors to Mariano Moreno's Buenos Aires public library in 1810. Manchester firms possibly connected with him are listed in *Dean's Manchester and Salford Directory for 1813* (Manchester, 1813) and Edward Bains and W. Parson (eds), *History, Director and Gazeteer of the County Palatinate of Lancaster* (Liverpool, 1824).

30. Lady Anne Macdonnell, *Reminiscences of Diplomatic Life, being stray memories of personalities and incidents connected with several European courts and also with life in South America fifty years ago* (A. & C. Black, London, 1913).

31. Körner, *Zimmermann*, pp. 98, 103; Latham, *States of the River Plate*, p. 316; Thomas Woodbine Hinchliff, *South American Sketches* (London, 1863), p. 78; *Bertram Wodehouse Currie, 1827–1896, Recollections, Letters, and Journals* (Roehampton, privately printed, 1901), II, p. lxviii.

32. William MacCann, *Two Thousand Miles Ride through the Argentine Provinces* (London, 1853), p. 7.

33. Körner, *Zimmermann*, pp. 103–5.

34. Walter Devereux Jones, *Hisp.-Amer. Hist. Rev.*, XL.1 (1960).

35. Robert Greenhill, 'Merchants and the Latin American Trades: an Introduction', in D. C. M. Platt (ed.), *Business Imperialism, 1840–1930: an Inquiry based on British Experience in Latin America* (Clarendon, Oxford, 1977), p. 172.

36. E. J. Míguez, 'British Interest in Argentine Land Development, 1870–1914: a Study of British Investment in Argentina' (unpublished D.Phil. thesis, St. Antony's College, Oxford, 1981), pp. 308–9n.

37. Ibid., p. 20.

38. Reber, *British Mercantile Houses*, p. 134.

39. Ibid., p. 47.

40. Ibid., p. 135.

41. Ibid., p. 114.

42. Loc. cit.; Buenos Aires Herald, *Gran Bretaña*.

43. M. G. Mulhall, *The English in South America* (Buenos Aires, 1878), Chapter LVIII, 'The Future'.

44. John Lynch, *Argentine Dictator: Juan Manuel de Rosas, 1829–1852* (Oxford, Clarendon Press, 1981), p. 45.

45. Ibid., p. 37.

46. With unerring political judgement, Joseph Conrad places just this ideology on the lips of Charles Gould, the Anglo-South American mine-owner in *Nostromo*: 'What is wanted here is law, good faith, order, security. Anyone can declaim about these things, but I pin my faith to material interests. Only let material interests once get a firm footing, and they are bound to impose the conditions on which alone they can continue to exist. That's how your money-making is justified here in the face of lawlessness and disorder. It is justified because the security which it demands must be shared with an oppressed people. A

better justice will come afterwards. That's your ray of hope.' Joseph Conrad, *Nostromo* (London, 1904; Penguin Books, 1963), p. 81.

47. Bartolomé Mitre, *Historia de Belgrano y de la independencia argentina* (4th edn, Buenos Aires, 1887), I, p. 50.

48. Samuel Wilcocke, *History of the Viceroyalty of Buenos Aires* (London, 1807), pp. 506–7.

49. 'Sir John Bowring [himself a Radical] has described how the Spanish music-hall hit of the 1820s which began "Yo que soy contrabandista", [I, who am a smuggler] was sung before members of the Royal Family, and was much applauded by them.' Richard Gatty, *Portrait of a Merchant Prince: James Morrison, 1789–1857* (Northallerton, privately printed, n.d., *circa* 1976), p. 74, citing Bowring's *Autobiographical Reflections* of 1877.

50. Brian Inglis, *The Opium War* (Hodder & Stoughton, London, 1976), p. 218.

51. Percival Spear, *Master of Bengal: Clive and his India* (Thames & Hudson, London, 1975), p. 41.

52. Ibid., p. 112.

53. P. J. Marshall, *East India Fortunes: the British in Bengal in the Eighteenth Century* (Clarendon, Oxford, 1976), p. 266.

54. Holden Furber, *John Company at Work: a Study of European Expansion in India in the late Eighteenth Century* (Harvard University Press, Cambridge, Mass., 1947; reprinted Octagon Books, New York, 1970), p. 194.

55. Pamela Nightingale, *Trade and Empire in Western India, 1784–1806* (Cambridge University Press, Cambridge, 1970), p. 134.

56. Ibid., pp. 171, 179, 184.

57. Amales Tripathi, *Trade and Finance in the Bengal Presidency, 1793–1833* (Oxford University Press, Calcutta, 1956; 2nd edn, 1979), p. 11.

58. Yen-P'ing Hao, *The Comprador in Nineteenth Century China: Bridge between East and West* (Harvard University Press, Cambridge, Mass., 1970), *passim*.

59. Ibid., pp. 120–49.

60. Marshall, *East India Fortunes*, p. 264.

61. Radhe Shyam Rungta, *Rise of Business Corporations in India, 1851–1900* (Cambridge University Press, Cambridge, 1970), p. 56, quoting an extract from Millburn's *Oriental Commerce*, quoted in S. K. Sen, *Studies in Economic Policy and Development of India, 1848–1926* (Calcutta, 1966), p. 54.

62. Ibid., p. 58.

63. Colin N. Crisswell, *The Taipans: Hong Kong's Merchant Princes* (Oxford University Press, Hong Kong, 1981), p. 21.

64. Rungta, *Business Corporations in India*, p. 77, n. 3.

65. Crisswell, *The Taipans*, p. 145.

66. Rungta, *Business Corporations in India*, p. 59.

67. Tripathi, *Trade and Finance*, p. 207.

68. Spear, *Master of Bengal*, pp. 72–3.

69. Furber, *John Company*, p. 329.
70. Ibid., p. 213 and Appendix A, pp. 327–42.
71. V. G. Kiernan, *The Lords of Human Kind: European Attitudes to the Outside World in the Imperial Age* (Weidenfeld & Nicolson, London, 1969; Pelican Books, 1972), p. 36.
72. Yen-P'ing Hao, *The Comprador*, Chapter 8.
73. Crisswell, *The Taipans*, p. 112.
74. Crisswell, pp. 200–1.
75. Ibid., p. 207.
76. Nightingale, *Trade and Empire*, p. 232.
77. Furber, *John Company*, p. 152.
78. Quoted in Furber, *John Company*, p. 159.
79. Tripathi, *Trade and Finance*, p. 30, quoting Scott MSS, Home Misc., 404, p. 160.
80. Eric Stokes, *The English Utilitarians and India* (Clarendon Press, Oxford, 1959), p. viii.
81. Stokes, *The English Utilitarians*, *passim*.
82. Yen-P'ing Hao, *The Comprador*, p. 193.
83. M. Dorothy George, *London Life in the Eighteenth Century* (Kegan Paul, London, 1925; Penguin Books, 1966), pp. 131 *et seq.*
84. Bill Williams, *The Making of Manchester Jewry, 1740–1875* (Manchester University Press, Manchester, 1976), p. 42.
85. Ibid., pp. 19 and 43.
86. Ibid., p. 43.
87. Ibid., pp. 45–7.
88. Ibid., p. 78; Chaim Bermant, *The Cousinhood* (Eyre & Spottiswoode, London, 1971), pp. 64–5, 91–100.
89. Bermant, *The Cousinhood*, pp. 49–50, 119–28.
90. Palmerston to Bethell, Lord Chancellor, 20 February 1864, quoted in Jasper Ridley, *Lord Palmerston* (Constable, London, 1970), p. 687.
91. Ethelreda Lewis (ed.), *The Life and Works of Alfred Aloysius Horn, I— The Ivory Coast in the Earlies* (Jonathan Cape, London, 1927), p. 29.
92. Stephen E. Koss, *Sir John Brunner: Radical Plutocrat, 1842–1919* (Cambridge University Press, London, 1970), pp. 32–3.
93. Arthur Behrend, *Portrait of a Family Firm: Bahr, Behrend & Co., 1793–1945* (Liverpool, privately printed, 1970).
94. Richard Cyril Lockett, *Memoirs of the Family of Lockett* (Liverpool?, privately printed, 1939), pp. 61–3.
95. Koss, *Brunner*, pp. 32–3.
96. J. L. Hammond and Barbara Hammond, *James Stansfeld: a Victorian Champion of Sex Equality* (Longmans, London, 1932), p. 23.
97. George Jacob Holyoake, *Sixty Years of an Agitator's Life* (3rd edn, T. Fisher Unwin, London, 1906), p. 49.
98. Ibid., pp. 102, 165; Minutes of the Garibaldi Committee, Holyoake Collection, Bishopgate Institute, reprinted in Edward Royle (ed.), *The Infidel Tradition: from Paine to Bradlaugh* (Macmillan, London, 1976) pp. 184–5 ; E. F. Richards (ed.), *Mazzini's Letters to an English Family* (3 vols., Bodley Head, London, 1922), *passim*. The Ashursts were the

English family of the title.

99. F. J. Ryland, *Specks on the Dusty Road* (Cornish Bros., Birmingham, 1937), p. 41. See also Arnold Bennett, *The Card* (Methuen, London, 1911), Chapter 1.

100. Jose Harris and Pat Thane, 'British and European Bankers, 1880–1914: an "Aristocratic Bourgeoisie"?', in Pat Thane, Geoffrey Crossick, and Roderick Floud (eds), *The Power of the Past: Essays for Eric Hobsbawm* (Cambridge University Press, Cambridge, 1984); see also works cited in Stanley Chapman, 'Aristocracy and Meritocracy in Merchant Banking', *Brit. J. Soc.*, 37, 2 (June, 1986), pp. 180–93. Chapman contests this view. Briefly, he argues that the importance of newcomers to the City has been neglected, arguing, persuasively, that many newly-arrived families of economic importance resisted the aristocratic style of the older houses. But there is a problem in the debate. For both Chapman and those he criticises seem inclined to assume that an aristocratic bourgeoisie was a part-time or amateur bourgeoisie. Thus, Chapman suggests: 'London was a competitive financial market in which any part-timers inevitably lost business before long.' (p. 190). This worries me. For it is apparent that some—Charles Morrison is an obvious example—combined aristocratic taste and connexions with punctilious attention to business. Men of this sort met born aristocrats who were coming to take a more obviously capitalistic attitude to the exploitation of their estates half-way. The issues of class and idleness are distinct.

101. Richard Gatty, *Portrait of a Merchant Prince: James Morrison, 1789–1857* (Northallerton, privately printed, n.d., *circa* 1976), espec. pp. 48–62, 255–66; William C. Lubenow, *The Politics of Government Growth: Early Victorian Attitudes towards State Intervention, 1833–1848* (Newton Abbot, David & Charles, 1971), pp. 127–30.

102. Gatty, *James Morrison*, p. 181.

103. Richards, *Mazzini's Letters*, II, p. 100.

104. 'Mr. Morris' 80th Birthday Celebration: Report of Proceedings' (London, privately printed). The relevant passage is quoted in Charles A. Jones, 'Great Capitalists and the Direction of British Overseas Investment in the Late Nineteenth Century: the Case of Argentina', *Bus. Hist.*, 22, 2 (July, 1980), p. 156. Archives of Mandatos y Agencias del Río de la Plata, Records of the River Plate Trust Loan and Agency Co. Ltd, letters to Mr. Toso, III, John Morris to José Toso.

105. Sheila Marriner, *Rathbones of Liverpool, 1845–73* (Liverpool University Press, Liverpool, 1961), p. 4.

CHAPTER 4

1. G. S. Graham, 'The Ascendancy of the Sailing Ship, 1850–85', *Econ. Hist. Rev.*, 2nd series, 11 (1956), pp. 74–88.

2. Andre E. Sayous, 'Partnerships in the Trade between Spain and America and also in the Spanish Colonies in the Sixteenth Century', *J.*

Econ. and Bus. Hist., 1 (1928–29), pp. 183–6.

3. Pierre Jeannin, *Merchants of the Sixteenth Century* (Harper & Row, New York, etc., 1972), p. 71.

4. Loc. cit.

5. Sayous, 'Partnerships', pp. 297–9.

6. B. W. Clapp, *John Owens, Manchester Merchant* (Manchester University Press, Manchester 1965), pp. 26–33, 54.

7. R. G. Wilson, 'The Fortunes of a Leeds Merchant House, 1780–1820', *Bus. Hist.*, 9 (1967), pp. 70–86.

8. Richard Gatty, *Portrait of a Merchant Prince: James Morrison, 1789–1857* (Northallerton, privately printed, n.d., *circa* 1976), pp. 155–68.

9. Ralph W. Hidy, 'The Organization and Functions of Anglo-American Merchant Bankers, 1815–60', *J. Econ. Hist.* (December Suppl. 1941), esp. p. 56.

10. Sheila Marriner, *Rathbones of Liverpool, 1845–73* (Liverpool University Press, Liverpool, 1961), p. 75, n. 3.

11. John Mayo, 'Before the Nitrate Era: British Commission Houses and the Chilean Economy, 1851–80', *J. Lat. Amer. Stud.*, 11, 2 (November 1979), pp. 283–302.

12. Max Hartwell, 'Dalgety and New Zealand Loan Company: History of the Company' (unpublished typescript, n.d., *circa* 1974, in the possession of Dalgety Ltd, London), Chapter 4, p. 2.

13. Clapp, *John Owens*, pp. 144 *et seq.*

14. Stuart Weems Bruchey, *Robert Oliver, Merchant of Baltimore, 1783–1819* (Johns Hopkins Press, Baltimore, 1956), pp. 360–1.

15. Marriner, *Rathbones*, p. 206.

16. Douglass C. North, 'Ocean Freight Rates and Economic Development, 1750–1913', *J. Econ. Hist.*, 18 (1958), pp. 537–55; G. S. Graham, 'The Ascendancy of the Sailing Ship, 1850–85', *Econ. Hist. Rev.*, 2nd series, 11 (1956), pp. 74–88.

17. R. G. Albion, 'Capital Movement and Transportation: British Shipping and Latin America, 1806–1914', *J. Econ. Hist.*, 11 (1951), pp. 361–74.

18. Graham, 'The Ascendancy of the Sailing Ship'.

19. George Carr Glyn giving evidence before the Select Committee on Commercial Distress, 1848, Q.1649, quoted in Shizuyu Nishimura, *The Decline of the Inland Bill of Exchange, 1855–1913* (Cambridge University Press, Cambridge, 1971), p. 78, n. 1.

20. Elva Tooker, *Nathan Trotter: Philadelphia Merchant, 1787–1853* (Harvard University Press, Cambridge, Mass., 1955), p. 84.

21. S. D. Chapman, 'The International Houses: the Continental Contribution to British Commerce, 1800–1860', *J. Euro. Econ. Hist.*, 6, 1 (Spring 1977) p. 14.

22. P. N. Davies, *Sir Alfred Jones: Shipping Entrepreneur par excellence* (Europa Publications, London, 1978), pp. 42–3.

23. Hugh Barty-King, *Girdle Round the Earth* (Heinemann, London, 1979); James Foreman-Peck, *The History of the World Economy: International*

Economic Relations since 1850 (Wheatsheaf Books, Brighton, 1983), pp. 69–70.

24. Radhe Shyam Rungta, *Rise of Business Corporations in India, 1851–1900* (Cambridge University Press, Cambridge, 1970); Guy Palmade, *French Capitalism in the Nineteenth Century* (David and Charles, Newton Abbot, 1972), p. 139.

25. Richard Graham, *British and the Onset of Modernization in Brazil, 1850–1914* (Cambridge University Press, Cambridge, 1972), p. 25; Roderick J. Barman, 'Business and Government in Imperial Brazil: the Experience of Viscount Mauá', *J. Lat. Amer. Stud.*, 13, 2 (November 1981), pp. 249–58; Stanley J. Stein, *The Brazilian Cotton Manufacture: Textile Enterprise in an Underdeveloped Area* (Harvard University Press, Cambridge, Mass., 1957).

26. Balfour, Williamson & Co. Ltd, Roman House, Wood Street, London EC2. Records of Balfour, Williamson & Co., Stephen Williamson's letter books, Wiliamson to Alexander Balfour, 1 September 1865, pp. 293–8.

27. Records of Balfour, Williamson & Co., Memorandum of Stephen Wiliamson, 31 December 1889.

28. Records of Balfour, Williamson & Co., Memorandum: 'Stephen Williamson's property as at 31 Dec. 1897'.

29. Rungta, *Rise of Business Corporations*, p. 216.

30. Stanley D. Chapman, *The Rise of Merchant Banking* (George Allen & Unwin, London, 1984), pp. 138–9.

31. Warren Dean, *The Industrialization of São Paulo, 1880–1945* (Texas University Press, Austin, Texas, 1969), pp. 23–4; Graham, *Britain and the Onset of Modernization in Brazil*, p. 84; D. C. M. Platt, *Latin American and British Trade, 1806–1914* (Adam & Charles Black, London, 1972), pp. 139–43; University College, Gower Street, London WC1: Records of the Bank of London and South America, DI (London and River Plate Bank Ltd, confidential letters, London to Buenos Aires), Warden to Todd, 9 March 1882.

32. Robert Greenhill, 'Merchants and the Latin American Trades: an Introduction', in D. C. M. Platt (ed.), *Business Imperialism, 1840–1930: an Inquiry Based on British Experience in Latin America* (Clarendon, Oxford, 1977), p. 164, quoting Greene to E. Johnston & Co., 18 May 1903, in Letter Book III of the Johnston Papers.

33. Eugene W. Ridings, 'Business, Nationality, and Dependency in Late Nineteenth Century Brazil', *J. Lat. Amer. Stud.*, 14, 1 (May 1982).

34. Records of the Bank of London and South America, D35 (London and River Plate Bank Ltd, confidential letters, Buenos Aires to London), 14 November 1879; Hilda Sabato, 'Wood Trade and Commercial Networks in Buenos Aires, 1840s to 1880s', *J. Lat. Amer. Stud.*, 15, 1 (May 1983), pp. 49–81.

35. Quoted in G. C. Allen and Audrey G. Donnithorne, *Western Enterprise in Far Eastern Economic Development: China and Japan* (George Allen & Unwin, London, 1954), p. 110.

36. Compton Mackenzie, *Realms of Silver: One Hundred Years of Banking*

in the East (Routledge & Kegan Paul, London, 1954), pp. 69–70. For a more technical aspect of the effects of improved transport on the financing of the China trade see Francis E. Hyde, *Far Eastern Trade, 1860–1914* (A. & C. Black, London, 1973), pp. 61–2; and Sheila Marriner, *Rathbones of Liverpool, 1845–73* (Liverpool University Press, Liverpool, 1961), p. 218.

37. Colin N. Crisswell, *The Taipans: Hong Kong's Merchant Princes* (Oxford University Press, Hong Kong, 1981), p. 120.

38. Frank B. Forbes, Shanghai, to M. Cordier, Paris, 17 August 1872, quoted in Yen P'ing Hao, *The Comprador in Nineteenth Century China: Bridge between East and West* (Harvard University Press, Cambridge, Mass., 1970), p. 21.

39. William MacCann, *Two Thousand Miles Ride through the Argentine Provinces* (London, 1853 pp. 73 ff.).

40. E. C. J. Stone, *Makers of Fortune: a Colonial Business Community and its Fall* (Auckland University Press and Oxford University Press, Auckland, 1973), p. 46.

41. *James Finlay & Company Limited: Manufacturers and East India Merchants, 1750–1950* (Jackson Son & Company, Glasgow, 1951), p. 78. For further evidence of changes in patterns of intermediation during periods when the rate of technological change was less evidently rapid see also Gordon Jackson, *Hull in the Eighteenth Century: a Study in Economic and Social History* (Oxford University Press, London, 1972), p. 124; and Elva Tooker, *Nathan Trotter*, p. 85.

42. Crisswell, *The Taipans*, p. 120; Vera Blinn Reber, *British Mercantile Houses in Buenos Aires, 1810–1880* (Harvard University Press, Cambridge, Mass., 1979), pp. 138–9).

43. Pierre Jeannin, *Merchants*, pp. 1–11; Henry Kamen, *A Concise History of Spain* (Thames & Hudson, London, 1973), p. 72.

44. Samuel H. Baron, 'Entrepreneurs and Entrepreneurship in Sixteenth and Seventeenth Century Russia', in Geoffrey Guroff and Fred V. Carstensen (eds), *Entrepreneurship in Imperial Russia and the Soviet Union* (Princeton University Press, Princeton, N.J., 1983), pp. 27–48.

45. Michael G. Mulhall, *The English in South America* (Buenos Aires, 1878), pp. 326–7.

46. Vera Blinn Reber, *British Mercantile Houses in Buenos Aires, 1810–1880* (Harvard University Press, Cambridge, Mass., 1979), pp. 108, 113.

47. Ralph W. Hidy, 'The Organization and Functions of Anglo-American Merchant Bankers, 1815–60', *J. Econ. Hist.* (December supp. 1941), pp. 58, 66.

48. John Crawfurd, *A Sketch of the Commercial Resources and Monetary and Mercantile System of British India, with Suggestions for their Improvement by means of Banking Establishments* (1837), reprinted in K. N. Chaudhuri (ed.), *The Economic Development of India under the East India Company, 1814–58: a Selection of Contemporary Writings* (Cambridge University Press, Cambridge, 1971), pp. 217–316.

49. On Dattani, see Iris Origo, *The Merchant of Prato* (Penguin, 1963).

50. Hughes & Ronald, for example, a Liverpool house established in 1840, which originally supplied wool for south-west Scotland to Yorkshire, survived, for a time at least, by moving promptly to deal in imported wools from Spanish America and the Far East. J. D. Bailey, *A Hundred Years of Pastoral Banking: a History of the Australian Mercantile Land and Finance Company, 1863–1963* (Clarendon Press, Oxford, 1966), pp. 16–17.
51. Warren Dean, *The Industrialization of São Paulo, 1880–1945* (Texas University Press, Austin, Texas, 1969), p. 20.
52. R. Munting, 'Ransomes in Russia: an English Engineering Company's Trade with Russia to 1917', *Econ. Hist. Rev.*, 2nd series, 31 (1978), pp. 257–69. The desire to provide a full product range was later to be among the reasons for amalgamation in the industry. See E. P. Neufeld, *A Global Corporation: a History of the International Development of Massey-Ferguson Ltd* (University of Toronto Press, Toronto, 1969).
53. Fred V. Carstensen, 'Foreign Participation in Russian Economic Life: Notes on British Enterprise, 1865–1914', in Geoffrey Guroff and Fred V. Carstensen (eds), *Entrepreneurship in Imperial Russia and the Soviet Union* (Princeton University Press, Princeton, N.J., 1983), pp. 140–58.
54. Ibid., and Munting, 'Ransomes in Russia'.
55. Sir Percival Griffiths, *A History of the Inchcape Group* (Inchcape & Co. Ltd, London, 1977), pp. 65–8.
56. Stanley J. Stein, *The Brazilian Cotton Manufacture: Textile Enterprise in an Underdeveloped Area, 1850–1950* (Harvard University Press, Cambridge, Mass., 1957), pp. 36–8.
57. Sir Harry Townend *et al.*, *A History of Shaw Wallace & Co. and Shaw Wallace & Co. Ltd* (Calcutta, privately printed for the company, 1965), p. 10.
58. Hyde, *Far Eastern Trade*, p. 45; Crisswell, *The Taipans*, p. 97.
59. E. R. J. Owen, *Cotton and the Egyptian Economy, 1820–1914: a Study in Trade and Development* (Clarendon Press, Oxford, 1969), p. 209.
60. T. Ellison, *The Cotton Trade of Great Britain* (London, 1886), pp. 174–86. See also L. E. Davis and D. C. North, *Institutional Change and American Economic Growth* (Cambridge University Press, Cambridge, 1971), pp. 193–7, who drew on Ellison and other sources in an interesting treatment of institutional responses to improved transport and communications with a clear theoretical focus on the reduction of transaction costs by what they term 'arrangemental innovation'.
61. Godfrey Harrison, *Borthwicks: a Century in the Meat Trade, 1863–1963* (London, privately printed for the company, 1963), esp. p. 61.
62. Jack Colin Crossley, 'The Location and Development of the Agricultural and Industrial Enterprises of Liebig's Extract of Meat Company in the River Plate Countries, 1865–1932' (University of Leicester, unpublished Ph.D. thesis, November 1973), Chapter 3, especially p. 106.
63. Ibid., Chapter 7.
64. Loc. cit.

65. L. E. Davis, 'The Capital Markets and Industrial Concentration: the United States and the United Kingdom—a comparative study', in *Purdue Faculty Papers in Economic History, 1965–1966* (Irwin Homewood, Ill., 1967), p. 666.

66. H. E. W. Braund, *Calling to Mind: being some account of the first hundred years (1870–1970) of Steel Brothers and Company Ltd* (Pergamon Press, Oxford, 1975), pp. 37–8.

67. Rosemary Thorp and Geoffrey Bertram, *Peru, 1890–1977: Growth and Policy in an Open Economy* (Columbia University Press, New York, 1978), pp. 52, 175.

68. Marika Vicziany, 'Bombay Merchants and Structural Changes in the Export Community, 1850–1880', in K. N. Chaudhuri and Clive Dewey (eds), *Economy and Society* (Oxford University Press, Delhi and New York, 1979), p. 163.

69. Hyde, *Far Eastern Trade*, p. 81.

70. José Bianco, *Don Bernardo de Irigoyen, etadista y pioneer, 1822–1906* (Buenos Aires, 1927), p. 143.

71. Hilda Sabato, 'Wool Trade and Commercial Networks in Buenos Aires, 1840s to 1880s,' *J. Lat. Amer. Stud.*, 15, 1 (May 1983), pp. 66, 73.

72. Reber, *British Mercantile House*, p. 139.

73. Alan Barnard, *Visions and Profits: Studies in the Business Career of Thomas Sutcliffe Mort* (Melbourne University Press, Melbourne, 1961).

74. Ibid., p. 145.

75. Ibid., p. 58.

76. Bailey, *A Hundred Years of Pastoral Banking*.

77. Max Hartwell, 'Dalgety and New Zealand Loan Company: History of the Company', (unpublished typescript held by Dalgety Ltd, London).

78. The Holts, for example, preferred Swires to established houses in the East. Francis E. Hyde and J. R. Harris, *Blue Funnel: a History of Alfred Holt and Company of Liverpool from 1865 to 1914* (Liverpool University Press, Liverpool, 1957), pp. 33–66.

79. Kwang-ching Liu, 'British-Chinese Steamship Rivalry in China, 1873–85', in C. D. Cowan (ed.), *The Economic Development of China and Japan: Studies in Economic History and Political Economy* (George Allen & Unwin, London, 1964); Sheila Marriner and Francis E. Hyde, *The Senior John Samuel Swire, 1825–98: Management in Far Eastern Shipping Trades* (Liverpool Univerity Press, Liverpool, 1967), pp. 58–66; Yen P'ing Hao, *The Comprador in Nineteenth Century China*, pp. 116–26.

80. T. S. Mort in *Sydney Morning Herald*, 19 February 1857, quoted in Alan Barnard, *Visions and Profits: Studies in the Business Career of Thomas Sutcliffe Mort* (Melbourne University Press for the Australian National University, Melbourne, 1961), p. 77.

81. *Bengal Hurkau*, 2 February 1844, quoted in Blair B. Kling, 'The Origin of the Managing Agency in India', *J. Asian Stud.*, 26, 1 (November 1966), p. 42.

82. Kling, 'Managing Agency in India, pp. 37–42.

83. Nigel Cameron, *Power: the Story of China Light* (Oxford University Press, Hong Kong, 1982).
84. Roderick J. Barman, 'Business and Government in Imperial Brazil: the Experience of Baron Mauá', *J. Lat. Amer. Stud.*, 13, 2 (November 1981), p. 259.
85. Loc. cit.
86. On the sale of shares, see the archives of the Bank of London and South America, at University College, London. GI (London and Brazilian Bank Ltd, head office extras to Rio de Janeiro branch), Beaton to Gordon, 11/44, October 1873. Beaton noted that Mauá was selling almost all of his shares in the London and Brazilian and in other companies. For Mauá I have relied principally upon Anyda Marchant, 'A New Portrait of Mauá the Banker: a Man of Business in Nineteenth Century Brazil', *Hisp.-Amer. Hist. Rev.*, 30, 4 (November 1950), pp. 411–31; Anyda Marchant, *Viscount Mauá and the Empire of Brazil a biography of Irineu Evangelista De Sousa, 1813–99* (University of California Press, Berkeley, Cal., 1965); and Barman, 'Business and Government in Imperial Brazil'.
87. Baring Papers, in the Guildhall Library, City of London. HC 16/1.
88. Loc. cit.
89. Baring Papers, HC 16/2.
90. Records of the Sun Insurance Office Ltd, held by the company at 63 Threadneedle Street, London EC2. Foreign Notebooks, Buenos Aires, etc., pp. 5–6, *circa* 1865.
91. Bank of London and South America, D70 (London and River Plate Bank Ltd, confidential letters, head office to Montevideo), 8 October 1870. It is possible that at this stage the Buenos Aires house was trading as Wanklyn & Co., and only the London house as Lumb Wanklyn & Co. Reber lists the partners in the Buenos Aires house, in 1869, as Ambrosio Lezica, with $200,000, Edward Lumb, also with $200,000, and Alfred Lumb and Frederick Wanklyn, with $100,000 each, making a total of about £120,000. Vera Blinn Reber, *British Mercantile Houses in Buenos Aires, 1810–1880* (Harvard University Press, Cambridge, Mass., and London, 1979), p. 122.
92. Reber, *British Mercantile Houses*, p. 122.
93. Public Record Office, BT 31 1736/6406.
94. Records of Mocatta & Goldsmidt Ltd, 16 Finsbury Circus, London EC2. Personal diary of Abraham de Mattos Mocatta, 1871–2.
95. Alexander Isaac, 1778/79–1863 was buried in the Hambro synagogue burial ground, Hackney. He was a man of some substance, living in Russell Square. Of nine children born to Alexander and his wife Sophia, 1790–1865, only six survived their parents, including Benjamin, 1822–1905, Leon Joseph, 1826–1906, and Frederick Simeon, 1828–1915. Buenos Aires and Montevideo houses were established under the name L. J. Isaac & Co. in about 1858. By 1866 they were reported to be 'very respectable'. Sun, foreign notebooks, Buenos Aires, etc., p. 9. The relationship of Alexander Isaac of Montevideo to the London family is not clear. Information on the family is derived from

records held by the Jewish Museum and Central Library, Woburn House, Upper Woburn Place, London WC1H 0EP.

96. There is an interesting overlap here with early British investment in Anglo-South African joint-stock companies. Seven of the London backers of the Mercantile Bank, controlling between them just over a quarter of the 1000 founders' shares and almost 8000 ordinary shares, were also to be found, some ten years later, amongst the first to invest in South African diamond mines, land and public utilities. These were Julius Beer, F. S. Isaac, Emile d'Erlanger, L. F. Floersheim, Henry Oppenheim, M. J. Posno and Hermann de Stern. In about 1882 these seven held shares to a paid-up nominal value of £23,464 in ten lots in five companies: the London and South African Exploration Co., the Central Mining Co. of Dorstfontein, the Cape Stock Farming Co., the Kimberley Water Works, and the Orion Diamond Mining Co. The history of informal investment syndicates has yet to be written. This one plainly centred on the Mosenthals. Public Record Office, BT 31 1577/5168, 2689/14444, 2688/14439, 14654/14271 and 2831/15551.

97. Bank of London and South America, D70, Smithers to Jones, 22 and 28 June 1872.

98. Bank of London and South America, D86 (London and River Plate Bank Ltd, Rosario to Buenos Aires, private Letters), Weldon to Smithers, 17 June 1872.

99. *Bankers' Magazine* (1874), p. 477.

100. Baring Papers, HC4.1.65, 26 December 1876 and 14 January 1878.

101. Bank of London and South America, D35 (London and River Plate Bank Ltd., Buenos Aires to London, confidential letters), 15 March 1875 and 29 October 1874.

102. *Bankers' Magazine* (1875), pp. 406–7; Bank of London and South America, D1), 25 March 1875.

103. Bank of London and South America, D70, 3 March 1875.

104. Bank of London and South America, D70, 24 February 1876.

105. Loc. cit.

106. Falconer Larkworthy, *Ninety-One Years* (Mills & Boon, London, 1924); R. J. Hanham, 'New Zealand Promoters and British Investors, 1860–1895', in R. Chapman and K. Sinclair (eds), *Studies of a Small Democracy* (Paul's, for the University of Auckland, Hamilton, N.Z., 1963); R. C. Stone, *Makers of Fortune: a Colonial Business Community and its Fall* (Auckland University Press and Oxford University Press, Auckland, 1973).

107. Blair B. Kling, 'The Origin of the Managing Agency in India', *J. Asian Stud.*, 26, 1 (November 1966), p. 47.

108. Griffiths, *Inchcape Group*, pp. 38–9.

109. Cameron, *The Story of China Light*, p. 112.

110. Barman, 'The Experience of Baron Mauá', p. 240; Anyda Marchant, 'A New Portrait of Mauá the Banker: a Man of Business in Nineteenth Century Brazil', *Hisp.-Amer. Hist. Rev.*, 30, 4 (November 1950), pp. 411–31.

111. Archives of Mandatos y Agencias del Río de la Plata (now destroyed).

Records of the English Bank of the River Plate Ltd. Confidential letter, Buenos Aires to head office, 10 October 1885.

112. Archives of the Bank of London and South America, at University College, London. D70 (London and River Plate Bank Ltd, London to Montevideo), 7 August 1883.

113. See above p. 114 and below p. 157.

114. Donna J. Guy, 'Tucuman Sugar Politics and the Generation of Eighty', *The Americas*, 32 (1975–76), p. 571.

115. Bank of London and South America, D35 (London and River Plate Bank Ltd, confidential letters, Buenos Aires to London), 4 January 1894.

116. Bank of London and South America, D35, 12 May 1899.

117. Loc. cit. At this point the London and River Plate Bank was lending to Tornquists at 7 per cent. Mandatos archives, Records of the River Plate Trust Loan and Agency Company Ltd, F. H. Chevallier Boutell to James Anderson, 18 October 1901.

118. Guy, 'Tucuman Sugar Politics', p. 579.

119. Mandatos archives. Records of the River Plate Trust Loan and Agency Co. Ltd, F. H. Chevallier Boutell to John Morris, 8 August 1897.

120. Guy, 'Tucuman Sugar Politics', p. 579.

CHAPTER 5

1. Sir Percival Griffiths, *A History of the Inchcape Group* (Inchcape & Co. Ltd, London, 1977), p. 48.

2. Francis E. Hyde and J. R. Harris, *Blue Funnel: a History of Alfred Holt and Company of Liverpool from 1865 to 1914* (Liverpool University Press, Liverpool, 1957).

3. A. H. John, *A Liverpool Merchant House: Being the History of Alfred Booth and Company, 1863–1958* (George Allen & Unwin, London, 1959).

4. Sheila Marriner and Francis E. Hyde, *The Senior: John Samuel Swire, 1825–98: Management in Far Eastern Shipping Trades* (Liverpool University Press, Liverpool, 1967), pp. 10–12.

5. Ibid., pp. 20–1.

6. Ibid., p. 60.

7. Ibid., p. 82.

8. Manuel A. Fernandez, 'The Development of the Chilean Economy and its British Connections, 1895–1914' (unpublished Ph.D. thesis, Glasgow, 1978, 2 vols.), p. 249.

9. Bill Albert, *An Essay on the Peruvian Sugar Industry, 1880–1920, and the Letters of Ronald Gordon, Administrator of the British Sugar Company in Canete, 1914–1920* (School of Social Studies, University of East Anglia, Norwich, 1976), pp. 219a–245a; Robert Greenhill, 'The Nitrate and Iodine Trades, 1880–1914', in D. C. M. Platt (ed.), *Business Imperialism, 1840–1930: an Inquiry based on British Experience in Latin America* (Clarendon, Oxford, 1977), pp. 236–9. See also, on nitrates,

Harold Blakemore, *British Nitrates and Chilean Politics, 1886–1896: Balmaceda and Chile's Crucial Transition: 1870–1891* (New York University Press, New York and London, 1982).

10. Rosemary Thorp and Geoffrey Bertram, *Peru, 1890–1977: Growth and Policy in an Open Economy* (Columbia University Press, New York, 1978), p. 52.

11. Albert, *Essay*, p. 222a.

12. Wallis Hunt, *Heirs of Great Adventure: the History of Balfour Williamson & Company Limited* (Balfour Williamson & Co., London, 1951, 1960), II, pp. 15–19.

13. Robert Greenhill, 'Merchants and the Latin American Trades: an Introduction', in D. C. M. Platt (ed.), *Business Imperialism*, p. 179.

14. Rory Miller, 'Small Business in the Peruvian Oil Industry: Lobitos Oilfields Limited before 1934', *Bus. Hist. Rev.*, 56, 3 (Autumn 1982), pp. 400–23.

15. *Balfour Williamson & Company and Allied Firms: Memoirs of a Merchant House* (London, for private circulation, 1929), and see Greenhill, 'Merchants and the Latin American Trades', in Platt, *Business Imperialism*, pp. 179–80, who provides further Latin American examples of adaptations similar to those of Balfour Williamson.

16. Richard Graham, *Britain and the Onset of Modernization in Brazil, 1850–1914* (Cambridge University Press, Cambridge, 1972), pp. 141, 144.

17. S. D. Chapman, 'British-Based Investment Groups before 1914' (unpublished paper, 1984), p. 16, citing S. Thompstone, 'Ludwig Knoop, the Arkwright of Russia', *Textile History*, 15 (1984); Fred V. Carstensen, 'Foreign Participation in Russian Economic Life: Notes on British Enterprise, 1865–1914', in Geoffrey Guroff and Fred V. Carstensen (eds), *Entrepreneurship in Imperial Russia and the Soviet Union* (Princeton University Press, Princeton, N.J., 1983), p. 147.

18. *James Finlay & Company Limited: Manufacturers and East India Merchants, 1750–1950* (Jackson, Son & Co., Glasgow, 1951), p. 105.

19. Sir Harry Townend *et al.*, *A History of Shaw Wallace & Co. and Shaw Wallace & Co. Ltd* (Calcutta, the Company, 1965).

20. Richard Graham, 'A British Industry in Brazil: Rio Flour Mills, 1886–1920', *Bus. Hist.*, 8, 1 (January 1966).

21. Robert Henriques, *Marcus Samuel, First Viscount Bearsted and Founder of the 'Shell' Transport and Trading Company, 1853–1927* (Barrie and Rockliff, London, 1960, p. 164.

22. Ibid.

23. Robert V. Kubicek, *Economic Imperialism in Theory and Practice: the Case of South African Gold Mining Finance, 1886–1914* (Duke, Durham, N.C., 1979), p. 56.

24. Ibid., p. 79; John Martin, 'Group Administration in the Gold Mining Industry of the Witwatersrand', *Econ. J.* (1929), pp. 536–53; and see Duncan Innes, *Anglo-American and the Rise of Modern South Africa* (Heinemann, London, 1984), pp. 53–7; Peter Richardson and Jean-

Jacques Van Helten, 'The Development of the South African Gold-Mining Industry, 1895–1918', *Econ. Hist. Rev*, 2nd series, 37, 3 (August 1984), pp. 319–40.

25. Eric Rosenthal (comp.), *South African Dictionary of National Biography* (Warne, London, 1966); George Thomas Amphlett, *History of the Standard Bank of South Africa Ltd., 1862–1913* (Robert Maclehose, Glasgow, 1914), p. 11; E. H. D. Arndt, *Banking and Currency Development in South Africa, 1652–1927* (Juta & Co., Cape Town and Johannesburg, 1928).

26. Innes, *Anglo-American*, Chapter 1.

27. PRO BT31 1577/5168.

28. PRO BT31 2831/15551.

29. Innes, *Anglo-American*, pp. 38–9.

30. PRO BT31 3242/19013.

31. Agnes H. Hicks, *The Story of the Forestal* (The Forestal Land, Timber and Railways Co. Ltd, London, 1956), pp. 4–7.

32. Ibid.

33. PRO BT31 14745/18547.

34. J. Valerie Fifer, 'The Empire Builders: a History of the Bolivian Rubber Boom and the Rise of the House of Suarez', *J. Lat. Amer. Stud.*, 2 (1970), pp. 113–46.

35. I am grateful to the company for allowing me to see Max Hartwell's unpublished history of Dalgety.

36. One rather engaging exception was Robert Tertius Campbell, who made a fortune in Australia and returned to England in 1859, acquiring Buscot Park, near Faringdon, Oxfordshire. There he proceeded to develop a highly and inappropriately mechanised sugar beet project, with six miles of narrow gauge railway, an artificial fertiliser plant, a gas works, a private telegraph system, concrete farm buildings, a distillery and steam ploughs. Nothing could have been less English, or in greater contrast with the cultivated rusticity of the Rothschilds or the quieter country style of the Morrisons. See *The Faringdon Collection: Buscot Park* (Curwen Press, for the Trustees of the Faringdon Collection, 1975), p. 3.

37. G. C. W. Joel, *One Hundred Years of Coffee: E. Johnston & Co. Ltd* (London, privately printed, 1942).

38. Sheila Marriner, *Rathbones of Liverpool, 1845–73* (Liverpool University Press, Liverpool, 1961), p. 216.

39. Sheila Marriner and Francis E. Hyde, *The Senior, John Samuel Swire, 1825–98: Management in Far Eastern Trades* (Liverpool University Press, Liverpool, 1967), p. 19.

40. [Liverpool] *Journal of Commerce*, 28 March 1928.

41. John, *Alfred Booth and Company*.

42. Townend, *Shaw Wallace & Co.*; Paul H. Emden, *Money Powers of Europe in the Nineteenth and Twentieth Centuries* (Sampson Low Marston & Co. Ltd, London, n.d.), p. 381; Chaim Bermant, *The Cousinhood: the Anglo-Jewish Gentry* (Eyre & Spottiswoode, London, 1971), p. 227.

43. Bermant, *The Cousinhood*, pp. 223–38.
44. Ibid., p. 234, quoting R. R. James (ed.), *The Diaries of Sir Henry Channon* (Penguin Books, 1970), p. 250.
45. Ibid., p. 236.
46. Kubicek, *Economic Imperialism*, p. 196.
47. Ibid., p. 132, citing T. Gutsche, *No Ordinary Woman: the Life and Times of Florence Phillips* (Cape Town, 1966).
48. Leonore Davidoff, *The Best Circles: Social Etiquette and the Season* (Croom Helm, London, 1973), pp. 56, 59.
49. PRO BT31 4136/26668.
50. Henriques, *Marcus Samuel*; and on the difficulties encountered by a London-based company mining in the Andes in the 1820s see F. B. Head, *Reports Relating to the Failure of the Rio Plata Mining Association* (London, 1827); and Grosvenor Bunster, *Observations on Captain Head's 'Reports'* (London, 1827).
51. H. S. Ashton, 1918, in Townend, *Shaw Wallace & Co.*
52. R. V. Clements, 'British-Controlled Enterprise in the West between 1870 and 1900 and Some Agrarian Reactions', *Agric. Hist.*, 27 (October 1953), pp. 132–41, provides a slightly more elaborate taxonomy.
53. Radhe Shyam Rungta, *Rise of Business Corporations in India, 1851–1900* (Cambridge University Press, Cambridge, 1970), pp. 221–2.
54. Ibid., pp. 222–6. On the balance between Indian and British registration and ownership in Anglo-Indian companies, see N.Z. Ahmed, 'Some Aspects of the History of British Investment in the Private Sector of the Indian Economy, 1874–1914' (unpublished M.Sc.(Econ.) dissertation, London, 1955).
55. Francis E. Hyde, *Far Eastern Trade, 1860–1914* (A. & C. Black, London, 1973), p. 59.
56. Blair B. Kling, 'The Origin of the Managing Agency in India', *J. Asian Stud.* 26, 1 (November 1966).
57. H. A. Antrobus, *A History of the Assam Company, 1839–1953* (T. & A. Constable, Edinburgh, 1957), especially Chapters 6–12, pp. 35–162.
58. *The Anglo-African*, 5 February 1863, quoted by E. H. D. Arndt, *Banking and Currency Development in South Africa*, p. 287.
59. G. T. Amphlett, *History of the Standard Bank of South Africa, Ltd*, Chapter 2.
60. Robert V. Kubicek, *Economic Imperialism in Theory and Practice*, pp. 88–111.
61. Ibid., pp. 56–83.
62. Ibid., p. 196.
63. David Joslin, *A Century of Banking in Latin America* (Oxford University Press, London, 1963), p. 28.
64. Records of the Department of Trade and Industry, Companies House, 55–71 City Road, London EC1. Annual Returns to the Registrar of Companies. File 2854.
65. Archives of the Bank of London and South America, University College, London. D82 (London and River Plate Bank, printed annual reports) 18 December 1863; D91 ('letters from the late Henry Bruce')

Bruce to David Parish Robertson, 6 November 1862 and 29 September 1862.

66. BOLSA D91, 8 July 1864.

67. BOLSA D75 (London and River Plate Bank, Buenos Aires to various, 1890–92), Rodney Fennesy to Edward Ross Duffield, 30 January 1891.

68. H. S. Ferns, *Britain and Argentina in the Nineteenth Century* (Clarendon, Oxford, 1960), p. 333.

69. *Directory of Directors*, 1880, 1890.

70. John Galsworthy, *The Man of Property* (London 1906; Penguin Books, 1951), p. 19.

71. PRO BT31 4536/29687.

72. Juan Oddone, *La burgesia terrateniente argentina* (Buenos Aires, 1930), pp. 185–6.

73. PRO BT31 1736/6406.

74. BOLSA D68 (London and River Plate Bank, Montevideo to London), 27 March 1876.

75. Records of the Department of Trade and Industry, Annual Returns to the Registrar of Companies, file 15740 (River and Mercantile Trust Ltd).

76. Charles Jones, 'Great Capitalists and the Direction of British Overseas Investment in the Late Nineteenth Century: the Case of Argentina', *Bus. Hist.*, 22, 2 (July 1980); Charles Jones, 'Who Invested in Argentina and Uruguay?', *Bus. Arch.*, 48 (November 1982), pp. 1–24.

77. T. C. Coram, 'The Role of British Capital in the Development of the United States, *circa* 1600–1914' (unpublished M.Sc.(Econ.) dissertation, University of Southampton, 1967), p. 282.

78. W. P. Kennedy, 'Institutional Response to Economic Growth: capital markets in Britain to 1914', in Leslie Hannah (ed.), *Management Strategy and Business Development* (Macmillan, London, 1976), pp. 151–83.

79. J. C. Gilbert, *A History of Investment Trusts in Dundee, 1873–1938* (P. S. King, London, 1939), p. 10; B. L. Anderson, 'The Attorney and the Early Capital Market in Lancashire', in François Crouzet, *Capital Formation in the Industrial Revolution* (Methuen, London, 1972), pp. 223–55, first published as Chapter 3 of J. R. Harris (ed.), *Liverpool and Merseyside: Essays in the Economic and Social History of the Port and its Hinterland* (Frank Cass, London, 1969); and see above, p. 173.

80. Peter J. Buckley and Brian R. Roberts, *European Direct Investment in the U.S.A. before World War I* (Macmillan, London, 1982), p. 63.

81. R. V. Clements, 'The Farmer's Attitude Towards British Direct Investment in American Industry', *J. Econ. Hist.*, 20 (1955), p. 158.

82. William Curry Holden, *The Spur Ranch: a Study of the Inclosed Ranch Phase of the Cattle Industry in Texas* (Christopher Publishing House, Boston, Mass., 1934).

83. C. A. Jones, 'British Financial Institutions in Argentina, 1860–1914' (unpublished Ph.D. dissertation, University of Cambridge, 1973), pp. 145–9, is based on the archives of Mandatos y Agencias del Río de la Plata, now destroyed. The notes made by Linda and Charles Jones in

these archives in 1971 survive, and are available in a microfiche edition: Charles Jones, *The River Plate Trust Company Archives* (Oxford Microform, Oxford, 1984).

84. The Morrisons were active in the United States during the middle decades of the century, but it is not clear how directly their interests there were managed or how successful they were.

85. Donald G. Paterson, *British Direct Investment in Canada, 1890–1914* (University of Toronto Press, Toronto and Buffalo, 1976), pp. 101–2.

86. Buckley and Roberts, *European Direct Investment*, p. 4.

87. Coram, 'The Role of British Capital', p. 326. Since I wrote these words an isolated letter has come to light in the offices of Ashurst, Morris, Crisp, confirming this interpretation. It is reproduced here by kind permission of the firm. The letter reads:

Ashurst, Morris, Crisp & Co.　　　　　　　　　6, Old Jewry
　　　　　　　　　　　　　　　　　　　　　London E.C.
　　　　　　　　　　　　　　　　　　　　　19 Nov. 1889

Dear Crisp,

Before I leave I want to tell you my views about business of the class of Nelsons' original Co, the Rosario Water Works etc.

As you know, I have carried through both these things and others, on a somewhat similar basis, partly in connection with the Trust Co, and partly independently of them: as for instance in Nelson's Company.

The principle on which I have carried through these matters has been that no one is to get a farthing profit except out of success, actual cost being advanced for works etc by the capitalists, to be represented by debentures as a first charge and the surplus to be taken in ordinary bonus shares, the amount of which to be dependent upon actual working results, after it has been fully tested.

I also carried through an ingenious scheme in both the cases I have referred to for increasing the capital, without having to pay transfer duty on the increased amount, which in Nelson's case would have been multiplying the original capital by ten.

It is in a class of business which if conducted with great judgement and care is not only good in itself but becomes the parent of other concerns, as is notably illustrated in Nelson's case. On the other hand it is business which ought never to be taken up by anyone in an office like ours unless they can give a great deal of personal time and attention to it, not only to its inception but to its development, until it has been actually proved and the concern converted into a public company, which is the ultimate aim in the event of success.

Not only would it require a great deal of time and attention in this way but it also involves an enormous amount of responsibility. You know my great indisposition to recommend anything. Certainly I never would do so as regards ordinary companies but in these private combinations one cannot help taking the responsibility because you have to bring your own friends and connections into the syndicate. So long as those prove successful they will always be disposed to follow one but one failure might destroy the magic of it for a very long time.

My chief object in writing this is to say that I don't think anyone ought to take it up when I am away. In the first place it is very engrossing and requires great experience to judge of it, and time and attention which no one but myself could give to it, but having now had some special experience in that class of business I think that whenever a thing is so thoroughly good as to bear the kind of investigation required I should not be indisposed to look into it, believing that it is a good thing for office like ours who to be able to handle things of that kind, not in the usual way of company-promoters but in a thoroughly sound way on the principle I have indicated. If therefore anything (which I hope will not be the case) of a superlative class should come into the office while I am away I don't object to it being submitted to me if it will not keep until I come back. I have now on hand the case of Queen Anne's Mansion Electric Supply Company which I am thoroughly threshing out and on the lines I have indicated, and which so far as I can see at present is likely to prove a very good thing. I have found no difficulty whatever in getting the syndicate together and in fact, through the success which attended the other things I have referred to, the difficulty is to limit the choice. Here again there is a great responsibility and one must avoid being tempted thereby into taking up anything excepting under the conditions I have suggested. I write this to you, but of course I intend it for Willie and Ashurst also, so that we may all be in accord on the subject. I should like to have a little talk with you, if you have time before I leave to read this letter, which I would have made shorter, but I have been obliged to dictate it while very busy.

Yours
Morris

88. Roger V. Clements, 'British-Controlled Enterprise', *Agric. Hist.*, p. 53.
89. S. J. Butlin, *Australia and New Zealand Bank: the Bank of Australasia and the Union Bank of Australia Limited, 1828–1951* (Longmans, London, 1961), p. 241.
90. Falconer Larkworthy, *Ninety-one Years* (Mills & Boon, London, 1924), p. 219.
91. Trust and Agency Company of Australasia Ltd, 4 London Wall Buildings, London EC2M 5UJ. Board Minutes, IX, 27 December 1913; Sun Insurance Office, foreign notebooks, Buenos Aires, I, p. 134, Whitehead to head office, 3 April 1914; J. D. Bailey, *A Hundred Years of Pastoral Banking: a History of the Australian Mercantile Land & Finance Company, 1863–1963* (Clarendon, Oxford, 1966), p. 205.
92. Charles Jones, 'Insurance Companies', in D. C. M. Platt (ed.), *Business Imperialism, 1840–1930: an Inquiry Based on British Experience in Latin America* (Clarendon, Oxford, 1977), pp. 70–3.
93. *Sydney Morning Herald*, September 1853, quoted in A. J. S. Baster, *The Imperial Banks* (P. S. King & Son, London, 1929), p. 140.

94. E. T. and M. G. Mulhall, *Handbook of the River Plate* (Buenos Aires, 1869), I, p. 9.

95. T. C. Barker and Michael Robbins, *A History of London Transport: Passenger Travel and the Development of the Metropolis* (Allen & Unwin, London, 1963, 1974), p. 38.

96. *James Finlay & Company Limited*, Max Hartwell, 'Dalgety and New Zealand Loan Company: History of the Company' (unpublished typescript, n.d. *circa* 1974), Chapter 7; Bailey, *Pastoral Banking*; Jack Colin Crossley, 'The Location and Development of the Agricultural and Industrial Enterprises of Liebig's Extract of Meat Company in the River Plate Countries, 1865–1932' (unpublished Ph.D. thesis, University of Leicester, 1973), p. 104.

97. Charles Jones, 'Commercial Banks and Mortgage Companies', in Platt, *Business Imperialism*, p. 28.

98. Baster, *Imperial Banks*.

99. Ibid.

100. Arndt, *Banking and Currency Development in South Africa*, p. 308.

101. Charles A. Jones, 'Personalism, Indebtedness, and Venality: the Political Environment of British Firms in Santa Fé Province, 1865–1900', *Ibero-Amer. Arch.*, N.F. Jg9 H.3/4 (1983), pp. 381–99.

102. Marika Vicziany, 'Bombay Merchants and Structural Changes in the Export Community, 1850–1880', in K. N. Chaudhuri and Clive Dewey (eds), *Economy and Society* (Oxford University Press, Delhi and New York, 1979), p. 163, describes the marginalisation of non-European merchants in the bombay cotton trade after 1870. See Robert Greenhill, 'The Brazilian Coffee Trade', in Platt, *Business Imperialism*, p. 206; and Eugene W. Ridings, 'Business, Nationality & Dependency in Late Nineteenth Century Brazil', *J. Lat. Amer. Stud.*, 14, 1 (May 1982), p. 87, for the squeezing of Brazilian middlemen by British coffee exporters, and Greenhill and Crossley's 'The River Plate Beef Trade', also in Platt, *Business Imperialism*, for details of the monopolistic practices of foreign meat packers in Argentina (pp. 300–20). See also Charles Jones on banking in Platt, *Business Imperialism*, pp. 26–7.

103. John Mayo, 'Before the Nitrate Era: British Commission Houses and Chilean Economy, 1851–80', *J. Lat. Amer. Stud.*, 11, 2 (November 1979), p. 301; Charles Jones, 'Commercial Banks and Mortgage Companies', in Platt, *Business Imperialism*, p. 51.

104. T. F. Dod, in Townend, *Shaw Wallace*, p. 72.

105. Sun Insurance Office, foreign notebooks, Buenos Aires I, H. S. Whiting to head office, 22 May 1914.

106. Charles A. Jones, 'Competition and Structural Change in the Buenos Aires Fire Insurance Market: the Local Board of Agents, 1875–1921', in Oliver M. Westall (ed.), *The Historian and the Business of Insurance* (Manchester University Press, Manchester, 1984), pp. 114–29.

107. Dod in Townend, *Shaw Wallace*, p. 74.

108. Griffiths, *The Inchcape Group*, p. 64.

109. T. A. B. Corley, 'Communications, Entrepreneurship and the Managing Agency System: the Burmah Oil Co., 1886–1928'

(unpublished paper, *circa* 1980).

110. Rory Miller, 'Small Business in the Peruvian Oil Industry: Lobitos Oilfields Limited before 1934', *Bus. Hist. Rev.*, 56, 3 (Autumn 1982), pp. 400–23.

111. Corley, 'Communications, Entrepreneurship and the Managing Agency System', p. 19.

112. Townend, *Shaw Wallace*, p. 197.

113. Ibid., p. 55.

114. Miller, 'Small Business', p. 414. The quotation, which reflects the views of Standard Oil management at the time, is from Henrietta M. Larson *et al.*, *New Horizons, 1927–1950* (Harper & Row, New York and London, 1971), Volume 3 of a *History of Standard Oil Company* (New Jersey), pp. 326–8.

115. Yen P'ing Hao, *The Comprador in Nineteenth-Century China: Bridge between East and West* (Harvard University Press, Cambridge, Mass., 1970) p. 62; on British American Tobacco in China see Richard Dobson, *China Cycle* (Macmillan, London, 1946). Dobson, later Sir Richard, worked in China for BAT as a young man in the 1930s and subsequently became chairman of the company.

116. Henriques, *Marcus Samuel*, p. 392; Alan Barnard, *Visions and Profits: Studies in the Business Career of Thomas Sutcliffe Mort* (Melbourne University Press for Australian National University, Melbourne, 1961), p. 135, attributes Mort's relative loss of position in the Australian wool business to very similar failings.

117. Archives of the Bank of London and South America, letters of Robert A. Thurburn to his father.

118. Reminiscences of the lives of mid-nineteenth-century clerks overseas are numerous, but have never been systematically studied. See Larkworthy, *Ninety-one Years*; Charles Darbyshire, *My Life in the Argentine Republic* (Warne & Co., London and New York, 1917); the diaries of Walter Heald—John Rylands MSS.1217, 4 vols., 1866–70; and the letters of Robert Thurburn (see note 117, above).

119. See above, p. 114. Another case is that of Robert Barclay, a salesman for James Finlay & Co., who set up Robert Barclay & Co. of Buenos Aires in 1860 with a credit of £14,000 from Finlays. *James Finlay & Co.*

120. B. L. Anderson, 'The Social Economy of Late Victorian Clerks', in Geoffrey Crossick (ed.), *The Lower Middle Class in Britain, 1870–1914* (Croom Helm, London, 1977), pp. 113–33.

121. See above, p. 95; also G. C. W. Joel, *One Hundred Years of Coffee: E. Johnston & Co. Ltd* (London, privately printed, 1942), p. 23. E. Johnston & Co. incorporated in 1906.

122. On the general pattern of the transformation from managing agency to corporate group in India see S. K. Basu, *The Managing Agency System in Prospect and Retrospect* (Calcutta, 1958), pp. 13, 82. On the originally private character of nominally public companies in India see P. S. Lokanathan, *Industrial Organization in India* (George Allen & Unwin, London, 1935), p. 27, also Charles A. Jones, 'Great Capitalists and the Direction of British Overseas Investment in the Late

Nineteenth Century: the Case of Argentina', *Bus. Hist.*, 22, 2 (July 1980); and Charles Jones, 'Who Invested in Argentina and Uruguay?', *Bus. Arch.*, 48 (November 1982).
123. Townend, *Shaw Wallace & Co.*, p. 201.
124. Sir Charles Milner, first chairman of Shaw, Wallace & Co. Ltd, quoted in Townend, Chapter 22.
125. Griffiths, *The Inchcape Group*, pp. 116 *et seq.*
126. Ibid., p. 48. The early group system reached its apogee in shipping. See Edwin Green and Michael Moss, *A Business of National Importance: the Royal Mail Shipping Group, 1902–37* (Methuen, London and New York, 1982), and P. N. Davies, 'Group Enterprise: strengths and hazards—business history and the teaching of business management', in Sheila Marriner (ed.), *Business and Businessmen: Studies in Business, Economic and Accounting History* (Liverpool University Press, Liverpool, 1978).

CHAPTER 6

1. Charles Morrison, *An Essay on the Relations between Labour and Capital* (Longman, London, 1854), p. 126.
2. John Galsworthy, *The Forsyte Saga* (Penguin, 1978), p. 596.
3. A. O. Hirschman, *The Passions and the Interests* (Princeton University Press, Princeton, N.J., 1977), *passim.*
4. Jacques Savary, *Le parfait negociant*, quoted in Hirschman, op. cit., p. 59.
5. 'Free trade is a Divine Law: if it were not, the world would have been differently created. One country has cotton, another wine, another coal, which is proof that, according to the Divine Order of things, men should fraternize and exchange their goods and thus further Peace and Goodwill on Earth.' S. Schwabe, *Reminiscences of Richard Cobden* (London, 1895), p. viii, quoted in Peter Cain, 'Capitalism, War and Internationalism in the thought of Richard Cobden', *Brit. J. Inter. Stud.*, 5 (1979), p. 240.
6. P. N. Davies, *Sir Alfred Jones: Shipping Entrepreneur par excellence* (Europa Publications, London, 1978), pp. 66 and 102.
7. H. G. Wells, *Tono Bungay* (Macmillan, London, 1909; Pan Books, 1975), p. 55.
8. J. A. Hobson, *Imperialism: a Study* (Nisbet, London, 1902).
9. Archives of Mandatos y Agencias del Río de la Plata. Records of the River Plate Trust Loan and Agency Co. Ltd, managers' monthly reports, May 1903.
10. On this, see J. M. Roberts, *The Mythology of the Secret Societies* (Secker & Warburg, London, 1972; Paladin, 1974), especially Chapter 10.
11. Arthur Conan Doyle, *The Adventures of Sherlock Holmes*, XIX—'The Adventure of the Final Problem', in *The Strand Magazine*, VI (July–December, 1893), pp. 560–1.
12. G. K. Chesterton, in *Illustrated London News*, 13 June 1936, reprinted in

G. K. Chesterton, *The Man Who was Thursday* (Penguin Books, 1974), p. 185.

13. Wells, *Tono Bungay*, p. 185.
14. W. D. Rubinstein, 'The Victorian Middle Classes: Wealth, Occupation, and Geography', *Econ. Hist. Rev.*, 2nd series, 30, 4 (November 1977), p. 621.
15. John Morley, *The Life of Richard Cobden* (London, 1879; 1905 edn) p. 134.
16. Ibid., p. 946. Cobden to Hargreaves, 10 April 1883.
17. Ruth Brandon, *The Dollar Princesses: the American Invasion of the European Aristocracy, 1870–1914* (Weidenfeld & Nicolson, London, 1980), especially Chapter 2. More broadly, on the revival of enthusiasm for chivalry, see Mark Girouard, *The Return to Camelot: Chivalry and the English Gentleman* (Yale University Press, New Haven and London, 1981).
18. Morley, *Cobden*, p. 663, Cobden to Parker.
19. *James Finlay & Company Limited: Manufacturers and East India Merchants 1750–1950* (Jackson, Son & Co., Glasgow, 1951), p. 106.
20. V. G. Kiernan, *The Lords of Human Kind: European Attitudes to the Outside World in the Imperial Age* (Weidenfeld & Nicolson, London, 1969; Pelican Books, 1972), pp. 62–3.
21. Mandatos, River Plate Trust Loan and Agency, manager's monthly reports, May 1903.
22. Quoted in Harold Pollins, *Economic History of the Jews in England* (Associated University Presses, London, Toronto, and East Brunswick, N.J., 1984).
23. Mandatos, River Plate Trust Loan and Agency, managers' monthly reports, May 1903.
24. Galsworthy, *The Forsyte Saga* (Penguin, 1978), pp. 559–60.
25. Charles Morrison, quoted in Richard Gatty, *Portrait of a Merchant Prince: James Morrison, 1789–1857* (Northallerton, privately printed, n.d., *circa* 1976), p. 203.
26. Morrison, *Labour and Capital*, p. 127.
27. The balance of local and foreign competitive advantage has a long history. Dutch historians dealing with the seventeenth century distinguish between commercial industries (*verkeersindustrien*) in the trading towns (especially Amsterdam) which required knowledge of foreign processes and overseas markets, and more local industries based on domestic consumption (*fabrieken*) in Leiden and other cities. See Violet Barbour, *Capitalism in Amsterdam in the Seventeenth Century* (Johns Hopkins Press, Baltimore, 1950; 1963), p. 67.
28. Edward Reynold, *Trade and Economic Change on the Gold Coast, 1807–1874* (Longmans, Harlow, 1974), p. 106.
29. Ibid., p. 113.
30. A. G. Hopkins, 'Innovation in a Colonial Context: African Origins of the Nigerian Cocoa-farming industry, 1880–1920', in Clive Dewey and A. G. Hopkins (eds), *The Imperial Impact: Studies in the Economic History of Africa and India* (Athlone, London, 1978), pp. 83–96.

31. Satchi Ponnambalam, *Sri Lanka: the National Question and the Tamil Liberation Struggle* (Tamil Information Centre and Zed Books, London, 1983), p. 58.
32. Lord Frederick Hamilton, *Here, There and Everywhere* (Hodder & Stoughton, London, 1921; 20th edn, 1937), p. 17.
33. E. J. Míguez, 'British Interest in Argentine Land Development, 1870–1914: a Study of British Investment in Argentina' (unpublished D.Phil. thesis, Oxford, 1981), p. 75; Vera Blinn Reber, *British Mercantile Houses in Buenos Aires, 1810–1880* (Harvard University Press, Cambridge, Mass. and London, 1979), pp. 138–9.
34. Helga Kaye, *The Tycoon and the President: the Life and Times of Alois Hugo Nellmapius, 1847–1892* (Macmillan, Johannesburg, 1978); J. S. Marais, *The Fall of Kruger's Republic*, (Clarendon, Oxford, 1961), pp. 24–7.
35. Roderick J. Barman, 'Business and Government in Imperial Brazil: the Experience of Baron Mauá', *J. Lat. Amer. Stud.*, 13, 2 (November 1981).
36. Mark Wasserman, 'Foreign Investment in Mexico, 1876–1910: a Case Study in the Role of Regional Elites', *The Americas*, 36 (1979–80), pp. 3–21.
37. A. J. S. Baster, *The Imperial Banks* (King & Co., London, 1929), p. 112 and *passim*.
38. R. K. Hazari, 'The Implications of the Managing Agency System in Indian Development', in Ashok V. Bhuleshkar (ed.), *Indian Economic Thought and Development* (Popular Prakashan, Bombay, 1969), p. 212 and *passim*.
39. Roger V. Clements, 'The Farmer's Attitude towards British Direct Investment in American Industry', *J. Econ. Hist.*, 20 (1955), p. 151.
40. Roger V. Clements, 'British Investment and American Legislative Restrictions in the Trans-Mississippi West, 1880–1900', *Mis. V. Hist. Rev.*, 42 (September 1955), p. 218 and *passim*.
41. Ibid., p. 225.
42. Geoffrey Harrison, *Borthwicks: a Century in the Meat Trade, 1863–1963*, pp. 126–8.
43. David Joslin, *A Century of Banking in Latin America* (Oxford University Press, London, 1963), pp. 43–50; Ezequiel Gallo, 'El gobierno de Santa Fé vs. el Banco de Londres y Río de la Plata, 1876', in *Revista Latinoamericana de Sociología*, 7, 2–3 (Buenos Aires, 1971), pp. 147–74; E. H. D. Arndt, *Banking and Currency Development in South Africa, 1652–1927* (Juta & Co. Cape Town, and Johannesburg, 1928), pp. 302–19.
44. Ibid.
45. Charles Jones, 'Commercial Banks and Mortgage Companies', in D. C. M. Platt (ed.), *Business Imperialism, 1840–1930: an Inquiry based on British Experience in Latin America* (Clarendon, Oxford, 1977), p. 44.
46. Stephen E. Koss, *Sir John Brunner, Radical Plutocrat, 1842–1919* (Cambridge University Press, London, 1970), pp. 10, 193.
47. Gatty, *Morrison*, pp. 267–73; William C. Lubenow, *The Politics of Government Growth: Early Victorian Attitudes toward State Intervention,*

1833–1848 (David & Charles, Newton Abbott, 1971), pp. 126–8 and *passim.*

48. Koss, *Brunner*, p. 233.
49. Olive Anderson, *A Liberal State at War: English Politics and Economics during the Crimean War* (Macmillan, London, 1967), p. 104.
50. Ibid., pp. 117–18.
51. Ibid., p. 107.
52. Charles A. Jones, *Britain and the Dominions: a guide to business and related records* (G. K. Hall & Co., Boston, Mass., 1978), p. 97.
53. Robert Henriques, *Marcus Samuel, First Lord Bearsted and Founder of the 'Shell' Transport and Trading Company, 1853–1927* (Barrie & Rockliff, London, 1960), pp. 280–88, 526 *et seq.*
54. Cf. Duncan Crow, *A Man of Push and Go: the Life of George Macaulay Booth* (Rupert Hart-Davis, London, 1965). For the earlier history of Alfred Booth & Co., see above, p. 143.
55. W. J. Reader, 'Imperial Chemical Industries and the State, 1926–1945', in Barry Supple (ed.), *Essays on British Business History* (Clarendon, Oxford, 1977), pp. 227–43.
56. Ibid.
57. Wells, *Tono Bungay*, p. 214.
58. This is a complicated subject with an extensive literature. See Anderson, *Liberal State at War*, p. 129 *et seq.*; Valerie E. Chancellor, *History for their Masters: Opinion in the English History Textbook, 1800–1914* (Adams & Dart, Bath, 1970); Girouard, *Return to Chivalry*; David Masson (ed.), Thomas de Quincey: *Political Economy and Politics* (Black, London, 1897; reprinted, Kelley, New York, 1970), pp. 295–312, 'Falsification of English History'.
59. Anthony Trollope, *The Small House at Arlington* (London, 1864), Chapter 12; Anthony Trollope, *Phineas Redux* (London, 1873; Oxford University Press, London, 1973), p. 215.
60. Michael Trinick, *Castle Drogo* (National Trust, 1975); Andrew Saint and Sheila Pettit, *Cragside Hall* (National Trust, n.d.).
61. Morley, *Cobden*, p. 630, Cobden to Bright, 5 January 1855.
62. W. D. Rubinstein, 'Men of Property; Some Aspects of Occupation, Inheritance, and Power among Top British Wealthholders', in Philip Stanworth and Anthony Goddens (eds), *Elites and Power in British Society* (Cambridge University Press, Cambridge, 1974), pp. 169–72.
63. Henriques, *Marcus Samuel*, p. 427.
64. Ibid., pp. 455 *et seq.* In his later encounter with Fascism Deterding developed an appreciation of ceremony.
65. Jose Harris and Pat Thane, 'British and European Bankers, 1880–1914: an "aristocratic bourgeoisie"?', in Pat Thane, Geoffrey Crossick and Roderick Floud (eds), *The Power of the Past: Essays for Eric Hobsbawm* (Cambridge University Press, Cambridge, 1984). But see also a recent objection to this thesis from S. D. Chapman in his 'Aristocracy and Meritocracy in Merchant Banking', *Brit. J. Soc.*, 37, 2 (June 1986), pp. 180–93.
66. W. D. Rubinstein, *Men of Property: the Very Wealthy in Britain Since the*

Industrial Revolution (Croom Helm, London, 1981), pp. 44, 103.

67. John Flint, *Cecil Rhodes* (Hutchinson, London, 1976), Chapter 6; John S. Galbraith, *Crown and Charter: the Early Years of the British South Africa Company* (University of California Press, Berkeley, Cal., 1974); John S. Galbraith, *Mackinnon and East Africa, 1878–1895: a Study in the 'New Imperialism'* (Cambridge University Press, Cambridge, 1972).

68. Galbraith, *Mackinnon*; Sir Percival Griffiths, *A History of the Inchcape Group* (Inchcape & Co. Ltd, London, 1977), pp. 55 *et seq.*

69. Flint, *Rhodes.*

70. Fritz Stern, *Gold and Iron: Bismarck, Bleichröder, and the Building of the German Empire* (George Allen & Unwin, London, 1977), pp. 394–435.

71. Mandatos, River Plate Trust Loan and Agency, Chevallier Boutell's private letters, Chevallier Boutell to James Anderson, 15 January 1897.

72. Davies, *Sir Alfred Jones*, p. 68.

73. H. E. W. Braund, *Calling to Mind: being some account of the first hundred years (1870–1970) of Steel Brothers and Company Limited* (Pergamon, Press, Oxford, 1975).

74. Records of the Phoenix Insurance Co. Ltd, Phoenix House, King William Street, London EC4. 'Report of Victory Committee (1942) on Post-War Development Overseas'.

Name Index

Subject Index